**The John W...
Christian Perfection Library**

Volume Three

THE
JOHN WESLEY READER
ON CHRISTIAN PERFECTION

1725 — 1791

Edited By
Mark K. Olson

Truth In Heart
8071 Main Street
Fenwick, MI 48834

(989) 637-4179

TruthInHeart.com

2008

Wesley, John 1703-1791
Olson, Mark K. 1957-

The John Wesley Reader On Christian Perfection
(The John Wesley Christian Perfection Library. Volume III)

Reproduction of Wesley's text is from:

The Works of John Wesley, Third Edition, Editor: Thomas Jackson. London: Wesleyan Methodist Book Room, 1872.

The Works of John Wesley: The Bicentennial Edition, 34 projected volumes. Nashville: Abingdon Press. 1984-Present.

Explanatory Notes Upon The New Testament, 2 Volumes. Grand Rapids: Baker Book House. 1983, Reprint.

The Letters of the Rev. John Wesley, 8 Volumes. Editor: John Telford. London: Epworth Press. 1931.

Unless otherwise noted, all Scripture quotations are from *The Holy Bible, The King James Version.*

ISBN- 10: 1-932370-90-0 Hardcover
ISBN- 13: 978-1-932370-90-4

Library of Congress Control Number: 2008905868

To order more copies of this book:
Truth In Heart
TruthInHeart.com
8071 Main St.
Fenwick, MI 48834
(989) 637-4179

The John Wesley Reader On Christian Perfection

1725 – 1791

Edited By

Mark K. Olson

Volume Three
of
The John Wesley
Christian Perfection Library

The John Wesley
Christian Perfection Library
in
Five Volumes

VOLUME ONE
JOHN WESLEY'S 'A PLAIN ACCOUNT OF CHRISTIAN PERFECTION'
THE ANNOTATED EDITION
(Released 2005)

VOLUME TWO
JOHN WESLEY'S THEOLOGY OF CHRISTIAN PERFECTION
DEVELOPMENTS IN DOCTRINE & THEOLOGICAL SYSTEM
(Released 2007)

VOLUME THREE
THE JOHN WESLEY READER ON CHRISTIAN PERFECTION
1725 – 1791
(Released 2008)

VOLUME FOUR
JOHN WESLEY'S DOCTRINE OF CHRISTIAN PERFECTION
SYSTEMATIC FORMULATION FOR CONTEMPORARY RELEVANCE

VOLUME FIVE
JOHN WESLEY'S PREACHING ON CHRISTIAN PERFECTION
FOR THE 21ST CENTURY

John Wesley Booklets also available by the publisher:

Thoughts on Christian Perfection
Farther Thoughts on Christian Perfection
(Both are fully annotated)

BY
MARK K. OLSON

TRUTHINHEART.COM

Table of Contents

List of Abbreviations

John Wesley's Writings

Works J   The Works of John Wesley, 14 Volumes. Editor: Thomas Jackson (volume: page number).

Works B   The Works of John Wesley, Bicentennial Edition. Abingdon Press (volume: page number).

Telford   The Letters of the Rev. John Wesley, 8 Volumes. Editor: John Telford (volume: page number).

Outler   Outler, Albert *John Wesley.* New York: Oxford University Press. 1964, (page number).

Latin Terms

Ars Moriendi   art of dying
Ordo salutis   order of salvation (faith journey)

Old Testament:

Genesis	Gen	Ecclesiastes	Ecc
Exodus	Ex	Song of Songs	SS
Leviticus	Lev	Isaiah	Is
Numbers	Num	Jeremiah	Jer
Deuteronomy	Deut	Lamentations	Lam
Joshua	Josh	Ezekiel	Eze
Judges	Jdg	Daniel	Dan
Ruth	Ruth	Hosea	Hos
1 Samuel	1 Sam	Joel	Joel
2 Samuel	2 Sam	Amos	Am
1 Kings	1 Kgs	Obediah	Ob
2 Kings	2 Kgs	Jonah	Jon
1 Chronicles	1 Ch	Micah	Mic
2 Chronicles	2 Ch	Nahum	Nah

Ezra	Ezra	Habakkuk	Hab
Nehemiah	Neh	Zephaniah	Zep
Esther	Es	Haggai	Hag
Job	Job	Zechariah	Zec
Psalms	Ps	Malachi	Mal
Proverbs	Pr		

New Testament:

Matthew	Matt
Mark	Mk
Luke	Lk
John	Jn
Acts	Acts
Romans	Rom
1 Corinthians	1 Cor
2 Corinthians	2 Cor
Galatians	Gal
Ephesians	Eph
Philippians	Php
Colossians	Col
1 Thessalonians	1 Th
2 Thessalonians	2 Th
1 Timothy	1 Tim
2 Timothy	2 Tim
Titus	Tit
Philemon	Phm
Hebrews	Heb
James	Ja
1 Peter	1 Pet
2 Peter	2 Pet
1 John	1 Jn
2 John	2 Jn
3 John	3 Jn
Jude	Jude
Revelation	Rev

Introduction

John Wesley (1703-1791) is widely recognized as the chief architect and source of inspiration for the modern doctrine of Christian perfection. From the year 1725, when Wesley was "exceedingly affected" and resolved to "dedicate all (his) life to God," holiness became the DNA of his spiritual temperament. For the next sixty-six years Wesley taught and proclaimed a gospel of holy love, graciously given to sinful humanity in Jesus Christ, for the recovery of the divine image lost by the first Adam. Yet this vision of perfect love did not take shape over night. The path Wesley journeyed in developing his theology of holiness was often arduous, at times turbulent, became personally painful at specific junctures, and was long. It took Wesley many years to work through the particulars of his theological principles and finally integrate them into a holistic theological system. The purpose of this *Reader* is to tell the story, in Wesley's own words, how he developed his mature theology of Christian perfection. By placing Wesley's writings on the subject, in their chronological order, the student of Wesley can examine what he believed at specific periods of his career, and how his theology of perfect love took shape over time.

Wesley lived a full life and enjoyed a long ministerial career. In fact, his career stretches nearly seven decades (hence the subtitle: 1725-1791). At present no comprehensive reader on the subject is available that covers the entire length of his career. Though *The Plain Account of Christian Perfection* (1766) includes several of Wesley's writings, spanning approximately four decades, in reality the *Plain Account* does not present Wesley's views as they developed over time. As Thomas Jackson, early editor of the *Plain Account*, made plain:

> It is not to be understood, that Mr. Wesley's sentiments concerning Christian Perfection were in any measure changed after the year 1777. This tract

underwent several revisions and enlargements during his life-time; and in every successive edition the date of the most recent revision was specified. The last revision appears to have been made in the year 1777; and since that period, this date has been generally continued on the title-page of the several editions of the pamphlet.[1]

Instead, Wesley's primary motive for writing the *Plain Account* was apologetic. In the wake of the 1760's perfection revival and ensuing schism, Wesley felt the need to defend himself against mounting criticism that he had been inconsistent in his perfection views. Critics rose from within the Methodist ranks and from without. Their central charge was that Wesley had changed his views over time. So in 1765 Wesley compiled a couple sermons along with a number of other writings, most of which were heavily edited, to show he had been consistent in his principles over time. But as recent research has shown, Wesley's perfection theology did evolve throughout his life. In a prior volume of this series I thoroughly explore this doctrinal evolution in detail.[2] The goal of this *Reader* is to show this development by placing Wesley's writings in their chronological order, allowing for comparative study and reflection. It is my hope that the Wesley of different periods will be more appreciated and better understood.

This leads to another reason why this *Reader* is necessary. There is a tendency within Wesley studies to ignore the chronological development of his thought embedded in his sermons and writings. Often, Wesley is quoted while ignoring the chronological and historical context. This has led to mistaken notions as to what Wesley believed about perfect love and Christian holiness at a given time. By reading Wesley's writings

---

[1] Works J 11:366.
[2] Volume two of the series: *John Wesley's Theology of Christian Perfection: Developments in Doctrine & Theological System.* Fenwick: Truth in Heart, 2007.

Introduction

in their proper sequence fresh insights begin to open up for the reader. Writings from one period of his career can be compared to writings of another. This allows for patterns of change to become more visible. It also makes clear the unchanging principles that guided his theological development. We gain a much deeper appreciation for what Wesley believed (and wrote) at a given time, and why he believed it. It is the hope of this editor that this chronological *Reader* will help students of Wesley to clarify the developing nuances found in his doctrine of full salvation.

Guiding Principles

Wesley was a prolific writer and publisher. This is especially true regarding the topic at hand. Christian perfection was Wesley's most beloved theme and he wrote on it often. No single book could include everything he wrote; nor would this be advantageous. Too much material would only bury the reader in details. Therefore, a process of selection and editing was essential to make this *Reader* fulfill its purpose. The following steps guided the process.

First, the *Reader* is organized according to standard divisions of Wesley's career: early (1725-1738), middle (1738-1767), and late (1768-1791). But two adjustments were made to better highlight his doctrinal development.[3] In 1738 Wesley moved through a series of major theological changes that requires an additional section be added. Then Wesley's middle period is

---

[3] See my *John Wesley's Theology of Christian Perfection* for a fuller treatment of my reasons for doing so. In that volume Wesley's doctrinal evolution is organized according to his core understanding of the gospel in each era: The Gospel of Holiness (early), The Gospel of Faith Alone (Aldersgate), The Gospel of Two Works of Grace (middle), and The Gospel of Universal Holiness (late). The middle period was further divided into two sections as in this volume to highlight the unique features of his perfection theology in each section.

divided into two parts to bring out the doctrinal transitions that happened in each era. So the *Reader* has five sections instead of three.

Second, a landmark sermon was chosen that summarizes and expresses the theology of each period. The five sermons are *The Circumcision of the Heart* (1733), *Salvation By Faith* (1738), *Christian Perfection* (1741), *The Scripture Way of Salvation* (1765), and *On Working Out Our Own Salvation* (1785). A comparative study of these five sermons in their chronological order offers important insights into Wesley's theological development and the nuances that shaped his doctrine of perfect love.

Then, other sermons were chosen that played a significant role in Wesley's doctrinal evolution. Next, selections from Wesley's journal, letters, *Explanatory Notes Upon the New Testament*, and other writings were chosen because they help tell the story how his theology of perfection took shape over his long career. Several selections from the journal are included because they are necessary to telling the story, since Wesley's doctrine develops in step with his own faith journey. In the end, this *Reader* offers the student of Wesley a comprehensive sample of his views on full salvation in a chronological format covering his entire career.

A word should be said about punctuation. Since writings were selected from both the Jackson edition of Wesley's works (Works J) and the Bicentennial edition (Works B), and the two editions do not use the same styles of punctuation, I adjusted the latter to conform to the former in style. My purpose was to maintain evenness in the text for the reader.

Last, each section begins with a series of study questions to alert the reader to significant themes and motifs in that section. These can be used for personal or group study. The introductory comments in each chapter further serve to place the selection within its historical context and to inform the reader of which major specific themes and motifs to look for.

Introduction

The John Wesley Christian Perfection Library

With the release of this third volume the series is one more step toward completion. Together, the first three volumes offer one of the most comprehensive and complete studies on Wesley's doctrine of Christian perfection available today. Each volume serves a specific purpose.

Volume one offers a thorough study on Wesley's mature theology of perfection as presented in *The Plain Account of Christian Perfection*. The annotations are filled with pertinent comments from many Wesley scholars and specialists, and include over 150 quotations from Wesley himself. No other book presents a more thorough study of Wesley perfection theology as outlined in the *Plain Account*.

Volume two probes into the reasons why Wesley's perfection theology took the path it did, and how it took shape through his career. No stone is left unturned as his early, middle and late periods are mined for critical insights into his motivations and those key junctures in his faith journey that profoundly shaped his spiritual DNA and theology. One of the unique features of volume two is the in-depth survey of Wesley's early theological system (early period). This era has been neglected too long to the detriment of correctly grasping why Wesley did radical surgery on his theology upon his return to England in 1738. Aldersgate and its aftermath are examined with startling conclusions into the reasons why Wesley continued to struggle with doubt following his "heart warming" conversion on May 24. This volume further explores why Wesley's perfection theology shifted in emphasis in the mid to late sixties to form his mature theological system in the 1780's. All together, volume two offers unsurpassed insights into the evolution of Wesley's doctrine of Christian perfection.

Volume three complements the other two volumes by including material from the Wesley corpus not included in the *Plain Account*. In this way a broader sample of Wesley's views can be studied and appreciated. The *Reader* also presents those writings discussed in volume two in their historical order and context. Again, this empowers the reader to study these particular writings in their chronological context. Combined, the first three volumes of the series give the reader unsurpassed access into Wesley's theology of holiness.

A brief word should be said about the last two projected volumes. Wesley was no systematic thinker. His most comprehensive work on the subject, the *Plain Account*, includes only a select number of writings from his early and middle periods. So volume four will draw upon the text of the *Plain Account* to present Wesley's mature doctrine of holiness in a systematic format. This volume will be titled: *John Wesley's Doctrine of Christian Perfection: Systematic Formulation for Contemporary Relevance*. Wesley's views will be compared to that of the Holiness Movement, both past and present, to identify shifts in Wesleyan thought on the subject of holiness. Also, each chapter will include a study guide by which the reader can develop their own views according to scripture, reason, tradition and experience. In this way the reader can build their own biblical and systematic theology of holiness, drawing upon Wesley and the Holiness Movement for inspiration.

It requires no insight to say that the world has changed dramatically since Wesley's day. The need to communicate the scripture truth of heart holiness is arguably greater now than ever before. Yet many holiness organizations are stymied in their ability to present a cogent message of holiness today.[4] While I do not pretend to think I can solve the issues that confront us, I do believe a study into how Wesley promoted his message could be helpful to his descendants today. Thus, volume five, *John Wesley's Preaching of Christian Perfection for the 21st Century*, will explore the variety of means he used to communicate to his generation. Maybe there is something we can learn from this

---

[4] By saying this I cast no aspersions. The reasons are many and complex. The statement just reflects current reality. My own denomination (The Church of the Nazarene) is currently wrestling with the issue (Quanstrom, Mark R. *A Century of Holiness*. Beacon Hill: Kansas City. 2004).

Introduction

saint of holy love on how best to teach and pass on the blessed truth of scripture holiness.

To close, it is with joy that this *Reader* is offered to seekers of holiness. John Wesley firmly believed that God can so transform the believer's dispositional nature in this life that his love, even his perfect love, can become the natural and habitual characteristic of that person's life. Yet, Wesley also affirmed that a life perfected in love is still characterized by ignorance, mistake, temptation and trial—all the human frailties which are inescapable in this present age. To this end John Wesley gave himself completely and without reserve. To this end he encouraged all his people to pray:

> Almighty God, unto whom all hearts be open, all desires known, and from whom all secrets are hid; cleanse the thoughts of our hearts by the inspiration of thy Holy Spirit, that we may perfectly love thee, and worthily magnify thy holy Name, through Christ our Lord. Amen.[5]

---

[5] White, Jame F. *John Wesley's Prayer Book: The Sunday Service of the Methodists in North America.* OSL Publications: Akron, 1991; 125.

Section One

The Early Period

1725 – 1738

Questions to Consider for
John Wesley's Early Period

1. Why is the *ars moriendi* motif so important for early Wesley?

2. What are Wesley's early views on forgiveness and assurance? How do his views on forgiveness shape his early doctrine of holiness?

3. When is Christian perfection attained? Do Wesley's views develop during the early period?

4. Note how Wesley defines perfection in his early period. What is the essential idea he is seeking to communicate?

5. How did Wesley define sin in his early period?

6. What is the relationship between infirmities and sin? How do Wesley's views shape his understanding on the attainability of holiness?

7. Reflect on how perfect love is attained. How would you state Wesley's position?

8. Does Wesley in his early period have a clear-cut understanding of the faith journey (*ordo salutis*)?

9. What is the relationship between the single intention and the new birth?

10. What impact did the storms at sea have on Wesley' doctrinal development?

Ars Moriendi
1725

We begin with excerpts from Wesley's first two written sermons. These homilies place Wesley's early views on perfection within the ars moriendi *(art of dying) motif. Take note how Wesley defines sin and its deliverance at death, how he connects happiness to holiness, and how he understands the kingdom of God and his righteousness. Source: Works B 4:211-214; 219-220.*

There the wicked cease from troubling;
there the weary are at rest.

Job 3:17

It is not my design to enter into any particular inquiry whether the happiness of the just immediately after death be the same with that they will enjoy when united again to their bodies; or whether, as seems most agreeable to Holy Writ, it receives a new accession at the great day. Sure we are that it is infinitely superior to any happiness it is possible to arrive at in this world. They are delivered from all those cares, afflictions, and dangers, all that anguish and anxiety, which is unavoidably their portion as long as they remain in this transitory life. They are exempted from sorrow, need, and sickness, and from a possibility of any future adversity, and enjoy a perfect quiet and rest from their labours. They shall hunger no more, neither thirst any more; neither shall the sun light on them; nor any heat: the Lord God shall wipe all tears from their eyes, and sorrow and sighing shall flee away.

Add to this that they are freed from the tyranny of sin, a yoke they could never hope to cast off entirely as long as they carried about them those mortal bodies in which the seeds of corruption were so deeply implanted. The law of our members is now continually warring against the law of our mind, and even when we would do good, evil is present with us. But we lay down these infirmities with this veil of flesh, and the spirit will then be able as well as willing to perform its duty; and the more sensible we are of our present weakness, the more shall we rejoice at our deliverance from it. What a satisfaction must it be to a good man to perceive the good works he had begun in this life continued and perfected in himself, to find every one of those Christian virtues with which he had endeavoured to adorn his soul improved and drawn out to its utmost extent!

And it will be no small addition to his happiness that he has a lively sense of the farther glory reserved for him. St. Peter observes that pious men, even in manifold temptations, rejoice with joy unspeakable and full of glory when they contemplate the inheritance of which they will one day be made partakers. How inconceivable then must be their joy when they see it no longer through a glass darkly, but have a full and clear prospect of that crown of righteousness which the Lord, the righteous Judge, has appointed for them; when they are no longer tormented with fears of falling away and coming short of the reward they have in view, being already possessed of a partial happiness, as an earnest of one more complete and perfect.

Now if the reward of the just even before the day of final retribution will be so inexpressibly, so inconceivably great and glorious; if their happiness be so great already, and will nevertheless be still greater, what shall we say of the state of just men made perfect? When to the absence of all evil shall be added the presence of all the good that a Being of infinite wisdom and power is able to bestow? When God shall make them possess the fullness of joy at his own right hand for evermore, and drink of the rivers of pleasure in the new Jerusalem? Very excellent things are indeed spoken of thee, O thou city of God! But who, even with the tongue of men and angels, can worthily describe what eye hath not seen nor ear heard, neither hath it entered into the heart of man to conceive!

Seeing, then, all these things are for our sakes; seeing we have the promise of perfect happiness annexed to our obedience, of "an inheritance incorruptible, undefiled, and that fadeth not away;" "what manner of men ought we to be in all holy conversation and godliness!" What diligence, even according to human prudence, should we use to make our calling and election sure! With what unconcern should we encounter all temporal afflictions, with what patience, yea, cheerfulness, shall we face death itself, so terrible to the natural man, when we are assured that all these things work together for our good, and will entitle us to an eternal weight of glory! When we are defamed, reviled, or despitefully treated by men, let us comfort ourselves with the firm persuasion that we shall soon rest where the wicked cease from troubling. If we are at any time oppressed with a sense of our infirmities, or discouraged by the mortifying reflection that this body, however now set off with outward advantages or adorned with the bloom of youth and beauty, must shortly be resolved into its principles of dust and ashes; let us reflect at the same time that God will not leave our soul in hell, but in his own good time reunite it to its ancient companion; and that then this corruptible shall put on incorruption, and this mortal be clothed with immortality; finally, that though after our skin worms destroy this body, yet even in our flesh shall we see God.

Seek ye first the kingdom of God, and his righteousness,
and all these things shall be added unto you.
Matthew 6:33

The kingdom which our blessed Lord here requires us to seek is that which he himself assures us is not of this world. All things here are subject to corruption or decay. But the crown which God has prepared for those who diligently seek it is incorruptible and fadeth not away. But lest we should imagine any to have a claim to these eternal mansions beside those that do the will of their heavenly Father, we are expressly commanded to seek his righteousness as well as his kingdom: which word, though in the strictest sense it contains only our duty to our neighbour, yet implies here, as in many other places of Holy Scripture, the sum of the Christian religion. Whatever virtues are recommended to us by reason, especially as assisted by revelation, whatsoever things are lovely, whatsoever things are pure—in a word, the whole of our duty both towards God, ourselves, and our neighbour—are here included in the word "righteousness." And although this may in one sense be said to be ours, as being in some measure owing to our own endeavours, working together with the Holy Spirit of God, yet is it very justly ascribed to him and termed his righteousness, since he is the confirmer and perfecter, as well as the infuser of it.

The attainment of this, and the kingdom of God, which is no other way attainable, we are here directed to make our first, as well as our chief study; to consider in the beginning of every undertaking whether it be proper or likely in any degree to promote the glory of God, or peace and goodwill among men—the great end and design of all religion; in a word (it not being my purpose to descend to particular duties) to let it be always our first care to observe those great commandments under which our Saviour comprises the whole duty of a Christian, "Thou shalt love the Lord thy God with all thy heart, with all thy soul, and with all thy mind": with the whole bias of thy understanding, thy will, and thy affections; and, "Thou shalt love thy neighbour," that is, every man, "as thyself."

Forgiveness & Assurance
1725

Important to Wesley's early doctrine of holiness was his belief in the present forgiveness of sin, though at this time he did not equate forgiveness with present justification. This will come later when he embraces his new gospel in 1738 (Section Two). Still, this insight is critical to properly grasp how early Wesley correlated perfection to eternal salvation. Source: Telford.

To his Mother
June 18, 1725.

Wesley quotes Thomas `a Kempis:

> *A true penitent must all the days of his life pray for pardon and never think the work completed till he dies. Whether God has forgiven us or no we know not, therefore still be sorrowful for ever having sinned.*

I take the more notice of this last sentence, because it seems to contradict his own words in the next section, where he says that by the Lord's Supper all the members are united to one another and to Christ the head: the Holy Ghost confers on us the graces we pray for, and our souls receive into them the seeds of an immortal nature. Now, surely these graces are not of so little force, as that we can't perceive whether we have them or no; and if we dwell in Christ, and Christ in us, which He will not do till we are regenerate, certainly we must be sensible of it. If his opinion be true, I must own I have always been in a great error; for I imagined that when I communicated worthily, i.e. with faith, humility, and thankfulness, my preceding sins were *ipso facto* forgiven me. I mean, so forgiven that, unless I fell into them again, I might be secure of their ever rising in judgment against me at least in the other world. But if we can never have any certainty of our being in a state of salvation, good reason it is that every moment should be spent not in joy but fear and trembling; and then undoubtedly in this life *we are* of all men most miserable!

God deliver us from such a fearful expectation as this! Humility is undoubtedly necessary to salvation; and if all these things are essential to humility, who can be humble, who can be saved?

Seeking After Holiness
1730-31

The following letters offer further insights into Wesley's early perfection theology. The first letter explores the correlation between sanctification and final forgiveness. Wesley's point, though muddled in expression, is not that forgiveness is sanctification, but that sanctification serves as the ground for forgiveness at the final judgment (note Wesley's comment at the end). This letter must be read in light of the prior one. Both letters reveal that early Wesley already held to two senses of forgiveness, one present and one future, with the latter intertwined with full sanctification.

The second letter addresses how perfection is attained through the means of grace, and the third one examines the nature of genuine love to God. The fourth letter gives clarification to Wesley's early views on sin and holiness. Note the distinctions made between habitual and single acts of sin, and the degree of deliverance attainable in this life. These are significant qualifiers in Wesley's early doctrine of inward holiness. Source: Telford.

To his Mother
February 28, 1730.

As faith is distinguished from other species of assent, from knowledge particularly, by the difference of the evidence it is built on, may we not find the same foundation for distinguishing hope from faith as well as from knowledge? Is not the evidence on which we build it less simple than that of faith, and less demonstrative than the arguments that create knowledge? It seems to have one of its feet fixed on the Word of God, the other on our opinion of our own sincerity, and so to be a persuasion that we shall enjoy the good things of God, grounded on His promises made to sincere Christians, and on an opinion that we are sincere Christians ourselves. Agreeably to this, Bishop Taylor himself says in his Rules for Dying: "We are to be curious of our duty and confident of the article of remission of sins, and the conclusion of those promises will be that we shall be full of hopes of a prosperous resurrection." Every one, therefore, who inquires into the grounds of his own hope reasons in this manner:

If God be true, and I am sincere, then I am to hope;
But God is true, and I am sincere (there is the pinch);
Therefore I am to hope.

What I so much like is his account of the pardon of sins, which is the clearest I ever met with:

Pardon of sins in the gospel is sanctification. Christ came to take away our sins, by turning every one of us from our iniquities (Acts 3:26). And there is not in the nature of the thing any expectation of pardon, or sign or signification of it, but so far as the thing itself discovers itself. As we hate sin, grow in grace, and arrive at the state of holiness, which is also a state of repentance and imperfection, but yet of sincerity of heart and diligent endeavor; in the same degree we are to judge concerning the forgiveness of sins. For, indeed, that is the evangelical forgiveness, and it signifies our pardon, because it effects it, or rather it is in the nature of the thing, so that we are to inquire into no hidden records. Forgiveness of sins is not a secret sentence, a word, or a record, but it is a state of change effected upon us; and upon ourselves we are to look for it, to read it and understand it. (*Holy Dying*, chap. v. sect. 5)

In all this he appears to steer in the middle road exactly, to give assurance of pardon to the penitent, but to no one else.

To Mary Granville
December 12, 1730.

Madam,

I could say that if our ultimate end is the love of God, to which the several particular Christian virtues lead us, so the means leading to these are to communicate every possible time, and, whatsoever we do, to pray without ceasing; not to be content with our solemn devotions, whether public or private, but at all times and in all places to make fervent returns "by ejaculations" and "abrupt intercourses of the mind with God" to thrust "these between all our other employments," if it be only by a word, a thought, a look, always remembering:

> *If I but lift my eyes, my suit is made!*
> *Thou canst no more not hear than Thou canst die!*

To account what of frailty remains after this a necessary encumbrance of flesh and blood, such an one as God out of His mercy to us will not yet remove, as seeing it to be useful though grievous; yet still to hope that since we seek Him "in a time when He may be found," before the great water-flood hath overwhelmed us, He will in His good time "quell the raging of this sea, and still the waves thereof when they arise." To you, who know them so well, I can but just mention these considerations, which I would press upon another: yet let me beg you to believe that though I want the power I have the most sincere desire of approving myself.

To Mary Pendarves
February 11, 1731

Who (Mrs. Pendarves) can be a fitter person than one that knows it by experience to tell me the full force of that glorious rule, 'Set your affections on things above, and not on things of the earth'? Is it equivalent to 'Thou shalt love the Lord thy God with all thy heart, soul, and strength'? But what is it to love God? Is not to love anything the same as habitually to delight in it? Is not, then, the purport of both these injunctions this, that we delight in the Creator more than His creatures; that we take more pleasure in Him than in anything He has made, and rejoice in nothing so much as in serving Him; that (to take Mr. Pascal's expression) while the generality of men use God and enjoy the world, we on the contrary only use the world while we enjoy God?

To Ann Granville
October 3, 1731

One that is generous, charitable, and devout, that has an easy fortune and many sincere friends, is yet unhappy; something lurking within poisons all the sweets, nor can she taste any of the goodness she enjoys. She strives against it, but in vain. She spends her strength, but to no purpose—her enemy still renews his strength—nature even:

> *When 'gainst his head her sacred arms she bent*
> *Strict watch, and fast severe, and prayer omnipotent.*

Still he pursues her prayer; still he wounds her doubts and scruples of various sorts, so as to make the very ways of pleasantness uneasy and the path of life like that which leads to destruction.

And is there no help? Yes. If Selima can believe, all things are possible to her that believeth. The shield of faith will yet repel all darts, if she can be taught to use it skillfully; if the eyes of her understanding can be enlightened to see what is the hope of her calling: to know that our hope is sincerity, not perfection; not to do well, but to do our best. If God were to mark all that is done amiss, who could abide it? Not the great Apostle himself, who, even when he had finished his course on earth and was ripe for paradise, yet mentions himself as not having already attained that height, not being already perfect.

Perfect, indeed, he was from sin, strictly speaking, which is a voluntary breach of a known law; at least from habits of such sin: as to single acts, he knew whom he had believed. He knew who had promised to forgive these, not seven times but seventy times seven. Nay, a thousand times a thousand, if they sincerely desire it, shall all sins be forgiven unto the sons of men. We need except none; no, not the sin against the Holy Ghost, for in truth this phrase is nowhere in the whole sacred book. "The sin against the Holy Ghost" is a term invented by the devil to perplex those whom he cannot destroy. The term used by God is the blasphemy against the Holy Ghost, a phrase that instantly shuts out all thoughts and accusations, for blasphemy must be a speech; and what speech it is Christ has expressly told us in Mark 3:22, 29, 30: "He hath Beelzebub, and by the prince of the devils casteth He out devils."

Shall He not cast out by the finger of God that anxiety which they have instilled in His servant? Shall He not avenge her that cries to Him day and night, though (for wise reasons) He bear long with her enemies? I trust He shall avenge her speedily. At last, if she ceases not to cry unto Him to deliver her from her weakness, then let her be assured it shall not be in vain: for God is in the cry, but not in the weakness.

I do not say that she shall immediately be delivered: nor yet are her good dispositions lost; seeing there is a reward for suffering as well as for acting, and blessed are they that endure temptation. God has given them a means of improving their good dispositions, which is not given to the rest of the world; a means which supplies the want of activity and gives them all the advantage of a busy life without the dangers. This is the surest, it is the shortest way, as to all virtue, so particularly to humility, the distinguishing virtue of Christians, the sole inlet to all virtue.

The Circumcision of the Heart
1733

This is the landmark sermon of Wesley's early period. Hence it demands a careful reading. By late 1732 criticism around Oxford was mounting against the methodical practices of Wesley's Holy Club. In response he carefully crafted this homily and preached it at St. Mary's on January 1, 1733.

The reader should pay close attention to how perfection is defined, explained and defended in this homily. Also, note how Wesley explains humility, faith, hope and love. These four virtues serve as stages in Wesley's early ordo salutis. But his understanding of the latter three virtues will change significantly over time (cf. footnote at I.7). Moreover, be attentive to the robust pneumatology in this sermon, grounded on the atonement of Christ, offering assurance to the single-minded Christian. The Holy Spirit will take on a more pronounced role in Wesley's perfection theology after this. Source: Works J 5:202-212.

> Circumcision is that of the heart, in the spirit
> and not in the letter.
>
> Romans 2:29

1. It is the melancholy remark of an excellent man, that he who now preaches the most essential duties of Christianity, runs the hazard of being esteemed, by a great part of his hearers, "a setter forth of new doctrines." Most men have so lived away the substance of that religion, the profession whereof they still retain, that no sooner are any of those truths proposed which difference the Spirit of Christ from the spirit of the world, than they cry out, "Thou bringest strange things to our ears; we would know what these things mean"—Though he is only preaching to them "Jesus and the resurrection," with the necessary consequence of it, If Christ be risen, ye ought then to die unto the world, and to live wholly unto God.

2. A hard saying this to the natural man, who is alive unto the world, and dead unto God; and one that he will not readily be

The Circumcision of the Heart

persuaded to receive as the truth of God, unless it be so qualified in the interpretation, as to have neither use nor significancy left. He "receiveth not the" words "of the Spirit of God," taken in their plain and obvious meaning; "they are foolishness unto him: Neither" indeed "can he know them, because they are spiritually discerned"—They are perceivable only by that spiritual sense, which in him was never yet awakened; for want of which he must reject, as idle fancies of men, what are both the wisdom and the power of God.

3. That "circumcision is that of the heart, in the spirit, and not in the letter;" that the distinguishing mark of a true follower of Christ, of one who is in a state of acceptance with God, is not either outward circumcision, or baptism, or any other outward form, but a right state of soul, a mind and spirit renewed after the image of Him that created it; is one of those important truths that can only he spiritually discerned. And this the Apostle himself intimates in the next words, "Whose praise is not of men, but of God." As if he had said, "Expect not, whoever thou art, who thus followest thy great Master, that the world, the men who follow him not, will say, 'Well done, good and faithful servant!' Know that the circumcision of the heart, the seal of thy calling, is foolishness with the world. Be content to wait for thy applause till the day of thy Lord's appearing. In that day shalt thou have praise of God, in the great assembly of men and angels."

I design, First, particularly to inquire, wherein this circumcision of the heart consists; and, Secondly, to mention some reflections that naturally arise from such an inquiry.

I. 1. I am, First, to inquire, wherein that circumcision of the heart consists, which will receive the praise of God. In general we may observe, it is that *habitual disposition* of soul which, in the sacred writings, is termed holiness; and which directly implies, the being cleansed from sin, "from all filthiness both of flesh and spirit;" and, by consequence, the being endued with those virtues which

15

were also in Christ Jesus; the being so "renewed in the spirit of our mind," as to be "perfect as our Father in heaven is perfect."

2. To be more particular: Circumcision of heart implies humility, faith, hope, and charity. Humility, a right judgment of ourselves, cleanses our minds from those high conceits of our own perfections, from that undue opinion of our own abilities and attainments, which are the genuine fruit of a corrupted nature. This entirely cuts off that vain thought, "I am rich, and wise, and have need of nothing;" and convinces us that we are by nature "wretched, and poor, and miserable, and blind, and naked." It convinces us, that in our best estate we are, of ourselves, all sin and vanity; that confusion, and ignorance, and error reign over our understanding; that unreasonable, earthly, sensual, devilish passions usurp authority over our will; in a word, that there is no whole part in our soul, that all the foundations of our nature are out of course.

3. At the same time we are convinced, that we are not sufficient of ourselves to help ourselves; that, without the Spirit of God, we can do nothing but add sin to sin; that it is He alone who worketh in us by his almighty power, either to will or do that which is good; it being as impossible for us even to think a good thought, without the supernatural assistance of his Spirit, as to create ourselves, or to renew our whole souls in righteousness and true holiness.

4. A sure effect of our having formed this right judgment of the sinfulness and helplessness of our nature, is a disregard of that "honour which cometh of man," which is usually paid to some supposed excellency in us. He who knows himself, neither desires nor values the applause which he knows he deserves not. It is therefore "a very small thing with him, to be judged by man's judgment." He has all reason to think, by comparing what it has said, either for or against him, with what he feels in his own breast, that the world, as well as the god of this world, was "a liar

from the beginning." And even as to those who are not of the world; though he would choose, if it were the will of God, that they should account of him as of one desirous to be found a faithful steward of his Lord's goods, if haply this might be a means of enabling him to be of more use to his fellow-servants, yet as this is the one end of his wishing for their approbation, so he does not at all rest upon it: For he is assured, that whatever God wills, he can never want instruments to perform; since he is able, even of these stones, to raise up servants to do his pleasure.

5. This is that lowliness of mind, which they have learned of Christ, who follow his example and tread in his steps. And this knowledge of their disease, whereby they are more and more cleansed from one part of it, pride and vanity, disposes them to embrace, with a willing mind, the second thing implied in circumcision of the heart, that faith which alone is able to make them whole, which is the one medicine given under heaven to heal their sickness.

6. The best guide of the blind, the surest light of them that are in darkness, the most perfect instructor of the foolish, is faith. But it must be such a faith as is "mighty through God, to the pulling down of strong-holds,"—to the overturning all the prejudices of corrupt reason, all the false maxims revered among men, all evil customs and habits, all that "wisdom of the world which is foolishness with God;" as "casteth down imaginations," reasonings, "and every high thing that exalteth itself against the knowledge of God, and bringeth into captivity every thought to the obedience of Christ."

7. "All things are possible to him that" thus "believeth." "The eyes of his understanding being enlightened," he sees what is his calling; even to glorify God, who hath bought him with so high a price, in his body and in his spirit, which now are God's by redemption, as well as by creation. He feels what is "the exceeding greatness of his power," who, as he raised up Christ from the

dead, so is able to quicken us, dead in sin, "by his Spirit which dwelleth in us." "This is the victory which overcometh the world, even our faith;" that faith, which is not only an unshaken assent to all that God hath revealed in Scripture, and in particular to those important truths, "Jesus Christ came into the world to save sinners;" "He bare our sins in his own body on the tree;" "He is the propitiation for our sins, and not for ours only, but also for the sins of the whole world."[1]

8. Such a faith as this cannot fail to show evidently the power of Him that inspires it, by delivering his children from the yoke of sin, and "purging their consciences from dead works;" by strengthening them so, that they are no longer constrained to obey sin in the desires thereof; but instead of "yielding their members unto it, as instruments of unrighteousness," they now "yield themselves" entirely "unto God, as those that are alive from the dead."

9. Those who are thus by faith born of God, have also strong consolation through hope. This is the next thing which the circumcision of the heart implies; even the testimony of their own spirit with the Spirit which witnesses in their hearts that they are the children of God. Indeed it is the same Spirit who works in them that clear and cheerful confidence that their heart is upright to-

---

[1] In 1748 Wesley added the following addition to make the sermon more in line with his new understanding of the gospel:

But likewise the revelation of Christ in our hearts; a divine evidence or conviction of his love, his free, unmerited love to me a sinner; a sure confidence in his pardoning mercy, wrought in us by the Holy Ghost; a confidence, whereby every true believer is enabled to bear witness, "I know that my Redeemer liveth," that I have an "Advocate with the Father," and that "Jesus Christ the righteous" is my Lord, and "the propitiation for my sins,"—I know he hath "loved me, and given himself for me,"—He hath reconciled me, even me, to God; and I "have redemption through his blood, even the forgiveness of sins."

18

ward God; that good assurance, that they now do, through his grace, the things which are acceptable in his sight; that they are now in the path which leadeth to life, and shall, by the mercy of God, endure therein to the end. It is He who giveth them a lively expectation of receiving all good things at God's hand; a joyous prospect of that crown of glory, which is reserved in heaven for them. By this anchor a Christian is kept steady in the midst of the waves of this troublesome world, and preserved from striking upon either of those fatal rocks, presumption or despair. He is neither discouraged by the misconceived severity of his Lord, nor does he "despise the riches of his goodness." He neither apprehends the difficulties of the race set before him to be greater than he has strength to conquer, nor expects them to be so little as to yield in the conquest, till he has put forth all his strength. The experience he already has in the Christian warfare, as it assures him his "labour is not in vain," if "whatever his hand findeth to do, he doeth it with his might;" so it forbids his entertaining so vain a thought, as that he can otherwise gain any advantage, as that any virtue can be shown, any praise attained, by faint hearts and feeble hands; or, indeed, by any but those who pursue the same course with the great Apostle of the Gentiles: "I," says he, "so run, not as uncertainly; so fight I, not as one that beateth the air. But I keep under my body, and bring it into subjection; lest, by any means, when I have preached to others, I myself should be a castaway."

10. By the same discipline is every good soldier of Christ to inure himself to endure hardship. Confirmed and strengthened by this, he will be able not only to renounce the works of darkness, but every appetite too, and every affection, which is not subject to the law of God. For "every one," saith St. John, "who hath this hope, purifieth himself even as He is pure." It is his daily care, by the grace of God in Christ, and through the blood of the covenant, to purge the inmost recesses of his soul from the lusts that before possessed and defiled it; from uncleanness, and envy, and malice, and wrath; from every passion and temper that is after the flesh,

that either springs from or cherishes his native corruption. As well knowing, that he whose very body is the temple of God, ought to admit into it nothing common or unclean; and that holiness becometh that house for ever, where the Spirit of holiness vouchsafes to dwell.

11. Yet lackest thou one thing, whosoever thou art, that to a deep humility, and a steadfast faith, hast joined a lively hope, and thereby in a good measure cleansed thy heart from its inbred pollution. If thou wilt be perfect, add to all these, charity; add love, and thou hast the circumcision of the heart. "Love is the fulfilling of the law, the end of the commandment." Very excellent things are spoken of love; it is the essence, the spirit, the life of all virtue. It is not only the first and great command, but it is all the commandments in one. "Whatsoever things are just, whatsoever things are pure, whatsoever things are amiable," or honourable; "if there be any virtue, if there be any praise," they are all comprised in this one word, love. In this is perfection, and glory, and happiness. The royal law of heaven and earth is this, "Thou shalt love the Lord thy God with all thy heart, and with all thy soul, and with all thy mind, and with all thy strength."

12. Not that this forbids us to love anything besides God: It implies that we love our brother also. Nor yet does it forbid us (as some have strangely imagined) to take pleasure in any thing but God. To suppose this, is to suppose the Fountain of holiness is directly the author of sin; since he has inseparably annexed pleasure to the use of those creatures which are necessary to sustain the life he has given us. This, therefore, can never be the meaning of his command. What the real sense of it is, both our blessed Lord and his Apostles tell us too frequently, and too plainly, to be misunderstood. They all with one mouth bear witness, that the true meaning of those several declarations—"The Lord thy God is one Lord." "Thou shalt have no other gods but me." "Thou shalt love the Lord thy God with all thy strength." "Thou shalt cleave unto him." "The desire of thy soul shall be to

his name"—is no other than this: The one perfect Good shall be your one ultimate end. One thing shall ye desire for its own sake, the fruition of Him that is All in all. One happiness shall ye propose to your souls, even an union with Him that made them; the having "fellowship with the Father and the Son;" the being joined to the Lord in one Spirit. One design you are to pursue to the end of time, the enjoyment of God in time and in eternity. Desire other things, so far as they tend to this. Love the creature as it leads to the Creator. But in every step you take, be this the glorious point that terminates your view. Let every affection and thought, and word, and work, be subordinate to this. Whatever ye desire or fear, whatever ye seek or shun, whatever ye think, speak, or do, be it in order to your happiness in God, the sole End, as well as Source, of your being.

13. Have no end, no ultimate end, but God. Thus our Lord, "One thing is needful." And if thine eye be singly fixed on this one thing, "thy whole body shall be full of light." Thus St. Paul, "This one thing I do; I press toward the mark, for the prize of the high calling in Christ Jesus." Thus St. James, "Cleanse your hands, ye sinners, and purify your hearts, ye double-minded." Thus St. John, "Love not the world, neither the things that are in the world. For all that is in the world, the lust of the flesh, the lust of the eye, and the pride of life, is not of the Father, but is of the world." The seeking happiness in what gratifies either the desire of the flesh, by agreeably striking upon the outward senses; the desire of the eye, of the imagination, by its novelty, greatness, or beauty; or the pride of life, whether by pomp, grandeur, power, or, the usual consequence of them, applause and admiration—"is not of the Father," cometh not from, neither is approved by, the Father of spirits; "but of the world." It is the distinguishing mark of those who will not have Him to reign over them.

II. 1. Thus have I particularly inquired, what that circumcision of heart is, which will obtain the praise of God. I am, in the Second place, to mention some reflections that naturally arise from such an inquiry, as a plain rule whereby every man may judge of himself, whether he be of the world or of God.

And, First, it is clear from what has been said, that no man has a title to the praise of God, unless his heart is circumcised by humility; unless he is little, and base, and vile in his own eyes; unless he is deeply convinced of that inbred "corruption of his nature," "whereby he is very far gone from original righteousness," being prone to all evil, averse to all good, corrupt and abominable; having a "carnal mind which is enmity against God, and is not subject to the law of God, nor indeed can be;" unless he continually feels in his inmost soul, that without the Spirit of God resting upon him, he can neither think, nor desire, nor speak, nor act anything good, or well-pleasing in his sight. No man, I say, has a title to the praise of God, till he feels his want of God; nor indeed, till he seeketh that "honour which cometh of God only;" and neither desires nor pursues that which cometh of man, unless so far only as it tends to this.

2. Another truth, which naturally follows from what has been said, is, that none shall obtain the honour that cometh of God, unless his heart be circumcised by faith; even a "faith of the operation of God." Unless, refusing to be any longer led by his senses, appetites, or passions, or even by that blind leader of the blind, so idolized by the world, natural reason, he lives and walks by faith; directs every step, as "seeing Him that is invisible;" "looks not at the things that are seen, which are temporal, but at the things that are not seen, which are eternal;" and governs all his desires, designs, and thoughts, all his actions and conversations, as one who is entered in within the veil, where Jesus sits at the right hand of God.

3. It were to be wished, that they were better acquainted with this faith, who employ much of their time and pains in laying another foundation; in grounding religion on the eternal fitness of things, on the intrinsic excellence of virtue, and the beauty of actions

flowing from it; on the reasons, as they term them, of good and evil, and the relations of beings to each other. Either these accounts of the grounds of Christian duty coincide with the scriptural, or not. If they do, why are well-meaning men perplexed, and drawn from the weightier matters of the law, by a cloud of terms, whereby the easiest truths are explained into obscurity? If they are not, then it behoves them to consider who is the author of this new doctrine; whether he is likely to be an angel from heaven, who preacheth another gospel than that of Christ Jesus; though, if he were, God, not we, hath pronounced his sentence: "Let him be accursed."

4. Our gospel, as it knows no other foundation of good works than faith, or of faith than Christ, so it clearly informs us, we are not his disciples while we either deny him to be the Author, or his Spirit to be the Inspirer and Perfecter, both of our faith and works. "If any man have not the Spirit of Christ, he is none of his." He alone can quicken those who are dead unto God, can breathe into them the breath of Christian life, and so prevent, accompany, and follow them with his grace, as to bring their good desires to good effect. And, "as many as are thus led by the Spirit of God, they are the sons of God." This is God's short and plain account of true religion and virtue; and "other foundation can no man lay."

5. From what has been said, we may, Thirdly, learn, that none is truly "led by the Spirit," unless that "Spirit bear witness with his spirit, that he is a child of God;" unless he see the prize and the crown before him, and "rejoice in hope of the glory of God." So greatly have they erred who have taught that, in serving God, we ought not to have a view to our own happiness! Nay, but we are often and expressly taught of God, to have "respect unto the recompence of reward;" to balance the toil with the "joy set before us," these "light afflictions" with that "exceeding weight of glory." Yea, we are "aliens to the covenant of promise," we are "without God in the world," until God, "of his abundant mercy,

hath begotten us again unto a living hope of the inheritance incorruptible, undefiled, and that fadeth not away."

6. But if these things are so, it is high time for those persons to deal faithfully with their own souls, who are so far from finding in themselves this joyful assurance that they fulfil the terms, and shall obtain the promises, of that covenant, as to quarrel with the covenant itself, and blaspheme the terms of it, to complain, they are too severe; and that no man ever did or shall live up to them. What is this but to reproach God, as if he were a hard Master, requiring of his servants more than he enables them to perform?— as if he had mocked the helpless works of his hands, by binding them to impossibilities; by commanding them to overcome, where neither their own strength nor his grace was sufficient for them?

7. These blasphemers might almost persuade those to imagine themselves guiltless, who, in the contrary extreme, hope to fulfil the commands of God, without taking any pains at all. Vain hope! that a child of Adam should ever expect to see the kingdom of Christ and of God, without striving, without agonizing, first "to enter in at the strait gate"—that one who was "conceived and born in sin," and whose "inward parts are very wickedness," should once entertain a thought of being "purified as his Lord is pure," unless he tread in His steps, and "take up his cross daily;" unless he "cut off his right hand," and "pluck out the right eye, and cast it from him"—that he should ever dream of shaking of his old opinions, passions, tempers, of being "sanctified throughout in spirit, soul, and body," without a constant and continued course of general self-denial!

8. What less than this can we possibly infer from the above-cited words of St. Paul, who, living "in infirmities, in reproaches, in necessities, in persecutions, in distresses" for Christ's sake;— who, being full of "signs, and wonders," and mighty deeds, who, having been "caught up into the third heaven"—yet reckoned, as

a late author strongly expresses it, that all his virtues would be insecure, and even his salvation in danger, without this constant self-denial? "So run I," says he, "not as uncertainly; so fight, not as one that beateth the air." By which he plainly teaches us, that he who does not thus run, who does not thus deny himself daily, does run uncertainly, and fighteth to as little purpose as he that "beateth the air."

9. To as little purpose does he talk of "fighting the fight of faith," as vainly hope to attain the crown of incorruption, (as we may, Lastly, infer from the preceding observations,) whose heart is not circumcised by love. Love, cutting off both the lust of the flesh, the lust of the eye, and the pride of life, engaging the whole man, body, soul, and spirit, in the ardent pursuit of that one object, is so essential to a child of God, that, without it, whosoever liveth is counted dead before him. "Though I speak with the tongues of men and of angels, and have not love, I am as sounding brass, or a tinkling cymbal. Though I have the gift of prophecy, and understand all mysteries, and all knowledge; and though I have all faith, so as to remove mountains, and have not love, I am nothing." Nay, "though I give all my goods to feed the poor, and my body to be burned, and have not love, it profiteth me nothing."

10. Here, then, is the sum of the perfect law; this is the true circumcision of the heart. Let the spirit return to God that gave it, with the whole train of its affections. "Unto the place from whence all the rivers came," thither let them flow again. Other sacrifices from us he would not; but the living sacrifice of the heart he hath chosen. Let it be continually offered up to God through Christ, in flames of holy love. And let no creature be suffered to share with him: For he is a jealous God. His throne will he not divide with another: He will reign without a rival. Be no design, no desire admitted there, but what has Him for its ultimate object. This is the way wherein those children of God once walked, who, being dead, still speaks to us: "Desire not to live, but to praise his name: Let all your thoughts, words, and works,

tend to his glory. Set your heart firm on him and on other things only as they are in and from him. Let your soul be filled with so entire a love of him that you may love nothing but for his sake." "Have a pure intention of heart, a steadfast regard to his glory in all your actions." "Fix your eye upon the blessed hope of your calling, and make all the things of the world minister unto it." For then, and not till then, is that "mind in us which was also in Christ Jesus;" when, in every motion of our heart, in every word of our tongue, in every work of our hands, we "pursue nothing but in relation to him, and in subordination to his pleasure;" when we, too, neither think, nor speak, nor act, to fulfill our "own will, but the will of him that sent us;" when, whether we "eat, or drink, or whatever we do, we do all to the glory of God."

Preface to a Collection of Prayers
1733

Since Wesley was an ardent seeker of inward holiness, he became keenly interested in delineating the path to attaining such holiness. One way he did this was by making lists of Christian duties outlining stages of development. What is written here should be compared to what he wrote on humility, faith, hope and love in The Circumcision of the Heart. *Both express Wesley's early* ordo salutis. *We also see the imprint of his early pneumatology under the motif of Christ's indwelling. But note there is no evangelical explanation of the cross. Source: Sixth Edition, Works J 14:270-272. The first edition was in 1733.*

The intention of the collector of these prayers was, First, to have forms of prayer for every day in the week, each of which contained something of deprecation, petition, thanksgiving, and intercession. Secondly, to have such forms for those days which the Christian Church has ever judged peculiarly proper for religious rejoicing, as contained little of deprecation, but were explicit and large in acts of love and thanksgiving. Thirdly, to have such for those days which from the age of the Apostles have been set apart for religious mourning, as contained little of thanksgiving, but were full and express in acts of contrition and humiliation. Fourthly, to have intercessions every day for all those whom our own Church directs us to remember in our prayers. And, Fifthly, to comprise in the course of petitions for the week the whole scheme of our Christian duty.

Whoever follows the direction of our excellent Church, in the interpretation of the Holy Scriptures, by keeping close to that sense of them which the Catholic Fathers and ancient Bishops have delivered to succeeding generations, will easily see that the whole system of Christian duty is reducible to these five heads:

First: The renouncing ourselves. "If any man will come after me, let him renounce himself and follow me." This implies, 1. A thorough conviction that we are not our own; that we are not the proprietors of ourselves, or anything we enjoy; that we have no right to dispose of our goods, bodies, souls, or any of the actions or passions of them. 2. A solemn resolution to act suitably to this conviction: Not to live to ourselves; not to pursue our own desires; not to please ourselves; nor to suffer our own will to be any principle of action to us.

Secondly: Such a renunciation of ourselves naturally leads to the devoting of ourselves to God. As this implies, 1. A thorough conviction that we are God's; that He is the proprietor of all we are, and all we have; and that not only by right of creation, but of purchase; for He died for all, and therefore "died for all, that they which live should not henceforth live unto themselves, but unto Him that died for them."
2. A solemn resolution to act suitably to this conviction: To live unto God; to render unto God the things which are God's, even all we are, and all we have; to glorify Him in our bodies, and in our spirits, with all the powers and all the strength of each; and to make his will our sole principle of action.

Thirdly: Self-denial is the immediate consequence of this. For whosoever has determined to live no longer to the desires of men, but to the will of God, will soon find that he cannot be true to his purpose without denying himself, and taking up his cross daily. He will daily feel some desire which this one principle of action, the will of God, does not require him to indulge. In this, therefore, he must either deny himself, or so far deny the faith. He will daily meet with some means of drawing nearer to God, which are unpleasing to flesh and blood. In this, therefore, he must either take up his cross, or so far renounce his Master.

Fourthly: By a constant exercise of self-denial, the true follower of Christ continually advances in mortification. He is more and more dead to the world, and the things of the world, till at length he can say, with that perfect disciple of his Lord, Marquis de Renty: "I desire nothing but God." Or, with St. Paul: "I am crucified unto the world; I am dead with Christ; I live not, but Christ liveth in me."

Fifthly: Christ liveth in me. This is the fulfilling of the law, the last stage of Christian holiness: This maketh the man of God perfect. He that being dead to the world is alive to God; the desire of whose soul is unto his name; who has given Him his whole heart; who delights in Him, and in nothing else but what tends to Him; who, for his sake, burns with love to all mankind; who neither thinks, speaks, nor acts, but to fulfill his will, is on the last round of the ladder to heaven: Grace hath had its full work upon his soul: The next step he takes is into glory.

May the God of glory give unto us who have not already attained this, neither are already perfect, to do this one thing; forgetting those things which are behind, and reaching forth unto those things which are before, to press toward the mark for the prize of our high calling in Christ Jesus!

May He so enlighten our eyes, that we may reckon all things but loss for the excellency of the knowledge of Christ Jesus our Lord; and so stablish our hearts, that we may rejoice to suffer the loss of all things, and count them but dung, that we may win Christ!

The One Thing Needful
1734

The phrase one thing needful *is sprinkled throughout the Wesley corpus, but is defined differently in each period of his career. Here it expresses the essence of his early perfection theology: the inward transformation of the Christian's moral nature (holy tempers) into the image of God.* Imago Dei *became a basic staple in Wesley's theology, especially in his explication of full salvation. Be attentive to how Wesley articulates this process of renewal. Note his robust doctrine of original sin. Source: Works B 4:352-359.*

One thing is needful.

Luke 10:42

1. Could we suppose an intelligent being, entirely a stranger to the state of this world and its inhabitants, to take a view of their various enterprises and employments, and thence conjecture the end of their existence, he would surely conclude that these creatures were designed to be busied about many things. While he observed not only the infinite difference of the ends which different men were pursuing, but how vast a multitude of objects were successively pursued by almost every different person, he might fairly infer that for all these things were the sons of men placed upon the earth, even to gratify their several desires with sensual pleasure, or riches, or honour, or power.

2. How surprised then would he be to hear their Creator declare to all, without distinction, "One thing is needful!" But how much more when he knew that this one thing needful for men, their one business, the one end of their existence, was none of all those things which men were troubled about, none of all those ends they were pursuing, none of all those businesses wherein they were so deeply engaged, which filled their hearts and employed their hands. Nay, that it was an end not only distinct from but

30

contrary to them all—as contrary as light and darkness, heaven and hell, the kingdom of God and that of Satan!

3. The only thought he could form in their favour must be, that they had a surplusage of time at their command; that they therefore trifled a few hours, because they were assured of thousands of years wherein to work. But how beyond measure would he be amazed when he heard farther that these were creatures of a day; that as they yesterday arose out of the dust, so tomorrow they were to sink into it again; that the time they had for their great work was but a span long, a moment; and yet that they had no manner of assurance of not being snatched away in the midst of this moment, or indeed at the very beginning of it! When he saw that all men were placed on a narrow, weak, tottering bridge, whereof either end was swallowed up in eternity; that the waves and storms which went over it were continually bearing away one after another, in an hour when they looked not for it; and that they who yet stood, knew not but they should plunge into the great gulf the very next instant, but well knew that if they fell before they had finished their work they were lost, destroyed, undone—for ever: how would all utterance, nay, all thought, be lost! How would he express, how would he conceive the senselessness, the madness, of those creatures who, being in such a situation, could think of anything else, could talk of anything else, could do anything besides, could find time for any other design, or care, but that of ensuring the one thing needful!

4. It cannot, therefore, be an improper employment for us, first, to observe what this one thing needful is; and, secondly, to consider a few of the numberless reasons that prove this to be the one thing needful.

I. 1. We may observe what this one thing is, in which, 'tis true, many things are comprised—as are all the works of our callings, all that properly belong to our several stations in the world, insomuch that whoever neglects any of these so far neglects the one thing needful. And this indeed can no otherwise be pursued than by performing all the works of our calling, but performing them in such a manner as in and by every one to advance our great work.

2. Now this great work, this one thing needful, is the renewal of our fallen nature. In the image of God was man made, but a little lower than the angels. His nature was perfect, angelical, divine. He was an incorruptible picture of the God of glory. He bore his stamp on every part of his soul; the brightness of his Creator shone mightily upon him. But sin hath now effaced the image of God. He is no longer nearly allied to angels. He is sunk lower than the very beasts of the field. His soul is not only earthly and sensual, but devilish. Thus is the mighty fallen! The glory is departed from him! His brightness is swallowed up in utter darkness.

3. From the glorious liberty wherein he was made he is fallen into the basest bondage. The devil, whose slave he now is, to work his will, hath him so fast in prison that he cannot get forth. He hath bound him with a thousand chains, the heavy chains of his own vile affections. For every inordinate appetite, every unholy passion, as it is the express image of the god of this world, so it is the most galling yoke, the most grievous chain, that can bind a freeborn spirit. And with these is every child of Adam, everyone that is born into this world, so loaded that he cannot lift up an eye, a thought to heaven; that his whole soul cleaveth unto the dust!

4. But these chains of darkness under which we groan do not only hold us in on every side, but they are within us, too; they enter into our soul; they pierce through its inmost substance. Vile affections are not only so many chains, but likewise so many diseases. Our nature is distempered, as well as enslaved; the whole head is faint, and the whole heart sick. Our body, soul, and spirit, are infected, overspread, consumed, with the most fatal leprosy. We are all over, within and without, in the eye of God, full of

diseases, and wounds, and putrifying sores. Every one of our brutal passions and diabolical tempers, every kind of sensuality, pride, selfishness, is one of those deadly wounds, of those loathsome sores, full of corruption, and of all uncleanness.

5. To recover our first estate, from which we are thus fallen, is the one thing now needful—to re-exchange the image of Satan for the image of God, bondage for freedom, sickness for health. Our one great business is to rase out of our souls the likeness of our destroyer, and to be born again, to be formed anew after the likeness of our Creator. It is our one concern to shake off this servile yoke and to regain our native freedom; to throw off every chain, every passion and desire that does not suit an angelical nature. The one work we have to do is to return from the gates of death to perfect soundness; to have our diseases cured, our wounds healed, and our uncleanness done away.

II.1. Let us in the second place consider a few of the numberless reasons which prove that this is the one thing needful; so needful that this alone is to be had in view, and pursued at all times and in all places; not indeed by neglecting our temporal affairs, but by making them all minister unto it; by so conducting them all, that every step therein may be a step to this higher end.

2. Now, that the recovery of the image of God, of this glorious liberty, of this perfect soundness, is the one thing needful upon earth, appears first from hence, that the enjoyment of them was the one end of our creation. For to this end was man created, to love God; and to this end alone, even to love the Lord his God with all his heart, and soul, and mind, and strength. But love is the very image of God: it is the brightness of his glory. By love man is not only made like God, but in some sense one with him. "If any man love God, God loveth him, and cometh to him, and maketh his abode with him." He "dwelleth in God, and God in him;" and "he that is thus joined to the Lord is one spirit." Love is perfect freedom. As there is no fear, or pain, so there is no con-

straint in love. Whoever acts from this principle alone, he doth whatsoever he will. All his thoughts move freely; they follow the bent of his own mind, they run after the beloved object. All his words flow easy and unconstrained; for it is the abundance of the heart that dictates. All his actions are the result of pure choice: the thing he would, that he does, and that only. Love is the health of the soul, the full exertion of all its powers, the perfection of all its faculties. Therefore, since the enjoyment of these was the one end of our creation, the recovering of them is the one thing now needful.

3. May not the same truth appear, secondly, from hence, that this was the one end of our redemption; of all our blessed Lord did and suffered for us; of his incarnation, his life, his death? All these miracles of love were wrought with no other view than to restore us to health and freedom. Thus himself testifies of the end of his coming into the world: "The Spirit of the Lord is upon me; he hath sent me to heal the broken-hearted, to preach deliverance to the captives;" or, as the prophet expresses it, "to preach good tidings to the meek, to bind up the broken-hearted, to proclaim liberty to the captives, and the opening of the prison to them that are bound." For this only he lived, that he might heal every disease, every spiritual sickness of our nature. For this only he died, that he might deliver those who were all their lifetime subject to bondage. And it was in pursuance of the very same design that he gave us his merciful law. The end of his commandment, too, was only our health, liberty, perfection, or, to say all in one word, charity. All the parts of it centre in this one point, our renewal in the love of God; either enjoining what is necessary for our recovery thereof, or forbidding what is obstructive of it. Therefore this, being the one end of our redemption as well as our creation, is the one thing needful for us upon earth.

4. This is the one thing needful, thirdly, because it is the one end of all God's providential dispensations. Pleasure and pain, health and sickness, riches and poverty, honour and dishonour, friends

and enemies, are all bestowed by his unerring wisdom and goodness with a view to this one thing. The will of God, in allotting us
our several portions of all these, is solely our sanctification; our
recovery from that vile bondage, the love of his creatures, to the
free love of our Creator. All his providences, be they mild or severe, point at no other end than this. They are all designed either
to wean us from what is not, or to unite us to what is worthy our
affection. Are they pleasing? Then they are designed to lift up our
hearts to the Parent of all good. Are they painful? Then they are
means of rooting out those passions that forcibly withhold us
from him. So that all lead that same way, either directly or indirectly, either by gratitude or mortification. For to those that have
ears to hear, every loss, especially of what was nearest and dear-
est to them, speaks as clearly as if it were an articulate voice from
heaven, "Little children, keep yourselves from idols." Every pain
cries aloud, "Love not the world, neither the things of the world."
And every pleasure says, with a still small voice, "Thou shalt
love the Lord thy God with all thy heart."

5. To the same end are all the internal dispensations of God, all
the influences of his Holy Spirit. Whether he gives us joy or sorrow of heart, whether he inspires us with vigour and cheerfulness,
or permits us to sink into numbness of soul, into dryness and
heaviness, 'tis all with the same view, viz., to restore us to health,
to liberty, to holiness. These are all designed to heal those inbred
diseases of our nature, self-love, and the love of the world. They
are all given together with the daily bread of his external dispensations, to enable us to turn that into proper nourishment, and so
recover his love, the health of our souls. Therefore the renewal of
our nature in this love being not only the one end of our creation
and our redemption, but likewise of all the providences of God
over us, and all the operations of his Spirit in us, must be, as the
eternal wisdom of God hath declared, the one thing needful.

III. 1. How great reason is there, then, even in the Christian
world, to resume the Apostle's exhortation, "Awake, thou that

35

sleepest, and arise from the dead!" Hath not Christ given thee light? Why then sittest thou still in the shadow of death? What slumber is this which hangs on thy temples? Knowest thou not that only one thing is needful? What then are all these? Why hath any but that the least place in thy thoughts, the least share in thy affections? Is the entertainment of the senses the one thing needful? Or the gratifying the imagination with uncommon, or great, or beautiful objects? Our Lord saith not so. Saith he then that the one thing is to acquire a fortune, or to increase that thou hast already? I tell you, Nay: these may be the thoughts of those that dream, but they cannot [be those] of waking men. Is it to obtain honour, power, reputation, or (as the phrase is) to get preferment? Is the one thing to gain a large share in that fairest of the fruits of earth, learning? No. Though any of these may sometimes be conducive to, none of them is, the one thing needful. That is simply to escape out of the snare of the devil, to regain an angelical nature; to recover the image wherein we were formed; to be like the Most High. This, this alone, is the one end of our abode here; for this alone are we placed on the earth; for this alone did the Son of God pour out his blood; for this alone doth his Holy Spirit watch over us. One thing we have to do, to press towards this mark of the prize of our high calling; to emerge out of chains, diseases, death, into liberty, health, and life immortal!

2. Let us well observe, that our Lord doth not call this our main concern, our great business, the chief thing needful, but the one thing—all others being either parts of this or quite foreign to the end of life. On this then let us fix our single view, our pure unmixed intention; regarding nothing at all, small or great, but as it stands referred to this. We must use many means; but let us ever remember we have but one end. For as while our eye is single our whole body will be full of light, so, should it ever cease to be single, in that moment our whole body would be full of darkness.

3. Be we then continually jealous over our souls, that there be no mixture in our intention. Be it our one view in all our thoughts,

and words, and works, to be partakers of the divine nature, to re-gain the highest measure we can of that faith which works by love, and makes us become one spirit with God. I say, the highest measure we can; for who will plead for any abatement of health, liberty, life, and glory? Let us then labour to be made perfectly whole, to burst every bond in sunder; to attain the fullest con-quest over this body of death, the most entire renovation of our nature; knowing this, that when the Son of man shall send forth his angels to cast the double-minded into outer darkness, then shall the single of heart receive the one thing they sought, and shine forth as the sun in the kingdom of their Father!

Now to God the Father, God the Son, and God the Holy Ghost, be ascribed all honour and glory, adoration and worship, both now and for ever. Amen.

Holiness Defined
1734

In these brief definitions of authentic religion, holiness is defined as a temper of the heart, a ruling disposition in the soul. This same motif is found in The Circumcision of the Heart I.1 *and serves as the core definition of holiness in Wesley's perfection theology. What other motifs are present in these brief definitions? Source: Telford.*

To Richard Morgan, Sen.
January 15, 1734

Why, you say I am to incite him to live a sober, virtuous, and religious life. Nay, but first let us agree what religion is. I take religion to be, not the bare saying over so many prayers, morning and evening, in public or in private; not anything superadded now and then to a careless or worldly life; but a constant ruling habit of soul, a renewal of our minds in the image of God, a recovery of the divine likeness, a still-increasing conformity of heart and life to the pattern of our most holy Redeemer.

To Samuel Wesley, Sen.
December 10, 1734

By holiness I mean not fasting (as you seem to suppose), or bodily austerity, or any other external means of improvement, but the inward temper, to which all these are subservient, a renewal of the soul in the image of God. I mean a complex habit of lowliness, meekness, purity, faith, hope, and the love of God and man. And I therefore believe that, in the state wherein I am, I can most promote this holiness in myself, because I now enjoy several advantages which are almost peculiar to it.

The Trouble and Rest of Good Men
1735

This was Wesley's first published sermon and mirrors the motifs and text of his first homily ten years earlier (page 3). Written only days before his departure to America, it should be read in conjunction with The Circumcision of the Heart. *For as the latter homily might lead the reader to suppose that perfection can be attained in this life, this sermon settles the question beyond all doubt. In addition, take notice how sin and infirmities are correlated, and how perfection is developed around the theme of* rest. *Once again, Wesley's ars moriendi motif finds expression in this sermon. Source: Works J 7:365-372.*

There the wicked cease from troubling,
and there the weary be at rest.

Job 3:17

When God at first surveyed all the works he had made, "behold, they were very good." All were perfect in beauty; and man, the lord of all, was perfect in holiness. And as his holiness was, so was his happiness. Knowing no sin, he knew no pain; but when sin was conceived, it soon brought forth pain. The whole scene was changed in a moment. He now groaned under the weight of a mortal body, and, what was worse, a corrupted soul. That "spirit" which could have borne all his other "infirmities" was itself "wounded," and sick unto death. Thus, "in the day" wherein he sinned, he began to "die;" and thus "in the midst of life we are in death;" yea, "the whole creation groaneth together," being in bondage to sin, and therefore to misery.

The whole world is, indeed, in its present state, only one great infirmary. All that are therein are sick of sin; and their one business is to be healed. And for this very end, the great Physician of souls is continually present with them; marking all the diseases of every soul, "and giving medicines to heal its sickness." These medicines are often painful too: Not that God willingly afflicts his creatures, but he allots them just as much pain as is necessary to their health; and for that reason, because it is so.

The pain of cure must, then, be endured by every man, as well as the pain of sickness. And herein is manifest the infinite wisdom of Him who careth for us, that the very sickness of those with whom he converses may be a great means of every man's cure. The very wickedness of others is, in a thousand ways, conducive to a good man's holiness. They trouble him, it is true; but even that trouble is "health to his soul, and marrow to his bones." He suffers many things from them; but it is to this end, that he may be "made perfect through" those "sufferings."

But as perfect holiness is not found on earth, so neither is perfect happiness. Some remains of our disease will ever be felt, and some physic will be necessary to heal it. Therefore we must be, more or less, subject to the pain of cure, as well as the pain of sickness. And, accordingly, neither do "the wicked" here "cease from troubling," nor can "the weary be at rest."

Who, then, will "deliver" us "from the body of this death?" Death will deliver us. Death will set those free in a moment, who "were all their life-time subject to bondage." Death shall destroy at once the *whole body* of sin, and therewith its companion— pain. And therefore, "there the wicked cease from troubling; and there the weary be at rest." The Scriptures give us no account of the place where the souls of the just remain from death to the resurrection; but we have an account of their state in these words: In explaining which I shall consider,

I. How the wicked do here trouble good men; and,
II. How the weary are there at rest.

I. Let us consider, First, how the wicked here trouble good men. And this is a spacious field. Look round the world; take a view of all the troubles therein: How few are there of which the wicked are not the occasion! "From whence come wars and fightings among you?" Whence all the ills that embitter society; that often turn that highest of blessings into a curse, and make it "good for man to be alone?" "Come they not hence," from self-will, pride, inordinate affection? in one word, from wickedness? And can it be otherwise, so long as it remains upon earth? As well may "the Ethiopian change his skin," as a wicked man cease to trouble both himself and his neighbour, but especially good men: Inasmuch as, while he is wicked, he is continually injuring either them, or himself, or God.

1. First. Wicked men trouble those who serve God, by the injuries they do them. As at first, "he that was born after the flesh persecuted him that was born after the Spirit; even so it is now." And so it must be, till all things are fulfilled; "till heaven and earth pass away," "all that will live godly in Christ Jesus shall suffer persecution." For there is an irreconcilable enmity between the Spirit of Christ, and the spirit of the world. If the followers of Christ "were of the world, the world would love its own: But because they are not of the world, therefore the world hateth them." And this hatred they will not fail to show by their words: They will 'say all manner of evil against them falsely;" they will "find out many inventions" whereby even "the good that is in them may be evil spoken of;" and in a thousand instances lay to their charge the ill that they know not. From words, in due time, they proceed to deeds; treating the servants as their forefathers did their Master; wronging and despitefully using them in as many ways as fraud can invent, and force accomplish.

2. It is true, these troubles sit heaviest upon those who are yet weak in the faith; and the more of the Spirit of Christ any man gains, the lighter do they appear to him. So that to him who is truly renewed therein, who is full of the knowledge and love of God, all the wrongs of wicked men are not only no evils, but are matter of real and solid joy. But still, though he rejoices for his own sake, he cannot but grieve for theirs. He hath "great heaviness and continual sorrow in" his "heart, for" his "brethren according to the flesh," who are thus "treasuring up to themselves wrath against the day of wrath, and revelation of the righteous

judgment of God." His eyes weep for them in secret places; he is horribly afraid for them; yea, he "could wish to be accursed" himself, so they might inherit a blessing. And thus it is, that they who can not only slight, but rejoice in, the greatest injury done to them, yet are troubled at that which wicked men do to themselves, and the grievous misery that attends them.

3. How much more are they troubled at the injuries wicked men are continually offering to God! This was the circumstance which made "the contradiction of sinners" so severe a trial to our Lord himself: "He that despiseth me, despiseth Him that sent me." And how are these despisers now multiplied upon earth! who fear not the Son, neither the Father. How are we surrounded with those who blaspheme the Lord and his Anointed; either reviling the whole of his glorious gospel, or making him a liar as to some of the blessed truths which he hath graciously revealed therein! How many of those who profess to believe the whole, yet, in effect, preach another gospel; so disguising the essential doctrines thereof, by their new interpretations, as to retain the words only, but nothing of "the faith once delivered to the saints!" How many who have not yet made shipwreck of the faith, are strangers to the fruits of it! It hath not purified their hearts; it hath not overcome the world. They are yet "in the gall of bitterness, and in the bond of iniquity." They are still "lovers of themselves," lovers of the world, "lovers of pleasure," and not "lovers of God." Lovers of God! No. He "is not in all their thoughts." They delight not in Him; they thirst not after Him; they do not rejoice in doing his will, neither make their boast of his praise. O faith, working by love, whither art thou fled? Surely the Son of man did once plant thee upon earth. Where art thou now? Among the wealthy? No. "The deceitfulness of riches" there "chokes the word, and it becometh unfruitful." Among the poor? No. "The cares of the world" are there, so that it bringeth forth no fruit to perfection. However, there is nothing to prevent its growth among those who have "neither poverty nor riches":—Yes; "the desire of other things." And experience shows, by a thousand melancholy exam-

ples, that the allowed desire of anything, great or small, otherwise than as a means to the one thing needful, will by degrees banish the care of that out of the soul, and unfit it for every good word or work.

Such is the trouble—not to descend to particulars, which are endless—that wicked men occasion to the good. Such is the state of all good men while on earth: But it is not so with their souls in paradise. In the moment wherein they are loosed from the body, they know pain no more. Though they are not yet possessed of the "fulness of joy," yet all grief is done away. For "there the wicked cease from troubling; and there the weary are at rest."

II. 1. "There the weary are at rest,"—which was the Second thing to be considered, not only from those evils which prudence might have prevented, or piety removed, even in this life; but from those which were inseparable therefrom, which were their unavoidable portion on earth. They are now at rest, whom wicked men would not suffer to rest before: For into the seats of the spirits of just men, none but the spirits of the just can enter. They are at length hid from the scourge of the tongue: Their name is not here cast out as evil. Abraham, Isaac, and Jacob, and the Prophets, do not revile, or separate them from their company. They are no longer despitefully used, and persecuted; neither do they groan under the hand of the oppressor. No injustice, no malice, no fraud, is there; they are all "Israelites indeed, in whom there is no guile." There are no sinners against their own souls; therefore there is no painful pity, no fear for them. There are no blasphemers of God or of his word; no profaners of his name or of his Sabbaths; no denier of the Lord that bought him; none that tramples on the blood of the everlasting covenant: In a word, no earthly or sensual, no devilish spirit; none who do not love the Lord their God with all their heart.

2. There, therefore, "the weary are at rest" from all the troubles which the wicked occasioned; and indeed from all the other evils which are necessary in this world, either as the consequence of

43

sin, or for the cure of it. They are at rest, in the First place, from bodily pain. In order to judge of the greatness of this deliverance, let but those who have not felt it take a view of one who lies on a sick or death bed. Is this he that was "made a little lower than the angels?" How is the glory departed from him! His eye is dim and heavy; his cheek pale and wan; his tongue falters; his breast heaves and pants; his whole body is now distorted, and writhed to and fro; now moist, and cold, and motionless, like the earth to which it is going. And yet, all this which you see is but the shadow of what he feels. You see not the pain that tears his heart, that shoots through all his veins, and chases the flying soul through every part of her once-loved habitation. Could we see this too, how earnestly should we cry out, "O sin, what hast thou done! To what hast thou brought the noblest part of the visible creation! Was it for this the good God made man?" O no! Neither will he suffer it long. Yet a little while, and all the storms of life shall be over, and thou shalt be gathered into the storehouse of the dead; and "there the weary are at rest!"

3. They "are at rest" from all those infirmities and follies which they could not escape in this life. They are no longer exposed to the delusions of sense, or the dreams of imagination. They are not hindered from seeing the noblest truths, by inadvertence; nor do they ever lose the sight they have once gained, by inattention. They are not entangled with prejudice, nor ever misled by hasty or partial views of the object: And, consequently, no error is there. O blessed place, where truth alone can enter! truth unmixed, undisguised, enlightening every man that cometh into the world! where there is no difference of opinions; but all think alike; all are of one heart, and of one mind: Where that offspring of hell, controversy, which turneth this world upside down, can never come: Where those who have been sawn asunder thereby, and often cried out in the bitterness of their soul, "Peace, peace!" shall find what they then sought in vain, even a peace which none taketh from them.

44

4. And yet all this, inconceivably great as it is, is the least part of their deliverance. For in the moment wherein they shake off the flesh, they are delivered, not only from the troubling of the wicked, not only from pain and sickness, from folly and infirmity; but also from all sin. A deliverance this, in sight of which all the rest vanish away. This is the triumphal song which every one heareth when he enters the gates of paradise:—"Thou, being dead, sinnest no more. Sin hath no more dominion over thee. For in that thou diedst, thou diedst unto sin once; but in that thou livest, thou livest unto God."

5. There, then, "the weary are at rest." The blood of the Lamb hath healed all their sickness, hath washed them thoroughly from their wickedness, and cleansed them from their sin. The disease of their nature is cured; they are at length made whole; they are restored to perfect soundness. They no longer mourn the "flesh lusting against the Spirit;" the "law in their members" is now at an end, and no longer "wars against the law of their mind, and brings them into captivity to the law of sin." There is no root of bitterness left; no remains even of that sin which did "so easily beset them;" no forgetfulness of "Him in whom they live, and move, and have their being;" no ingratitude to their gracious Redeemer, who poured out his soul unto death for them; no unfaithfulness to that blessed Spirit who so long bore with their infirmities. In a word, no pride, no self-will is there; so that they who are "delivered from the bondage of corruption" may indeed say one to another, and that in an emphatical sense, "Beloved, now are we the children of God; and it doth not yet appear what we shall be; but we shall be like him, for we shall see him as he is."

6. Let us view, a little more nearly, the state of a Christian at his entrance into the other world. Suppose "the silver cord" of life just "loosed," and "the wheel broken at the cistern;" the heart can now beat no more; the blood ceases to move; the last breath flies off from the quivering lips, and the soul springs forth into eternity. What are the thoughts of such a soul that has just subdued

her last enemy, death? that sees the body of sin lying beneath her, and is new born into the world of spirits? How does she sing, "'O death, where is thy sting? O grave, where is thy victory? Thanks be unto God,' who hath given me 'the victory, through our Lord Jesus Christ!' O happy day, wherein I shall begin to live! wherein I shall taste my native freedom! When I was 'born of a woman' I had 'but a short time to live,' and that time was 'full of misery;' that corruptible body pressed me down, and enslaved me to sin and pain. But the snare is broken, and I am delivered. Henceforth I know them no more. That head is no more an aching head: Those eyes shall no more run down with tears: That heart shall no more pant with anguish or fear; be weighed down with sorrow or care: Those limbs shall no more be racked with pain: Yea, 'sin hath no more dominion over' me. At length, I have parted from thee, O my enemy; and I shall see thy face no more! I shall never more be unfaithful to my Lord, or offend the eyes of his glory: I am no longer that wavering, fickle, self-inconsistent creature, sinning and repenting, and sinning again. No. I shall never cease, day or night, to love and praise the Lord my God with all my heart, and with all my strength. But what are ye? Are 'all these ministering spirits sent forth to minister to' one 'heir of salvation?' Then, dust and ashes, farewell! I hear a voice from heaven saying, 'Come away, and rest from thy labours. Thy warfare is accomplished; thy sin is pardoned; and the days of thy mourning are ended.'"

7. My brethren, these truths need little application. Believe ye that these things are so? What, then, hath each of you to do, but to "lay aside every weight, and run with patience the race set before" him? To "count all things" else "but dung" and dross; especially those grand idols, learning and reputation, if they are pursued in any other measure, or with any other view, than as they conduce to the knowledge and love of God? To have this "one thing" continually in thine heart, "when thou sittest in thine house, and when thou walkest by the way, and when thou liest down, and when thou risest up?"—to have thy "loins" ever "girt,"

and thy "light burning?"—to serve the Lord thy God with all thy might; if by any means, when He requireth thy soul of thee, perhaps in an hour when thou lookest not for Him, thou mayest enter "where the wicked cease from troubling, and where the weary are at rest?"

Unwilling to Die
1735-36

These journal comments reveal the kind of perfection Wesley was seeking while en route to America: a confidence and readiness to enter God's holy presence at death. Wesley's unwillingness to die exposed the underbelly of his present hope: he came face to face with his un-sanctified heart. This explains why he so quickly changed his perfection theology upon his return to England. Source: Works J 1:17-26.

Journal

Tuesday, October 14, 1735. Mr. Benjamin Ingham, of Queen's College, Oxford, Mr. Charles Delamotte, son of a merchant, in London, who had offered himself some days before, my brother Charles Wesley, and myself, took boat for Gravesend, in order to embark for Georgia. Our end in leaving our native country was not to avoid want, (God having given us plenty of temporal blessings,) nor to gain the dung or dross of riches or honour; but singly this, to save our souls; to live wholly to the glory of God. In the afternoon we found the Simmonds off Gravesend, and immediately went on board.

Mon. 20. Believing the denying ourselves, even in the smallest instances, might, by the blessing of God, be helpful to us, we wholly left off the use of flesh and wine, and confined ourselves to vegetable food, chiefly rice and biscuit. In the afternoon, David Nitschman, Bishop of the Germans, and two others, began to learn English. O may we be, not only of one tongue, but of one mind and of one heart!

Fri. 24. Having a rolling sea, most of the passengers found the effects of it. Mr. Delamotte was exceeding sick for several days; Mr. Ingham, for about half an hour. My brother's head ached much. Hitherto it hath pleased God, the sea has not disordered me

Unwilling to Die

at all; nor have I been hindered one quarter of an hour from reading, writing, composing, or doing any business I could have done on shore.

During our stay in the Downs, some or other of us went, as often as we had opportunity, on board the ship that sailed in company with us, where also many were glad to join in prayer and hearing the word.

Fri. 31. We sailed out of the Downs. At eleven at night I was waked by a great noise. I soon found there was no danger. But the bare apprehension of it gave me a lively conviction what manner of men those ought to be who are every moment on the brink of eternity.

Thur. (November) 20. We fell down into Yarmouth road, but the next day were forced back into Cowes. During our stay here there were several storms; in one of which two ships in Yarmouth road were lost.

The continuance of the contrary winds gave my brother an opportunity of complying with the desire of the Minister of Cowes, and preaching there three or four times. The poor people flocked together in great numbers. We distributed a few little books among the more serious of them, which they received with all possible expressions of thankfulness.

Fri. 21. One recovering from a dangerous illness desired to be instructed in the nature of the Lord's supper. I thought it concerned her to be first instructed in the nature of Christianity; and, accordingly, fixed an hour a day to read with her in Mr. Law's Treatise on Christian Perfection.

Sun. 23. At night I was awaked by the tossing of the ship and roaring of the wind, and plainly showed I was *unfit*, for I was *unwilling*, to die.

Sat. (January) 17 (1736). Many people were very impatient at the contrary wind. At seven in the evening they were quieted by a storm. It rose higher and higher till nine. About nine the sea broke over us from stem to stern; burst through the windows of the state cabin, where three or four of us were, and covered us all over, though a bureau sheltered me from the main shock. About eleven I lay down in the great cabin, and in a short time fell asleep, though very uncertain whether I should wake alive, and much ashamed of my *unwillingness to die*. O how pure in heart must he be, who would rejoice to appear before God at a moment's warning! Toward morning, "He rebuked the winds and the sea, and there was a great calm."

Fri. 23. In the evening another storm began. In the morning it increased, so that they were forced to let the ship drive. I could not but say to myself, "How is it that thou hast no faith?" being still *unwilling to die*. About one in the afternoon, almost as soon as I had stepped out of the great cabin-door, the sea did not break as usual, but came with a full, smooth tide over the side of the ship. I was vaulted over with water in a moment, and so stunned that I scarce expected to lift up my head again, till the sea should give up her dead. But thanks be to God, I received no hurt at all. About midnight the storm ceased.

Sun. 25. At noon our third storm began. At four it was more violent than before. Now, indeed, we could say, "The waves of the sea were mighty, and raged horribly. They rose up to the heavens above, and" clave "down to hell beneath." The winds roared round about us, and (what I never heard before) whistled as distinctly as if it had been a human voice. The ship not only rocked to and fro with the utmost violence, but shook and jarred with so unequal, grating a motion, that one could not but with great difficulty keep one's hold of any thing, nor stand a moment without it. Every ten minutes came a shock against the stern or side of the ship, which one would think should dash the planks in pieces. At this time a child, privately baptized before, was brought to be received into the church. It put me in mind of Jeremiah's buying the field, when the Chaldeans were on the point of destroying Jerusalem, and seemed a pledge of the mercy God designed to show us, even in the land of the living.

Unwilling to Die

We spent two or three hours after prayers, in conversing suitably to the occasion, confirming one another in a calm submission to the wise, holy, gracious will of God. And now a storm did not appear so terrible as before. Blessed be the God of all consolation!

At seven I went to the Germans. I had long before observed the great seriousness of their behaviour. Of their humility they had given a continual proof, by performing those servile offices for the other passengers, which none of the English would undertake; for which they desired, and would receive no pay, saying, "it was good for their proud hearts," and "their loving Saviour had done more for them." And every day had given them occasion of showing a meekness which no injury could move. If they were pushed, struck, or thrown down, they rose again and went away; but no complaint was found in their mouth. There was now an opportunity of trying whether they were delivered from the spirit of fear, as well as from that of pride, anger, and revenge. In the midst of the psalm wherewith their service began, the sea broke over, split the main-sail in pieces, covered the ship, and poured in between the decks, as if the great deep had already swallowed us up. A terrible screaming began among the English. The Germans calmly sung on. I asked one of them afterwards, "Was you not afraid?" He answered, "I thank God, no." I asked, "But were not your women and children afraid?" He replied, mildly, "No, our women and children are not *afraid to die*."

From them I went to their crying, trembling neighbours, and pointed out to them the difference in the hour of trial, between him that feareth God, and him that feareth him not. At twelve the wind fell. This was the most glorious day which I have hitherto seen.

Sat. (February) 7. Mr. Oglethorpe returned from Savannah with Mr. Spangenberg, one of the Pastors of the Germans. I soon found what spirit he was of; and asked his advice with regard to my own conduct. He said, "My brother, I must first ask you one or two questions. Have you the witness within yourself? Does the

51

Spirit of God bear witness with your spirit, that you are a child of God?" I was surprised, and knew not what to answer. He observed it, and asked, "Do you know Jesus Christ?" I paused, and said, "I know he is the Saviour of the world." "True," replied he, "but do you know he has saved you?" I answered, "I hope he has died to save me." He only added, "Do you know yourself?" I said, "I do." But I fear they were vain words.

(Thur. February 26). At our return the next day, (Mr. Quincy being then in the house wherein we afterwards were,) Mr. Delamotte and I took up our lodging with the Germans. We had now an opportunity, day by day, of observing their whole behaviour. For we were in one room with them from morning to night, unless for the little time I spent in walking. They were always employed, always cheerful themselves, and in good humour with one another; they had put away all anger, and strife, and wrath, and bitterness, and clamour, and evil-speaking; they walked worthy of the vocation wherewith they were called, and adorned the Gospel of our Lord in all things.

A Single Intention
1736

This is a very important sermon in the evolution of Wesley's perfection theology. He wrote this homily only a few months after The Trouble and Rest of Good Men, *while en route to America. The significance is found in Wesley's positive affirmations concerning the single intention as the foundation for true religion and as the essence of adult conversion. Especially note his use of evangelical concepts and terminology to describe the single intention. Missing are the negative overtones concerning human nature found in earlier sermons (e.g. in* The Trouble and Rest of Good Men). *Perfection as inward holiness is now becoming more accessible to this life. Wesley is already moving down a path that will eventually lead to his new gospel. Source: Works B 4:372-377*

> The light of the body is the eye: if therefore thine eye
> be single, whole body shall be full of light. But if thine
> eye be evil, thy whole body shall be full of darkness.
>
> Matthew 6:22-23

1. The good providence of God hath at length brought you all unto the haven where you would be. This is the time which you have so long wished to find; this is the place you have so long desired to see. What then ought to be your thoughts, your designs, your resolutions, now God has given you your heart's desire? Consider well what ye have to do; now choose, whether ye will serve God or not. But consider withal that if ye do serve him, ye must do it with all your might. Consider that no man can serve two masters; ye cannot serve God and mammon. Either therefore ye must give God your whole heart, or none at all; he cannot, will not, be served by halves. Either wholly lay aside the thoughts of pleasing him, and choose you another master, or let the pleasing him be your one view in all your thoughts, all your words, and all your actions. Believe our Lord, you can find no middle way. The light of the body is the eye. If therefore thine eye be single, thy whole body shall be full of light. But if thine eye be not single, but evil, thy whole body shall be full of darkness.

I am persuaded there is not one of you here, from the least even to the greatest, who will not earnestly attend while in the name of that God who hath hitherto defended us, and is now present with us, I first briefly explain these important words of our Lord, and secondly, apply them to your present circumstances.

I.1. And, first, may the God who spoke them enable me so to explain them that the meaning thereof may sink deep into your hearts. "The light of the body is the eye;" that is, the intention is to the soul what the eye is to the body. As every part of the body is directed when and how to move by the eye, so every power of the soul is in all its motion directed by the intention. As every turn of the foot or hand depends on and is governed by the bodily eye, so on this eye of the mind depends every deliberate movement of the understanding and the affections, and consequently of whatever depends upon these, as do the very most both of our words and actions.

2. "If therefore thine eye be single;" that is, if thy intention be not divided between two ends; if in all thy thoughts, words, and works, thou hast one only view, namely, to serve and please God: "thy whole body shall be full of light." This single intention will be a light in all thy paths: all darkness and doubt will vanish before it. All will be plain before thy face. Thou wilt clearly see the way wherein thou shouldst go, and steadily walk in it.

3. "But if thine eye be evil," if thy intention be not single, if thou hast more ends than one in view; if, besides that of pleasing God, thou hast a design to please thyself, or to do thy own will; if thou aimest at anything beside the one thing needful, namely, a recovery of the image of God: "thy whole body shall be full of darkness;" thou wilt see no light, which way soever thou turnest. Thou wilt never be free from doubt and perplexity, never out of uncertainty and entanglement. As thou art continually aiming at what cannot be done, thou wilt be continually disappointed. The thick darkness of ignorance, guilt, and misery, will gather about

thee more and more, nor wilt thou be able, while encompassed with such a cloud, ever to recover the way of light and peace.

4. The sum is this: as long as thou hast but one end in all thy thoughts, and words, and actions—to please God, or which is all one, to improve in holiness, in the love of God and thy neighbour—so long thou shalt clearly see what conduces thereto. The God whom thou servest shall so watch over thee that light, and love, and peace shall guide all thy ways, and shine upon all thy paths. But no sooner shalt thou divide thy heart, and aim at anything beside holiness, than the light from which thou turnest away being withdrawn, thou shalt not know whither thou goest. Ignorance, sin, and misery shall overspread thee, till thou fall headlong into utter darkness.

II.1. To apply these words to your present circumstances was the next thing I proposed. In order to do which the more effectually I shall, by the assistance of God, first, give you some directions concerning singleness of intention, and secondly, exhort you to practice them.

2. I would not willingly believe that any of you need to be directed to have a single eye in your religious exercises. To aim at the favour or praise of men, or indeed at anything beside the mere pleasing of God, in communicating, prayer, or any other duty of the like nature, is such an affront both to God and man that we should be very cautious of charging anyone with it, yea, even in our heart. It may be enough therefore barely to mention to you that there is no name bad enough for the folly of those who in any of these solemn offices have any other view than to please God, and to save their own souls.

3. But you are not perhaps so well aware that the same singleness of intention is full as necessary in every part of your business as it is in your devotions; and yet this is the very truth. Unless your single view therein be to please God, and to be more holy, the

most lawful business becomes unlawful to you, and is an abomi-nation in his sight. For it is no more allowed a Christian to work with any other intention than it is to pray. And a mixture of any other does as much pollute our work as it does our prayers. Eve-rything that proceeds from and is suitable to this intention is holy, and just, and good, and everything which does not proceed from this is so far wicked and unholy. This, therefore, is the second direction I would give, to keep a single intention in all your busi-ness, which indeed turns all business into religion, which enno-bles every employment, and makes the meanest offices of life a reasonable sacrifice, acceptable to God through Jesus Christ.

4. Nor is a single eye less necessary in our refreshments than it is in our business and our devotions. As every creature of God is good if it be sanctified by the Spirit of God and by prayer, so without this sort of prayer at least, an intention to please God by using it, no creature is good, nor can be used without hurt to the user. And lest we should fancy meat and drink were too little things for God to regard, he has been pleased to cut up this pre-tence by the roots by giving you this third direction in express terms: "Whether ye eat or drink, or whatsoever ye do, do all to the glory of God."

5. "Whatsoever ye do?" That plainly takes in our diversions as well as refreshments. A fourth direction therefore equally neces-sary is, Let the same singleness of intention be preserved in these, likewise: go through these too with a single view to the will of God, not your own. It is his will you should use them in such a manner and measure as they prepare you for business or devo-tion. So far therefore as your present weakness makes them nec-essary to this end you are to use them, but no farther. And you will clearly see how far they are necessary to this, if this be the single end for which you use them.

6. One direction more is very necessary to be given before we close this head; and that is, that you are above all concerned to

keep a single eye in your conversations. Whether devotion or business be the subject thereof, or whether you converse for refreshment or diversion, in all these cases you are equally obliged to do all to the glory of God. Whatever conversation has not this aim cometh from the evil one. That is, an "idle word"—or conversation, rather, as the term should be translated. And of every such idle word, our Lord plainly tells us before, we shall give an account in the day of judgment.

7. I have now given you the plainest directions I could wherein this singleness of intention is to be preserved. Nothing remains but to exhort you instantly, zealously, and diligently to practice them.

8. The God of your fathers hath lately given you full proof that he hath not forsaken you or your children. Your eyes have seen that his ears are not heavy that they should not hear, neither his hand shortened that it cannot save. Ye have cried unto him in your trouble, and he hath delivered you out of your distress. He hath led you through the terrors of the great deep: he there made bare his mighty arm before you. At his word the stormy wind arose, and lifted up the waves thereof. We reeled to and fro, and staggered like drunken men, and were at our wit's end. But he "made the storm to cease, so that the waves thereof were still." "He hath prepared a table for you in the way wherein you went; even there with corn and wine hath he sustained you." Some of you he hath delivered out of sickness. To some he hath forbidden sickness to approach. To all of you who allowed them to be any blessings at all hath he given abundance of spiritual blessings. Yea, in these he hath been found of them that sought him not; he hath spoken to the heart even of those who asked not after him. And now, behold, to complete all, he hath brought you unto the haven where ye would be.

9. "What reward then will ye give unto the Lord, for all the benefits he hath done unto you?" What? Why, give him your hearts;

love him with all your souls; serve him with all your strength. Forget the things that are behind: riches, honour, power—in a word, whatever does not lead to God. Behold, all things about you are become new! Be ye likewise new creatures! From this hour at least let your eye be single: whatever ye speak, or think, or do, let God be your aim, and God only! Let your one end be to please and love God! In all your business, all your refreshments, all your diversions, all your conversations, as well as in all those which are commonly called religious duties, let your eye look straight forward to God. He that hath ears to hear, let him hear! Have one design, one desire, one hope! Even that the God whom we serve may be your God and your all, in time and in eternity! O be not of a double heart! Think of nothing else! Seek nothing else! To love God, and to be beloved by him, is enough. Be your eyes fixed on this one point, and your whole bodies shall be full of light. God shall continually lift up, and that more and more, the light of his countenance upon you. His Holy Spirit shall dwell in you, and shine more and more upon your souls unto the perfect day. He shall purify your hearts by faith from every earthly thought, every unholy affection. He shall establish your souls with so lively a hope as already lays hold on the prize of your high calling. He shall fill you with peace, and joy, and love! Love, the brightness of his glory, the express image of his person! Love which never rests, never faileth, but still spreads its flame, still goeth on conquering and to conquer, till what was but now a weak, foolish, wavering, sinful creature, be filled with all the fullness of God!

Early Testimonies
1736

*The following testimonies come from Wesley's journal and sermon
On Love (which is Wesley's retelling of Lascelles testimony). They illustrate the kind of perfection he was seeking while a missionary in
America. The reader should note Wesley's confession about being unfit
to die. Once again, he echoes what he first confessed during the storms
at sea. Source: Journal, Work J 1:32, 34, 36-37; On Love, Works B
4:387-388.*

Mr. Henry Lascelles
May-June, 1736

At the first service on Sunday, *May 30th*, were only five; at the
second, twenty-five. The next day I made Mr. Lassel's will; who,
notwithstanding his great weakness, was quite revived when any
mention was made of death or of eternity.

Sun. 6. Calling on Mr. Lassel, and asking how he did, "My departure," said he, "I hope is at hand." I asked, "Are you troubled at
that?" He replied, "O no; to depart, and to be with Christ, is far
better. I desire no more of this bad world. My hope and my joy
and my love is there." The next time I saw him he said, "I desire
nothing more, than for God to forgive my many and great sins. I
would be humble. I would be the humblest creature living. My
heart is humble and broken for my sins. Tell me, teach me, what
shall I do to please God? I would fain do whatever is His will." I
said, "It is His will you should suffer." He answered, "Then I will
suffer. I will gladly suffer whatever pleases Him."

Mon. 7. Finding him weaker, I asked, "Do you still desire to
die?" He said, "Yes; but I dare not pray for it, for fear I should
displease my heavenly Father. His will be done. Let Him work
His will, in my life, or in my death."

This day (the 20th), at half an hour past ten, God heard the prayer of his servant; and Mr. Lassel, according to his desire, was "dissolved that he might be with Christ."

Homily: On Love (1737)

It was in this place that I saw the other good soldier of Christ grappling with his last enemy, death. And it was indeed a spectacle worthy to be seen, of God and men and angels. Some of his last breath was spent in a psalm of praise to him who was then giving him the victory; in assurance whereof be began the triumph even in the heat of the battle. When asked, "Hast thou love?" he lifted up his eyes and hands, and answered, "Yes, yes!" with the whole strength he had left. To one that inquired if he was afraid of the devil, whom he had just mentioned as making his last attack upon him, he replied: "No, no: our loving Saviour hath conquered every enemy. He is with me. I fear nothing." Soon after he said, "The way to our loving Saviour is sharp—but it is short." Nor was it long before he fell into a sort of slumber, wherein his soul sweetly returned to God that gave it. Here, we may observe, was no mixture of any passion or temper contrary to charity. Therefore was there no misery, perfect love casting out whatever might have occasioned torment. And whosoever thou art who hast the like measure of love, thy last end shall be like his!

Margaret and Rebecca Bovey
July, 1736

Thur. 8. Mr. Oglethorpe being there again, and casually speaking of sudden death, Miss Becky said, "If it was the will of God, I should choose to die without a lingering illness." Her sister said, "Are you, then, always prepared to die?" She replied, "Jesus

Christ is always prepared to help me. And little stress is to be laid on such a preparation for death, as is made in a fit of sickness."

Sat. 10. Just as they had done drinking tea, Mrs. Margaret, seeing her colour change, asked if she was well? She did not return any answer; and Dr. Talser soon after going by, she desired him to step in, and said, "Sir, my sister, I fear, is not well." He looked earnestly at her, felt her pulse, and replied, "Well! Madam; your sister is dying!" However, he thought it not impossible bleeding might help. She bled about an ounce, leaned back, and died!

As soon as I heard of it I went to the house, and begged they would not lay her out immediately, there being a possibility, at least, she might only be in a swoon; of which indeed, there was some slight hope, she not only being as warm as ever, but having a fresh colour in her cheeks, and a few drops of blood starting out upon bending her arm; but there was no pulse and no breath; so that having waited some hours, we found her "spirit was indeed returned to God that gave it."

I never saw so beautiful a corpse in my life. Poor comfort to its late inhabitant! I was greatly surprised at her sister. There was, in all her behaviour, such an inexpressible mixture of tenderness and resignation. The first time I spoke to her, she said, "All my afflictions are nothing to this. I have lost not only a sister, but a friend. But it is the will of God. I rely on Him; and doubt not but He will support me under it."

This evening we had such a storm of thunder and lightning as I never saw before, even in Georgia. This voice of God, too, told me *I was not fit to die*; since I was afraid, rather than desirous of it. O when shall I wish to be dissolved and to be with Christ? When I love Him with all my heart.

Almost the whole town was the next evening at the funeral; where many, doubtless, made a world of good resolutions. O how little trace of most of these will be left in the morning! It is a true saying, "Hell is paved with good intentions."

Who Will Deliver Me?
1737-38

The evolution of Wesley's perfection theology is bound to his own spiritual journey. So these confessions offer important insights into the development of that theology upon the eve of his return to England. Once again, we see the motif of ars moriendi *taking center stage in Wesley's frustrations over his lack of attainment in holy tempers. He acknowledges the root problem stems from unbelief and pride. Significantly, these confessions articulate a kind of perfection grounded on a faith that transforms and saves in this present life. Wesley is now ready to listen to a different gospel message that will profoundly change his life and theology. Source: Works J 1:70-75.*

Journal

Thur. (December) 22 (1737). I took my leave of America, (though, if it please God, not for ever,) going on board the Samuel, Captain Percy, with a young gentleman who had been a few months in Carolina, one of my parishioners of Savannah, and a French-man, late of Purrysburg, who was escaped thence with the skin of his teeth.

Sat. 24. We sailed over Charles-Town bar, and about noon lost sight of land.

The next day the wind was fair, but high, as it was on Sunday, 25, when the sea affected me more than it had done in the sixteen weeks of our passage to America. I was obliged to lie down the greatest part of the day, being easy only in that posture.

Mon. 26. I began instructing a Negro lad in the principles of Christianity. The next day I resolved to break off living delicately, and return to my old simplicity of diet; and after I did so, neither my stomach nor my head much complained of the motion of the ship.

Wed. 28. Finding the unaccountable apprehensions of I know not what danger, (the wind being small, and the sea smooth,) which had been upon me several days, increase, I cried earnestly for help; and it pleased God, as in a moment, to restore peace to my soul.

Let me observe hereon, 1. That not one of these hours ought to pass out of my remembrance, till I attain another manner of spirit, a spirit equally willing to glorify God by life or by death. 2. That whoever is uneasy on any account (bodily pain alone excepted) carries in himself his own conviction, that he is so far an unbeliever. Is he uneasy at the apprehension of death? Then he believeth not, that "to die is gain." At any of the events of life? Then he hath not a firm belief, that "all things work together for" his "good." And if he bring the matter more close, he will always find, beside the general want of faith, every particular uneasiness is evidently owing to the want of some particular Christian temper.

First Confession

Sun. 8. In the fullness of my heart, I wrote the following words:

By the most infallible of proofs, inward feeling, I am convince:

Of unbelief; having no such faith in Christ as will prevent my heart from being troubled; which it could not be, if I believed in God, and rightly believed also in him.

Of pride, throughout my life past; inasmuch as I thought I had what I find I have not.

Of gross irrecollection; inasmuch as in a storm I cry to God every moment; in a calm, not.

Of levity and luxuriancy of spirit, recurring whenever the pressure is taken off, and appearing by my speaking words not tending to edify; but most by my manner of speaking of my enemies.

Lord, save, or I perish! Save me:

By such a faith as implies peace in life and in death.

By such humility, as may fill my heart from this hour for ever, with a piercing uninterrupted sense, *Nihil est quod hactenus feci*; having evidently built without a foundation.

By such a recollection as may cry to thee every moment, especially when all is calm: Give me faith, or I die; give me a lowly spirit; otherwise, *mihi non, sit suave vivere.*

By steadiness, seriousness, sobriety of spirit; avoiding, as fire, every word that tendeth not to edifying; and never speaking of any who oppose me, or sin against God, without all my own sins set in array before my face.

Fri. 13. We had a thorough storm, which obliged us to shut all close; the sea breaking over the ship continually. I was at first afraid; but cried to God, and was strengthened. Before ten, I lay down: I bless God, without fear.

Second Confession

Tues. 24. We spoke with two ships, outward-bound, from whom we had the welcome news, of our wanting but one hundred and sixty leagues of the Land's-end. My mind was now full of thought; part of which I writ down as follows:

I went to America, to convert the Indians; but O! Who shall convert me? Who, what is he that will deliver me from this evil heart of unbelief? I have a fair summer religion. I can talk well; nay, and believe myself, while no danger is near: But let *death* look me in the face, and my spirit is troubled. Nor can I say, "To die is gain":

I have a sin of fear, that when I've spun
My last thread, I shall perish on the shore!

I think, verily, if the Gospel be true, I am safe: For I not only have given, and do give, all my goods to feed the

64

poor; I not only give my body to be burned, drowned, or whatever God shall appoint for me; but I follow after charity, (though not as I ought, yet as I can,) if haply I may attain it. I now believe the Gospel is true. "I show my faith by my works," by staking my all upon it. I would do so again and again a thousand times, if the choice were still to make. Whoever sees me, sees I would be a Christian. Therefore "are my ways not like other men's ways." Therefore I have been, I am, I am content to be, "a by-word, a proverb of reproach." But in a storm I think, 'What if the Gospel be not true? Then thou art of all men most foolish. For what hast thou given thy goods, thy ease, thy friends, thy reputation, thy country, thy life? For what art thou wandering over the face of the earth—A dream, "a cunningly-devised fable!" O! who will deliver me from this *fear of death*? What shall I do? Where shall I fly from it? Should I fight against it by thinking, or by not thinking of it? A wise man advised me some time since, Be still, and go on. Perhaps this is best, to look upon it as my cross; when it comes, to let it humble me, and quicken all my good resolutions, especially that of praying without ceasing; and at other times, to take no thought about it, but quietly to go on "in the work of the Lord."

The John Wesley Reader on Christian Perfection

Section Two

The Aldersgate Period

1738

Questions to Consider for
John Wesley's Aldersgate Period

1. Does Wesley abandon the *ars moriendi* (art of dying) motif during his Aldersgate period?

2. What is Wesley's new gospel? What are its essential properties?

3. How do Wesley's views on forgiveness and assurance change from his early period? How do his views on forgiveness influence his doctrine of holiness?

4. When, according to Wesley, is Christian perfection attained? Did his views change from the early period?

5. What is the relationship between perfection and the new birth?

6. What did Wesley receive at the Aldersgate society meeting on May 24? Did he taste the gift of full salvation?

7. Note how Wesley defines perfection. What is the essential idea he is seeking to communicate in this period? What has changed, if anything? What remains consistent with his early period?

8. How does Wesley define sin? Which kind of sin is removed in the attainment of perfection? Which kind is not?

9. Reflect on how perfect love is attained. What is the relationship between divine grace and human agency?

10. How does Wesley define faith? What is the relationship between faith and perfection?

A Perfect Faith Needed
February 1, 1738

This confession serves as the post-script to Extract One of Wesley's Journal. Its purpose is apologetic: to explain why he had changed his gospel message so drastically after his return to England. Therefore, its contents confirm that Wesley did not pen it on February 1, but most likely several months later. It is placed here because this is where Wesley placed it in his journal and it appropriately begins this phase in his theological development.[2]

Wesley opens with a startling confession of his unconverted condition, and then proceeds to make a point-by-point repudiation of his Holy Club program. After this he plunges into a confession of personal sinfulness that easily matches his Aldersgate memorandum (below). He now describes his prior faith as sub-Christian. Utilizing the categories found in Salvation By Faith, *Wesley describes the kind of faith he needs—a perfect one. Note carefully the freedoms he lists as the fruits of this faith. Wesley is now collapsing perfection into the article of conversion (new birth). Source: Works J 1:75-77.*

Journal

It is now two years and almost four months since I left my native country, in order to teach the Georgian Indians the nature of Christianity: But what have I learned myself in the mean time? Why, (what I the least of all suspected,) that I who went to America to convert others, was never myself converted to God. "I am not mad," though I thus speak; but "I speak the words of truth and soberness;" if haply some of those who still dream may awake, and see, that as I am, so are they.

Are they read in philosophy? So was I. In ancient or modern tongues? So was I also. Are they versed in the science of divin-

---

[2] For a full discussion of when this confession was written, see my *John Wesley's Theology of Christian Perfection: Developments in Doctrine & Theological System*, 97-100, 390ff.

ity? I too have studied it many years. Can they talk fluently upon spiritual things? The very same could I do. Are they plenteous in alms? Behold, I gave all my goods to feed the poor. Do they give of their labour as well as of their substance? I have laboured more abundantly than they all. Are they willing to suffer for their brethren? I have thrown up my friends, reputation, ease, country; I have put my life in my hand, wandering into strange lands; I have given my body to be devoured by the deep, parched up with heat, consumed by toil and weariness, or whatsoever God should please to bring upon me. But does all this (be it more or less, it matters not) make me acceptable to God? Does all I ever did or can know, say, give, do, or suffer, justify me in his sight? Yea, or the constant use of all the means of grace? (Which, nevertheless, is meet, right, and our bounden duty.) Or that I know nothing of myself; that I am, as touching outward, moral righteousness blameless? Or (to come closer yet) the having a rational conviction of all the truths of Christianity? Does all this give me a claim to the holy, heavenly, divine character of a Christian? By no means. If the Oracles of God are true, if we are still to abide by "the law and the testimony;" all these things, though, when ennobled by faith in Christ, they are holy and just and good, yet without it are "dung and dross," meet only to be purged away by "the fire that never shall be quenched."

This, then, have I learned in the ends of the earth—That I "am fallen short of the glory of God": That my whole heart is "altogether corrupt and abominable;" and, consequently, my whole life; (seeing it cannot be, that an "evil tree" should "bring forth good fruit"). That "alienated" as I am from the life of God," I am "a child of wrath," an heir of hell: That my own works, my own sufferings, my own righteousness, are so far from reconciling me to an offended God, so far from making any atonement for the least of those sins, which "are more in number than the hairs of my head," that the most specious of them need an atonement themselves, or they cannot abide his righteous Judgment; that "having the sentence of death" in my heart, and having nothing in or of myself to plead, I have no hope, but that of being justified freely, "through the redemption that is in Jesus": I have no hope, but that if I seek I shall find Christ, and "be found in him not having my own righteousness, but that which is through the faith of Christ, the righteousness which is of God by faith" (Php 3:9).

If it be said, that I have faith, (for many such things have I heard, from many miserable comforters,) I answer, So have the devils, a sort of faith; but still they are strangers to the covenant of promise. So the apostles had even at Cana in Galilee, when Jesus first "manifested forth his glory;" even then they, in a sort, "believed on him;" but they had not then "the faith that overcometh the world." The faith I want is, "a sure trust and confidence in God, that, through the merits of Christ, my sins are forgiven, and I reconciled to the favour of God." I want that faith which St. Paul recommends to all the world, especially in his Epistle to the Romans: That faith which enables every one that hath it to cry out, "I live not; but Christ liveth in me; and the life which I now live, I live by faith in the Son of God, who loved me, and gave himself for me." I want that faith which none can have without knowing that he hath it; (though many imagine they have it, who have it not;) for whosoever hath it, is "freed from sin, the" whole "body of sin is destroyed" in him. He is freed from fear, "having peace with God through Christ, and rejoicing in hope of the glory of God." And he is freed from doubt, "having the love of God shed abroad in his heart, through the Holy Ghost which is given unto him;" which "Spirit itself beareth witness with his spirit, that he is a child of God."

A New Gospel Embraced
February-April, 1738

*When Wesley touched English soil on February 1 he was a differ-
ent man. Two and a half years earlier he had left to be a missionary to
America, fully confident he was qualified to lead others in the holy life.
But faced with his fears of death and the mixed results of his ministry in
America, Wesley now realized he was less perfect in heart than what he
had supposed. He now became open to hear a different gospel message; one grounded on faith alone in Christ alone, with the twin fruits
of happiness and holiness testifying to its authenticity. Perfection is
now formally linked to the article of conversion: to be born again is to
be perfected in holiness. Once again, note how Wesley defines assurance, salvation from sin, and the instantaneous reception of saving
faith. Source: Works J 1:84-93.*

Journal

Tue. (February) 7. (A day much to be remembered.) At the house
of Mr. Weinantz, a Dutch merchant, I met Peter Böhler, Schulius,
Richter, and Wenzel Neisser, just then landed from Germany.
Finding they had no acquaintance in England, I offered to pro-
cure them a lodging, and did so near Mr. Hutton's, where I then
was. And from this time I did not willingly lose any opportunity
of conversing with them while I stayed in London.

Fri. 17. I set out for Oxford with Peter Böhler... (Sunday) All
this time I conversed much with Peter Böhler, but I understood
him not; and least of all when he said, *Mi frater, mi frater, exco-
quenda est ista tua philosophia*—My brother, my brother, that
philosophy of yours must be purged away.

Sat. (March) 4. I found my brother at Oxford, recovering from
his pleurisy; and with him Peter Böhler. By whom (in the hand of
the great God) I was on Sunday the 5th clearly convinced of un-

belief, of the want of "that faith whereby alone we are saved," with the full, Christian salvation.

Immediately it struck into my mind, "Leave off preaching. How can you preach to others, who have not faith yourself?" I asked Böhler whether he thought I should leave it off or not. He answered, "By no means." I asked, "But what can I preach?" He said, "Preach faith till you have it, and then, because you have it, you will preach faith."

Accordingly, *Monday 6*, I began preaching this new doctrine, though my soul started back from the work. The first person to whom I offered salvation by faith alone was a prisoner under sentence of death. His name was Clifford. Peter Böhler had many times desired me to speak to him before. But I could not prevail on myself so to do, being still (as I had been many years) a zealous asserter of the impossibility of a death-bed repentance.

Thur. 23. I met Peter Böhler again, who now amazed me more and more, by the account he gave of the fruits of living faith—the holiness and happiness which he affirmed to attend it. The next morning I began the Greek Testament again, resolving to abide by "the law and the testimony," and being confident that God would hereby show me "whether" this "doctrine was of God."

Sat. (April) 22. I met Peter Böhler once more. I had now no objection to what he said of the nature of faith, viz., that it is (to use the words of our Church), "A sure trust and confidence which a man hath in God, that through the merits of Christ his sins are forgiven, and he reconciled to the favour of God." Neither could I deny either the happiness or holiness which he described as fruits of this living faith. "The Spirit itself beareth witness with our spirit that we are the children of God," and "He that believeth hath the witness in himself," fully convinced me of the former; as "Whatsoever is born of God doth not commit sin," and "Whosoever believeth is born of God," did of the latter. But I could not comprehend what he spoke of an instantaneous work. I could not understand how this faith should be given in a moment; how a man could at once be thus turned from darkness to light, from sin and misery to righteousness and joy in the Holy Ghost. I searched the Scriptures again touching this very thing, particularly the Acts of the Apostles: but to my utter astonishment found scarce any instances there of other than instantaneous conversions—scarce any other so slow as that of St. Paul, who was three days in the pangs of the new birth. I had but one retreat left, viz., "Thus, I grant, God wrought in the first ages of Christianity; but the times are changed. What reasons have I to believe he works in the same manner now?"

But on *Sunday 23*, I was beat out of this retreat too, by the concurring evidence of several living witnesses, who testified God had thus wrought in themselves; giving them in a moment such a faith in the blood of his Son as translated them out of darkness into light, out of sin and fear into holiness and happiness. Here ended my disputing. I could now only cry out, "Lord, help thou my unbelief!"

I asked P Böhler again whether I ought not to "refrain from teaching others." He said, "No; do not hide in the earth the talent God hath given you." Accordingly on *Tuesday 25*, I spoke clearly and fully at Blendon, to Mr. Delamotte's family, of the nature and fruits of faith. Mr. Broughton and my brother were there. Mr. Broughton's great objection was, he could never think that I had not faith, who had done and suffered such things. My brother was very angry, and told me I did not know what mischief I had done by talking thus. And indeed it did please God then to kindle a fire, which I trust shall never be extinguished.

(Wed. April 26) P Böhler walked with me a few miles, and exhorted me not to stop short of the grace of God. At Gerrards Cross I plainly declared to those whom God gave into my hands "the faith as it is in Jesus;" as I did the next day to a young man I overtook on the road, and in the evening to our friends at Oxford. A strange doctrine, which some, who did not care to contradict, yet knew not what to make of; but one or two, who were thoroughly bruised by sin, willingly heard, and received it gladly.

A New Gospel Embraced

In the day or two following I was much confirmed in "the truth that is after godliness" by hearing the experiences of Mr. Hutchins (of Pembroke College) and Mrs. Fox—two living witnesses that God can (at least, if he does not always) give that faith whereof cometh salvation in a moment, as lightning falling from heaven.

Wed. (May) 3. My brother had a long and particular conversation with Peter Böhler. And it now pleased God to open his eyes, so that he also saw clearly what was the nature of that one, true, living faith, whereby alone "through grace we are saved."

Thur. 4. Peter Böhler left London in order to embark for Carolina. O what a work hath God begun since his coming into England! Such an one as shall never come to an end till heaven and earth pass away.

My Heart Strangely Warmed
May 24, 1738

This is Wesley's famous Aldersgate memorandum. He here shares his story of how he came to faith in Christ crucified for assurance and salvation from sin. The reader should keep in mind that what Wesley writes here of his earlier faith journey is colored by his present convictions. Later in life he will add footnotes that challenge some of these conclusions.[3] Note how the themes of happiness and holiness are repeated over and over in the following testimony. Wesley's new gospel of faith alone in Christ alone received in an instant is now ratified by his own experience. Moreover, take cognizance of how Wesley links personal assurance to salvation from all sin, thus collapsing perfection into the article of conversion (cf. §14). Source: Works J 1:98-104.

What occurred on Wednesday 24, I think best to relate at large, after premising what may make it the better understood. Let him that cannot receive it ask of the Father of lights that he would give more light both to him and me.

1. I believe, till I was about ten years old I had not sinned away that "washing of the Holy Ghost" which was given me in baptism, having been strictly educated and carefully taught that I could only be saved *by universal obedience, by keeping all the commandments of God*, in the meaning of which I was diligently instructed. And those instructions, so far as they respected outward duties and sins, I gladly received and often thought of. But all that was said to me of inward obedience or holiness I neither understood nor remembered. So that I was indeed as ignorant of the true meaning of the law as I was of the gospel of Christ.

---

[3] In the 1770's Wesley added a number of footnotes to his 1738 journal qualifying his harsher judgments on his pre-Aldersgate spiritual condition. See Works B 18:214-215, 235, 242, 245, 248, 261.

2. The next six or seven years were spent at school; where, outward restraints being removed, I was much more negligent than before even of outward duties, and almost continually guilty of outward sins, which I knew to be such, though they were not scandalous in the eye of the world. However, I still read the Scriptures, and said my prayers, morning and evening. And what I now hoped to be saved by, was, (1) *not being so bad as other people*; (2) *having still a kindness for religion*; and (3) *reading the Bible, going to church, and saying my prayers.*

3. Being removed to the university for five years, I still said my prayers both in public and private, and read with the Scriptures several other books of religion, especially comments on the New Testament. Yet I had not all the while so much as a notion of inward holiness; nay, went on habitually and (for the most part) very contentedly, in some or other known sin: indeed with some intermissions and short struggles, especially before and after the Holy Communion, which I was obliged to receive thrice a year. I cannot well tell what I hoped to be saved by now, when I was continually sinning against the little light I had, unless by those transient fits of what many divines taught me to call "repentance."

4. When I was about twenty-two my father pressed me to enter into holy orders. At the same time, the providence of God directing me to Kempis's Christian Pattern, I began to see that true religion was seated in the heart and that God's law extended to all our thoughts as well as words and actions. I was, however, very angry at Kempis for being *too strict*, though I read him only in Dean Stanhope's translation. Yet I had frequently much sensible comfort in reading him, such as I was an utter stranger to before. And meeting likewise with a religious friend, which I had never had till now, I began to alter the whole form of my

conversation and to set in earnest upon *a new life*. I set apart an hour or two a day for religious retirement. I communicated every week. I watched against all sins, whether in word or deed. I began to aim at and pray for inward holiness. So that now, *doing so much and living so good a life*, I doubted not but I was a good Christian.

5. Removing soon after to another college, I executed a resolution which I was before convinced was of the utmost importance, shaking off at once all my trifling acquaintance. I began to see more and more the value of time. I applied myself closer to study. I watched more carefully against actual sins; I advised others to be religious, according to that scheme of religion by which I modeled my own life. But meeting now with Mr. Law's *Christian Perfection* and *Serious Call* (although I was much offended at many parts of both, yet) they convinced me more than ever of the exceeding height and breadth and depth of the law of God. The light flowed in so mightily upon my soul that everything appeared in a new view. I cried to God for help and resolved not to prolong the time of obeying him as I had never done before. And by my continued *endeavour to keep his whole law*, inward and outward, *to the utmost of my power*, I was persuaded that I should be accepted of him, and that I was even then in a state of salvation.

6. In 1730 I began visiting the prisons, assisting the poor and sick in town, and doing what other good I could by my presence or my little fortune to the bodies and souls of all men. To this end I abridged myself of all superfluities, and many that are called necessaries of life. I soon became 'a byword' for so doing, and I rejoiced that 'my name was cast out as evil.' The next spring I began observing the Wednesday and Friday fasts, commonly observed in the ancient church, tasting no food till three in

the afternoon. And now I knew not how to go any farther. I diligently strove against all sin. I omitted no sort of self-denial which I thought lawful. I carefully used, both in public and in private, all the means of grace at all opportunities. I omitted no occasion of doing good. I for that reason suffered evil. And all this I knew to be nothing unless as it was directed toward inward holiness. Accordingly this, the image of God, was what I aimed at in all, by doing his will, not my own. Yet when, after continuing some years in this course, I apprehended myself to be near death, I could not find that all this gave me any comfort, nor any assurance of acceptance with God. At this I was then not a little surprised, not imagining I had been all this time building on the sand, nor considering that "other foundation can no man lay than that which is laid by God, even Christ Jesus."

7. Soon after, a contemplative man convinced me still more than I was convinced before, that outward works are nothing, being alone; and in several conversations instructed me how to pursue inward holiness, or a union of the soul with God. But even of his instructions (though I then received them as the words of God) I cannot but now observe, (1) that he spoke so incautiously against *trusting in outward works* that he discouraged me from doing them at all; (2) that he recommended (as it were, to supply what was wanting in them) mental prayer, and the like exercises, as the most effectual means of purifying the soul and uniting it with God. Now these were, in truth, as much my own works as visiting the sick or clothing the naked, and the "union with God" thus pursued was as really *my own righteousness* as any I had before pursued under another name.

8. In this *refined* way of trusting to my own works and my own righteousness (so zealously inculcated by the mystic

writers), I dragged on heavily, finding no comfort or help therein, till the time of my leaving England. On ship-board, however, I was again active in outward works; where it pleased God of his free mercy to give me twenty-six of the Moravian brethren for companions, who en-deavoured to show me a more excellent way. But I under-stood it not at first. I was too learned and too wise. So that it seemed foolishness unto me. And I continued preach-ing, and following after, and trusting in that righteousness whereby no flesh can be justified.

9. All the time I was at Savannah I was thus 'beating the air'. Being ignorant of the righteousness of Christ, which by a living faith in him bringeth salvation "to every one that believeth," I sought to establish my own righteous-ness, and so laboured in the fire all my days. I was now properly "under the law;" I knew that "the law" of God was "spiritual;" "I consented to it that it was good." Yea, "I delighted in it, after the inner man." Yet was I "carnal, sold under sin." Every day was I constrained to cry out, "What I do, I allow not; for what I would I do not, but what I hate, that I do." "To will is indeed present with me; but how to perform that which is good, I find not." For "the good which I would, I do not; but the evil which I would not, that I do." "I find a law, that when I would do good, evil is present with me," even the "law in my mem-bers warring against the law of my mind," and still "bringing me into captivity to the law of sin."

10. In this vile, abject state of bondage to sin I was indeed fighting continually, but not conquering. Before, I had willingly served sin: now it was unwillingly, but still I served it. I fell and rose and fell again. Sometimes I was overcome and in heaviness. Sometimes I overcame and was in joy. For as in the former state I had some foretastes of the terrors of the law, so had I in this of the comforts of

the gospel. During this whole struggle between nature and grace (which had now continued above ten years) I had many remarkable returns to prayer, especially when I was in trouble; I had many sensible comforts, which are indeed no other than short anticipations of the life of faith. But I was still 'under the law', not 'under grace' (the state most who are called Christians are content to live and die in); for I was only 'striving with', not "freed from sin." Neither had I "the witness of the Spirit with my spirit." And indeed could not; for I "sought it not by faith, but (as it were) by the works of the law."

11. In my return to England, January 1738, being in imminent danger of death, and very uneasy on that account, I was strongly convinced that the cause of that uneasiness was unbelief, and that the gaining a true, living faith, was the "one thing needful" for me. But still I fixed not this faith on its right object: I meant only faith in God, not faith in or through Christ. Again, I knew not that I was *wholly void of this faith*, but only thought *I had not enough* of it. So that when Peter Böhler, whom God prepared for me as soon as I came to London, affirmed of true faith in Christ (which is but one) that it had those two fruits inseparably attending it, "dominion over sin, and constant peace from a sense of forgiveness," I was quite amazed, and looked upon it as a *new gospel*. If this was so, it was clear I had not faith. But I was not willing to be convinced of this. Therefore I disputed with all my might and laboured to prove that faith might be where these were not, especially where that sense of forgiveness was not. For all the Scriptures relating to this I had been long since taught to construe away, and to call all "Presbyterians" who spoke otherwise. Besides, I well saw no one could (in the nature of things) have such a sense of forgiveness and not feel it. But I felt it not. If then there was

no faith without this, all my pretensions to faith dropped at once.

12. When I met Peter Böhler again, he readily consented to put the dispute upon the issue which I desired, viz., Scripture and experience. I first consulted the Scripture. But when I set aside the glosses of men, and simply considered the words of God, comparing them together and endeavouring to illustrate the obscure by the plainer passages, I found they all made against me, and was forced to retreat to my last hold, that experience would never agree with the literal interpretation of those Scriptures. Nor could I therefore allow it to be the true till I found some living witnesses of it. He replied, he could show me such at any time; if I desired it, the next day. And accordingly the next day he came again with three others, all of whom testified of their own personal experience that a true, living faith in Christ is inseparable from a sense of pardon for all past, and freedom from all present sins. They added with one mouth that this faith was the gift, the free gift of God, and that he would surely bestow it upon every soul who earnestly and perseveringly sought it. I was now thoroughly convinced. And, by the grace of God, I resolved to seek it unto the end, (1) by absolutely renouncing all dependence, in whole or in part, upon my own works or righteousness, on which I had really grounded my hope of salvation, though I knew it not, from my youth up; (2) by adding to "the constant use of all the" other "means of grace," continual prayer for this very thing, justifying, saving faith, a full reliance on the blood of Christ shed for me; a trust in him as my Christ, as my sole justification, sanctification, and redemption.

13. I continued thus to seek it (though with strange indifference, dullness, and coldness, and unusually frequent relapses into sin) till Wednesday, May 24. I think it was

about five this morning that I opened my Testament on those words, "There are given unto us exceeding great and precious promises, even that ye should be partakers of the divine nature." Just as I went out I opened it again on those words, "Thou art not far from the kingdom of God." In the afternoon I was asked to go to St. Paul's. The anthem was, "Out of the deep have I called unto thee, O Lord. Lord, hear my voice. O let thine ears consider well the voice of my complaint. If thou, Lord, wilt be extreme to mark what is done amiss, O Lord, who may abide it? But there is mercy with thee; therefore thou shalt be feared...O Israel, trust in the Lord: For with the Lord there is mercy, and with him is plenteous redemption. And he shall redeem Israel from all his sins."

14. In the evening I went very unwillingly to a society in Aldersgate Street, where one was reading Luther's Preface to the Epistle to the Romans. About a quarter before nine, while he was describing the change which God works in the heart through faith in Christ, I felt my heart strangely warmed. I felt I did trust in Christ, Christ alone for salvation, and an assurance was given me that he had taken away *my* sins, even *mine*, and saved *me* from the law of sin and death.

15. I began to pray with all my might for those who had in a more especial manner despitefully used me and persecuted me. I then testified openly to all there what I now first felt in my heart. But it was not long before the enemy suggested, "This cannot be faith; for where is thy joy?" Then was I taught that *peace and victory over sin are essential to faith in the Captain of our salvation; but that as to the transports of joy that usually attend the beginning of it, especially in those who have mourned deeply, God sometimes giveth, sometimes withholdeth them, according to the counsels of his own will.*

83

16. After my return home I was much buffeted with temptations; but cried out, and they fled away. They returned again and again. I as often lifted up my eyes, and he "sent me help from his holy place." And herein I found the difference between this and my former state chiefly consisted. I was striving, yea fighting with all my might under the law, as well as under grace. But then I was sometimes, if not often, conquered; now, I was always conqueror.

17. Thursday, May 25. The moment I awaked, "Jesus, Master," was in my heart and in my mouth; and I found all my strength lay in keeping my eye fixed upon him, and my soul waiting on him continually. Being again in St. Paul's in the afternoon, I could taste the good word of God in the anthem, which began, "My song shall be always of the loving-kindness of the Lord: with my mouth will I ever be showing forth thy truth from one generation to another." Yet the enemy injected a fear, "If thou dost believe, why is there not a more sensible change?" I answered (yet not I), "That I know not. But this I know, I have *now peace with God*, and I sin not today, and Jesus my Master has forbid me to take thought for the morrow."

18. "But is not *any* sort of *fear*," continued the tempter, "a proof that thou dost not believe?" I desired my Master to answer for me, and opened his book upon those words of St. Paul, "Without were fightings, within were fears." Then inferred I, well may fears be within *me*; but I must go on, and tread them under my feet.

Salvation By Faith
June 11, 1738

This is another landmark sermon and serves as the manifesto for Wesley's new gospel. Preached at St. Mary's, Oxford, Wesley here articulates the nature of saving faith (trust in Christ's death and resurrection) and of present salvation from all sin. Concerning the latter, major developments in his doctrine of sin are for the first time presented here. Sin is now categorized under the headings of guilt and power, with the latter further divided into the sub-categories of habitual, willful, desire, and infirmity. These distinctions make it possible for Wesley to proclaim a message of present salvation from all sin in the article of conversion (cf. II.7). The reader should also take note of the scriptures Wesley used to support his message of full salvation. Later, his understanding of these same scripture texts will undergo development. Source: Works J 5:7-16.

> By grace ye are saved through faith.
>
> Ephesians 2:8

1. All the blessings which God hath bestowed upon man are of his mere grace, bounty, or favour: his free, undeserved favour, favour altogether undeserved, man having no claim to the least of his mercies. It was free grace that "formed man of the dust of the ground, and breathed into him a living soul," and stamped on that soul the image of God, and "put all things under his feet." The same free grace continues to us, at this day, life, and breath, and all things. For there is nothing we are, or have, or do, which can deserve the least thing at God's hand. "All our works thou, O God, hast wrought in us." These therefore are so many more instances of free mercy: and whatever righteousness may be found in man, this also is the gift of God.

2. Wherewithal then shall a sinful man atone for any the least of his sins? With his own works? No. Were they ever so many or holy, they are not his own, but God's. But indeed they are all un-

holy and sinful themselves, so that every one of them needs a fresh atonement. Only corrupt fruit grows on a corrupt tree. And his heart is altogether corrupt and abominable, being "come short of the glory of God," the glorious righteousness at first impressed on his soul, after the image of his great Creator. Therefore having nothing, neither righteousness nor works, to plead, his "mouth is utterly stopped before God."

3. If then sinful man find favour with God, it is "grace upon grace." If God vouchsafe still to pour fresh blessings upon us— yea, the greatest of all blessings, salvation—what can we say to these things but "Thanks be unto God for his unspeakable gift!" And thus it is. Herein "God commendeth his love toward us, in that, while we were yet sinners, Christ died" to save us. "By grace," then, "are ye saved through faith." Grace is the source, faith the condition, of salvation.

Now, that we fall not short of the grace of God, it concerns us carefully to inquire:

I. What faith it is through which we are saved.
II. What is the salvation which is through faith.
III. How we may answer some objections.

I. What faith it is through which we are saved.
1. And, first, it is not barely the faith of a heathen. Now God requireth of a heathen to believe "that God is, and that he is a rewarder of them that diligently seek him;" and that he is to be sought by "glorifying him as God by giving him thanks for all things," and by a careful practice of moral virtue, of justice, mercy, and truth, toward their fellow-creatures. A Greek or Roman, therefore, yea, a Scythian or Indian, was without excuse if he did not believe thus much: the being and attributes of God, a future state of reward and punishment, and the obligatory nature of moral virtue. For this is barely the faith of a heathen.

2. Nor, secondly, is it the faith of a devil, though this goes much farther than that of a heathen. For the devil believes, not only that there is a wise and powerful God, gracious to reward and just to punish, but also that Jesus is the Son of God, the Christ, the Saviour of the world. So we find him declaring in express terms: "I know thee who thou art, the Holy One of God." Nor can we doubt but that unhappy spirit believes all those words which came out of the mouth of the Holy One; yea, and whatsoever else was written by those holy men of old, of two of whom he was compelled to give that glorious testimony, "These men are the servants of the most high God, who show unto you the way of salvation." Thus much then the great enemy of God and man believes, and trembles in believing, that "God was made manifest in the flesh;" that he will "tread all enemies under his feet;" and that "all Scripture was given by inspiration of God." Thus far goeth the faith of a devil.

3. Thirdly, the faith through which we are saved, in that sense of the word which will hereafter be explained, is not barely that which the apostles themselves had while Christ was yet upon earth; though they so believed on him as to "leave all and follow him;" although they had then power to work miracles, "to heal all manner of sickness, and all manner of disease;" yea, they had then "power and authority over all devils": and which is beyond all this, were sent by their Master to "preach the kingdom of God." Yet after their return from doing all these mighty works their Lord himself terms them, "a faithless generation." He tells them "they could not cast out a devil, because of their unbelief." And when long after, supposing they had some already, they said unto him, "Increase our faith," he tells them plainly that of this faith they had none at all, no, not as a grain of mustard seed: "The Lord said, If ye had faith as a grain of mustard seed, ye might say unto this sycamine tree, Be thou plucked up by the roots, and be thou planted in the sea; and it should obey you."

4. What faith is it then through which we are saved? It may be answered: first, in general, it is a faith in Christ—Christ, and God through Christ, are the proper object of it. Herein therefore it is sufficiently, absolutely, distinguished from the faith either of ancient or modern heathens. And from the faith of a devil it is fully distinguished by this—it is not barely a speculative, rational thing, a cold, lifeless assent, a train of ideas in the head; but also a disposition of the heart. For thus saith the Scripture, "With the heart man believeth unto righteousness." And, "If thou shalt confess with thy mouth the Lord Jesus, and shalt believe with thy heart that God hath raised him from the dead, thou shalt be saved."

5. And herein does it differ from that faith which the apostles themselves had while our Lord was on earth, that it acknowledges the necessity and merit of his death, and the power of his resurrection. It acknowledges his death as the only sufficient means of redeeming man from death eternal, and his resurrection as the restoration of us all to life and immortality; inasmuch as he "was delivered for our sins, and rose again for our justification." Christian faith is then not only an assent to the whole gospel of Christ, but also a full reliance on the blood of Christ, a trust in the merits of his life, death, and resurrection; a recumbency upon him as our atonement and our life, as given for us, and living in us. It is a sure confidence which a man hath in God, that through the merits of Christ his sins are forgiven, and he reconciled to the favour of God; and in consequence hereof a closing with him and cleaving to him as our "wisdom, righteousness, sanctification, and redemption" or, in one word, our salvation.

II. What salvation it is which is through this faith is the second thing to be considered.

1. And, first, whatsoever else it imply, it is a present salvation. It is something attainable, yea, actually attained on earth, by those who are partakers of this faith. For thus saith the Apostle to the

believers at Ephesus, and in them to the believers of all ages, not, "Ye shall be" (though that also is true), but "Ye are saved through faith."

2. Ye are saved (to comprise all in one word) from sin. This is the salvation which is through faith. This is that great salvation foretold by the angel before God brought his first-begotten into the world: "Thou shalt call his name Jesus, for he shall save his people from their sins." And neither here nor in other parts of Holy Writ is there any limitation or restriction. All his people, or as it is elsewhere expressed, all that believe in him, he will save from all their sins: from original and actual, past and present sin, of the flesh and of the spirit. Through faith that is in him they are saved both from the guilt and from the power of it.

3. First, from the guilt of all past sin. For whereas "all the world is guilty before God;" insomuch that should he "be extreme to mark what is done amiss, there is none that could abide it;" and whereas "by the law is only the knowledge of sin," but no deliverance from it, so that "by fulfilling the deeds of the law no flesh can be justified in his sight;" now "the righteousness of God, which is by faith of Jesus Christ', 'is manifested unto all that believe." Now they are "justified freely by his grace through the redemption that is in Jesus Christ. Him God hath set forth to be a propitiation through faith in his blood, to declare his righteousness for (or by) the remission of the sins that are past." Now hath Christ "taken away the curse of the law, being made a curse for us." He hath "blotted out the handwriting that was against us, taking it out of the way, nailing it to his cross." "There is therefore no condemnation now to them which believe in Christ Jesus."

4. And being saved from guilt, they are saved from fear. Not indeed from a filial fear of offending, but from all servile fear, from that "fear which hath torment," from fear of punishment, from fear of the wrath of God, whom they now no longer regard as a severe master, but as an indulgent Father. "They have not re-

ceived again the spirit of bondage, but the Spirit of adoption, whereby they cry, Abba, Father: the Spirit itself also bearing witness with their spirit, that they are the children of God." They are also saved from the fear, though not from the possibility, of falling away from the grace of God, and coming short of the great and precious promises. They are "sealed with the Holy Spirit of promise, which is the earnest of their inheritance." Thus have they "peace with God through our Lord Jesus Christ...They rejoice in hope of the glory of God...And the love of God is shed abroad in their hearts through the Holy Ghost which is given unto them." And hereby they are 'persuaded' (though perhaps not all at all times, nor with the same fullness of persuasion) "that neither death, nor life, nor things present, nor things to come, nor height, nor depth, nor any other creature, shall be able to separate them from the love of God, which is in Christ Jesus our Lord."

5. Again, through this faith they are saved from the power of sin as well as from the guilt of it. So the Apostle declares, "Ye know that he was manifested to take away our sins, and in him is no sin. Whosoever abideth in him sinneth not." Again, "Little children, let no man deceive you. . . . He that committeth sin is of the devil." "Whosoever believeth is born of God." And, "Whosoever is born of God doth not commit sin; for his seed remaineth in him: and he cannot sin, because he is born of God." Once more, "We know that whosoever is born of God sinneth not; but he that is begotten of God keepeth himself, and that wicked one toucheth him not."

6. He that is by faith born of God sinneth not, (1), by any habitual sin, for all habitual sin is sin reigning; but sin cannot reign in any that believeth. Nor, (2), by any willful sin; for his will, while he abideth in the faith, is utterly set against all sin, and abhorreth it as deadly poison. Nor, (3), by any sinful desire; for he continually desireth the holy and perfect will of God; and any unholy desire he by the grace of God stifleth in the birth. Nor, (4), doth he sin by infirmities, whether in act, word, or thought; for his infirmities

have no concurrence of his will; and without this they are not properly sins. Thus, "He that is born of God doth not commit sin." And though he cannot say he hath not sinned, yet now "he sinneth not."

7. This then is the salvation which is through faith, even in the present world: a salvation from sin and the consequences of sin, both often expressed in the word "justification," which, taken in the largest sense, implies a deliverance from guilt and punishment, by the atonement of Christ actually applied to the soul of the sinner now believing on him, and a deliverance from the *whole body*[4] of sin, through Christ "formed in his heart." So that he who is thus justified or saved by faith is indeed "born again." He is "born again of the Spirit" unto a new "life which is hid with Christ in God." And as a "newborn babe he gladly receives sincere milk of the word, and grows thereby;" "going on in the might of the Lord his God," "from faith to faith," "from grace to grace," "until at length he comes unto a perfect man, unto the measure of the stature of the fullness of Christ."

III. The first usual objection to this is,
1. That to preach salvation or justification by faith only is to preach against holiness and good works. To which a short answer might be given: it would be so if we spake, as some do, of a faith which was separate from these. But we speak of a faith which is not so, but necessarily productive of all good works and all holiness.

2. But it may be of use to consider it more at large: especially since it is no new objection, but as old as St. Paul's time, for even then it was asked, "Do we not make void the law through faith?" We answer, first, all who preach not faith do manifestly make

---

[4] This is the original wording. In 1771 Wesley changed the words "whole body" to "power." The original wording is supplied here because it shows that in 1738 Wesley did link salvation from all sin to the new birth and saving faith.

void the law, either directly and grossly, by limitations and comments that eat out all the spirit of the text; or indirectly, by not pointing out the only means whereby it is possible to perform it. Whereas, secondly, "We establish the law," both by showing its full extent and spiritual meaning, and by calling all to that living way whereby "the righteousness of the law may be fulfilled in them." These, while they trust in the blood of Christ alone, use all the ordinances which he hath appointed, do all the "good works which he had before prepared that they should walk therein," and enjoy and manifest all holy and heavenly tempers, even the same "mind that was in Christ Jesus."

3. But does not preaching this faith lead men into pride? We answer, accidentally it may. Therefore ought every believer to be earnestly cautioned (in the words of the great Apostle): "Because of unbelief the first branches were broken off, and thou standest by faith. Be not high-minded, but fear. If God spared not the natural branches, take heed lest he spare not thee. Behold therefore the goodness and severity of God: on them which fell, severity; but toward thee, goodness, if thou continue in his goodness: otherwise thou also shalt be cut off." And while he continues therein, he will remember those words of St. Paul, foreseeing and answering this very objection: "Where is boasting, then? It is excluded. By what law? Of works? Nay; but by the law of faith." If a man were justified by his works, he would have whereof to glory. But there is no glorying for him "that worketh not, but believeth on him that justifieth the ungodly." To the same effect are the words both preceding and following the text: "God, who is rich in mercy,...even when we were dead in sins, hath quickened us together with Christ (by grace ye are saved),...that he might show the exceeding riches of his grace in his kindness toward us through Christ Jesus. For by grace ye are saved through faith: and that not of yourselves." Of yourselves cometh neither your faith nor your salvation. "It is the gift of God," the free, undeserved gift—the faith through which ye are saved, as well as the salvation which he of his own good pleasure, his mere favour, annexes

thereto. That ye believe is one instance of his grace; that believing, ye are saved, another. "Not of works, lest any man should boast." For all our works, all our righteousness, which were before our believing, merited nothing of God but condemnation, so far were they from deserving faith, which therefore, whenever given, is not "of works." Neither is salvation of the works we do when we believe. For "it is" then "God that worketh in us." And, therefore, that he giveth us a reward for what he himself worketh only commendeth the riches of his mercy, but leaveth us nothing whereof to glory.

4. However, may not the speaking thus of the mercy of God, as saving or justifying freely by faith only, encourage men in sin? Indeed it may and will; many will "continue in sin, that grace may abound". But their blood is upon their own head. The goodness of God ought to lead them to repentance, and so it will those who are sincere of heart. When they know there is yet forgiveness with him, they will cry aloud that he would blot out their sins also through faith which is in Jesus. And if they earnestly cry and faint not, if they seek him in all the means he hath appointed, if they refuse to be comforted till he come, he "will come, and will not tarry." And he can do much work in a short time. Many are the examples in the Acts of the Apostles of God's working this faith in men's hearts as quick as lightning falling from heaven. So in the same hour that Paul and Silas began to preach the jailer repented, believed, and was baptized—as were three thousand by St. Peter on the day of Pentecost, who all repented and believed at his first preaching. And, blessed be God, there are now many living proofs that he is still thus "mighty to save."

5. Yet to the same truth, placed in another view, a quite contrary objection is made: "If a man cannot be saved by all that he can do, this will drive men to despair." True, to despair of being saved by their own works, their own merits or righteousness. And so it ought; for none can trust in the merits of Christ till he has utterly renounced his own. He that "goeth about to establish his

own righteousness" cannot receive the righteousness of God. The righteousness which is of faith cannot be given him while he trusteth in that which is of the law.

6. But this, it is said, is an uncomfortable doctrine. The devil spoke like himself, that is, without either truth or shame, when he dared to suggest to men that it is such. 'Tis the only comfortable one, 'tis "very full of comfort," to all self-destroyed, self-condemned sinners. That "whosoever believeth on him shall not be ashamed;" that "the same Lord over all is rich unto all that call upon him"—here is comfort, high as heaven, stronger than death! What! Mercy for all? For Zaccheus, a public robber? For Mary Magdalene, a common harlot? Methinks I hear one say, "Then I, even I, may hope for mercy!" And so thou mayst, thou afflicted one, whom none hath comforted! God will not cast out thy prayer. Nay, perhaps he may say the next hour, "Be of good cheer, thy sins are forgiven thee;" so forgiven that they shall reign over thee no more; yea, and that "the Holy Spirit shall bear witness with thy spirit that thou art a child of God." O glad tidings! Tidings of great joy, which are sent unto all people. "Ho, everyone that thirsteth, come ye to the waters; come ye and buy without money, and without price." Whatsoever your sins be, "though red, like crimson," though "more than the hairs of your head," "return ye unto the Lord, and he will have mercy upon you, and to our God, for he will abundantly pardon."

7. When no more objections occur, then we are simply told that salvation by faith only ought not to be preached as the first doctrine, or at least not to be preached to all. But what saith the Holy Ghost? "Other foundation can no man lay than that which is laid, even Jesus Christ." So, then, "that whosoever believeth on him shall be saved" is and must be the foundation of all our preaching; that is, must be preached first. "Well, but not to all." To whom then are we not to preach it? Whom shall we except? The poor? Nay, they have a peculiar right to have the gospel preached unto them. The unlearned? No. God hath revealed these things

unto unlearned and ignorant men from the beginning. The young? By no means. "Suffer these" in any wise "to come unto Christ, and forbid them not." The sinners? Least of all. He "came not to call the righteous, but sinners to repentance." Why then, if any, we are to except the rich, the learned, the reputable, the moral men. And 'tis true, they too often except themselves from hearing; yet we must speak the words of our Lord. For thus the tenor of our commission runs: "Go and preach the gospel to every creature." If any man wrest it or any part of it to his destruction, he must bear his own burden. But still, "as the Lord liveth, whatsoever the Lord saith unto us, that we will speak."

8. At this time more especially will we speak, that "by grace ye are saved through faith": because never was the maintaining this doctrine more seasonable than it is at this day. Nothing but this can effectually prevent the increase of the Romish delusion among us. 'Tis endless to attack one by one all the errors of that Church. But salvation by faith strikes at the root, and all fall at once where this is established. It was this doctrine (which our Church justly calls "the strong rock and foundation of the Christian religion") that first drove popery out of these kingdoms, and 'tis this alone can keep it out. Nothing but this can give a check to that immorality which hath overspread the land as a flood. Can you empty the great deep drop by drop? Then you may reform us by dissuasives from particular vices. But let "the righteousness which is of God by faith" be brought in, and so shall its proud waves be stayed. Nothing but this can stop the mouths of those who "glory in their shame," "and openly deny the Lord that bought them." They can talk as sublimely of the law as he that hath it written by God in his heart. To hear them speak on this head might incline one to think they were not far from the kingdom of God. But take them out of the law into the gospel; begin with the righteousness of faith, with "Christ, the end of the law to everyone that believeth," and those who but now appeared almost if not altogether Christians stand confessed the sons of perdition,

as far from life and salvation (God be merciful unto them!) as the depth of hell from the height of heaven.

9. For this reason the adversary so rages whenever "salvation by faith" is declared to the world. For this reason did he stir up earth and hell to destroy those who first preached it. And for the same reason, knowing that faith alone could overturn the foundations of his kingdom, did he call forth all his forces, and employ all his arts of lies and calumny, to affright that glorious champion of the Lord of Hosts, Martin Luther, from reviving it. Nor can we wonder thereat. For as that man of God observes, "How would it enrage a proud strong man armed to be stopped and set at nought by a little child, coming against him with a reed in his hand!"— especially when he knew that little child would surely overthrow him and tread him under foot. "Even so, Lord Jesus!" Thus hath thy strength been ever "made perfect in weakness!" Go forth then, thou little child that believest in him, and his "right hand shall teach thee terrible things!" Though thou art helpless and weak as an infant of days, the strong man shall not be able to stand before thee. Thou shalt prevail over him, and subdue him, and overthrow him, and trample him under thy feet. Thou shalt march on under the great Captain of thy salvation "conquering and to conquer," until all thine enemies are destroyed, and "death is swallowed up in victory."

Now thanks be to God which giveth us the victory through our Lord Jesus Christ, to whom, with the Father and the Holy Ghost, be blessing and glory, and wisdom, and thanksgiving, and honour, and power, and might, for ever and ever. Amen

Victory Over Sin
October 13, 1738

When Wesley embraced his new gospel he became convinced that salvation from sin was instantly given in the new birth. Source: Works B 25:569.

To Benjamin Ingham

My Dear Brother,

God hath been wonderfully gracious to us ever since our return to England. Though there are many adversaries, yet a great door and effectual is opened; and we continue, through evil report and good report, to preach the gospel of Christ to all people, and earnestly to contend for the faith once delivered to the saints. Indeed, He hath given unto us many of our fiercest opposers, who now receive with meekness the ingrafted word. One of the bitterest of them could have no rest in his spirit till, on Saturday, the 30th of September, he was compelled to send for me, who knew him not so much as by face, and to tell me the secrets of his heart. He owned with many tears that, in spite of all his endeavors, he was still carnal, sold under sin; that he continually did the thing he would not, and was thereby convinced of the entire corruption of his whole nature; that the very night before, after the most solemn resolutions to the contrary, he had been guilty of gross drunkenness, and had no hope of escaping, having neither spirit nor strength left in him. We fell on our knees, and besought our Lord to bring this sinner unto God, who through His blood justifieth the ungodly. He arose, and his countenance was no longer sad; for he knew, and testified aloud, that he was passed from death unto life, and felt in himself that he was healed of his plague. And from that hour to this he hath had peace and joy in believing, and sin hath no more dominion over him.

Perfection in the New Birth
December, 1738

*In December Wesley wrote to the society in London to "know how
the work of God went among our brethren." In response he received
these two testimonies that explicitly link perfection to the new birth.
They thus illustrate Wesley's own confused beliefs at the time since he
published these testimonies in his journal. As we will learn in the next
section, it is little surprise that with his present beliefs on perfection
and the new birth Wesley struggled over questions of personal assurance following his Aldersgate conversion. Source: Works J 1:165-169.*

William Fish

My Dear Friend, whom I love in the truth,

I know my Saviour's voice, and my heart burns with love and
desire to follow him in the regeneration. I have no confidence in
the flesh. I loathe myself and love him only.

My dear brother, my spirit even at this moment rejoices in
God my Saviour, and the love which is shed abroad in my heart
by the Holy Ghost, destroys all self-love, so that I could lay down
my life for my brethren. I know that my Redeemer liveth, and
have confidence towards God that through his blood my sins are
forgiven. He hath begotten me of his own will and saves me from
sin, so that it has no dominion over me. His Spirit bears witness
with my spirit, that I am his child by adoption and grace. And this
is not for works of righteousness which I have done. For I am his
workmanship, created in Christ Jesus unto good works: so that all
boasting is excluded. It is now about eighteen years since Jesus
took possession of my heart. He then opened my eyes and said
unto me, "Be of good cheer, thy sins are forgiven thee."

My dear friend, bear with my relating after what manner I
was born of God. It was an instantaneous act. My whole heart
was filled with a divine power, drawing all the faculties of my

soul after Christ, which continued three or four nights and days. It was as a mighty rushing wind coming into the soul, enabling me from that moment to be more than conqueror over those corruptions which before I was always a slave to. Since that time the whole bent of my will hath been towards him day and night, even in my dreams. I know that I dwell in Christ, and Christ in me; I am bone of his bone, and flesh of his flesh. That you, and all who wait for his appearing, may find the consolation of Israel, is the earnest prayer of

Your affectionate brother in Christ,

From Another Friend

My most Dear and Honoured Father in Christ,

In the twentieth year of my age, 1737, God was pleased to open my eyes and to let me see that I did not live as became a child of God. I found my sins were great (though I was what they call a sober person) and that God kept an account of them all. However, I thought if I repented and led a good life, God would accept me. And so I went on for about half a year and had sometimes great joy. But last winter I began to find that whatever I did was nothing. My very tears I found were sin, and the enemy of souls laid so many things to my charge that sometimes I despaired of heaven. I continued in great doubts and fears till *April 9*, when I went out of town. Here for a time I was greatly transported, in meditating and seeing the glorious works of God, but in about three weeks I was violently assaulted again. God then offered a Saviour to me, but my self-righteousness kept me from laying hold on him.

On *Whitsunday* I went to receive the blessed sacrament, but with a heart as hard as a stone. Heavy laden I was indeed, when God was pleased to let me see a crucified Saviour. I saw there was a fountain opened in his side for me to wash in and to be clean. But alas! I was afraid to venture, fearing I should be too presumptuous. And I know, and am sure, I at that time refused the atonement which I might then have had. Yet I received great comfort. But in about nine days time my joy went out, as a lamp does for want of oil, and I fell into my old state, into a state of damnation. Yet I was not without hope, for ever after that time I could not despair of salvation: I had so clear a sight of the fountain opened in the side of our Lord. But still when I thought of death, or the day of judgment, it was a great terror to me. And yet I was afraid to venture to lay all my sins upon Christ.

This was not all. But whenever I retired to prayer I had a violent pain in my head. This only seized me when I began to pray earnestly, or to cry out aloud to Christ. But when I cried to him against this also, he gave me ease. Well, I found God did love me and did draw me to Christ. I hungered and thirsted after him and had an earnest desire to be clothed with his righteousness. But I was still afraid to go boldly to Christ and to claim him as my Saviour.

July 3. My dear sister came down to see me. She had received the atonement on St. Peter's Day. I told her I thought Christ died for me, but as to the assurance she mentioned I could say nothing.

July 5. She went. That night I went into the garden, and considering what she had told me, I saw him by faith, whose eyes are as a flame of fire, him who justifieth the ungodly. I told him I was ungodly, and it was for me that he died. His blood did I plead with great faith, to blot out the handwriting that was against me. I told my Saviour that he had promised to give rest to all that were heavy laden. This promise I claimed, and I saw him by faith stand condemned before God in my stead. I saw the fountain opened in his side. I found, as I hungered, he fed me: as my soul thirsted, he gave me out of that fountain to drink. And so strong was my faith that if I had had all the sins of the whole world laid upon me, I knew and was sure one drop of his blood was sufficient to atone for all. Well, I clave unto him, and he did wash me in his blood.

He hath clothed me with his righteousness and has presented me to his Father and my Father, to his God and my God, a pure, spotless virgin, as if I had never committed any sin. It is on Jesus I stand, the Saviour of sinners. It is he that hath loved me and given himself for me. I cleave unto him as my surety, and he is bound to pay God the debt. While I stand on this rock I am sure the gates of hell cannot prevail against me. It is by faith that I am justified and have peace with God through him. His blood has made reconciliation to God for me. It is by faith I have received the atonement. It is by faith that I have the Son of God and the Spirit of Christ dwelling in me. And what then shall separate me from the love of God which is in Christ Jesus my Lord?

You must think what a transport of joy I was then in, when I that was lost and undone, dropping into hell, felt a Redeemer come, who is "mighty to save," "to save unto the uttermost." Yet I did not receive the witness of the Spirit at that time. But in about half an hour the devil came with great power to tempt me. However, I minded him not, but went in and lay down pretty much composed in my mind. Now St. Paul says, "After ye believed, ye were sealed with the Spirit of promise." So it was with me. After I had believed on him that "justifieth the ungodly," I received that seal of the Spirit which is the "earnest of our inheritance." But at that time I did not know anything of this. My sins were forgiven, but I knew I was not yet born of God.

July 6. In the morning, being by myself, I found the work of the Spirit was very powerful upon me (although you know God does not deal with every soul in the same way). As my mother bore me with great pain, so did I feel great pain in my soul in being born of God. Indeed I thought the pains of death were upon me, and that my soul was then taking leave of the body. I thought I was going to him whom I saw with strong faith standing ready to receive me. In this violent agony I continued about four hours, and then I began to feel "the Spirit of God bearing witness with my spirit, that I was born of God." "Because I was a child of God he sent forth the Spirit of his Son into me, crying, Abba, Father."

For that is the cry of every newborn soul. O mighty, powerful, happy change! I who had nothing but devils ready to drag me to hell, now found I had angels to guard me to my reconciled Father and my Judge, who just before stood ready to condemn me, was now become my righteousness.

But I cannot express what God hath done for my soul. No; this is to be my everlasting employment, when I have put off this frail, sinful body, this corrupt, hellish nature of mine; when I join with that great multitude which no man can number, in singing praises to the Lamb that loved us and gave himself for us! O how powerful are the workings of the Almighty in a newborn soul! The love of God was shed abroad in my heart, and a flame kindled there, with pains so violent, yet so very ravishing, that my body was almost torn asunder. I loved. The Spirit cried strong in my heart. I sweated. I trembled. I fainted. I sung. I joined my voice with those that excel in strength. My soul was got up into the holy mount. I had no thoughts of coming down again into the body. I who not long before had called to the rocks to fall on me, and the mountains to cover me, could now call for nothing else but, "Come, Lord Jesus, come quickly."

Then I could cry out with great boldness, There, O God, is my surety! There, O death, is thy plague! There, O grave, is thy destruction! There, O serpent, is the seed that shall forever bruise thy head. O, I thought my head was a fountain of water! I was dissolved in love. "My Beloved is mine, and I am his." He has all charms. He has ravished my heart. He is my Comforter, my Friend, my All. He is now in his garden, feeding among the lilies. O, "I am sick of love." He is altogether lovely, "the chiefest among ten thousand." O how Jesus fills, Jesus extends, Jesus overwhelms the soul in which he dwells!

Section Three

The Middle Period

Part One

1738 – 1755

Questions to Consider for
John Wesley's Middle Period: Part One

1. Why begin this section with a study of Wesley's struggles? How did his struggles contribute to further development in his doctrine of Christian perfection?

2. Carefully read Christian David's testimony. What phrases and ideas did Wesley later incorporate into his own explication of perfect love?

3. How are justification, sanctification and the new birth defined in this period? Do his views develop through this period?

4. Once again, note how Wesley defines perfection in this section. What is the essential idea he is seeking to communicate? What has changed? What remains constant?

5. How is Christian perfection attained? What are the major stages of growth to perfect love?

6. How is sin defined in this period? What distinctions does Wesley make in his understanding of sin? What has changed from the prior periods?

7. What scripture arguments does Wesley use to articulate and defend his views on full salvation? Does Wesley's use of 1 John 3:9 in relation to perfection change over time?

8. Finally, when does Wesley embrace the idea of two works of grace (perfection as a second work of grace)?

Struggles Over Assurance
May-June, 1738

To fully appreciate why Wesley embraced a gospel of two works of grace, we must return to those heady days following his Aldersgate conversion; when he testified to receiving an assurance of acceptance and a deliverance from the "law of sin and death" (happiness and holiness). The fact is Wesley continued to wrestle with doubts regarding his salvation. These doubts became the existential testing ground for the claim that in the new birth the believer is delivered from all sin. Source: Works B 18:253-254.

Journal

Mon. 29. I set out for Dummer with Mr. Wolf, one of the first-fruits of Peter Böhler's ministry in England. I was much strengthened by the grace of God in him: yet was his state so far above mine that I was often tempted to doubt whether we had one faith. But, without much reasoning about it, I held here: "Though his be strong and mine weak, yet that God hath given some degree of faith even to me I know by its fruits. For I have constant peace, not one uneasy thought. And I have freedom from sin, not one unholy desire."

Yet on Wednesday did I grieve the Spirit of God, not only by not "watching unto prayer," but likewise by speaking with sharpness instead of tender love, of one that was not sound in the faith. Immediately God hid his face and I was troubled; and in this heaviness I continued till the next morning, June 1, when it pleased God, while I was exhorting another, to give comfort to my soul, and (after I had spent some time in prayer) to direct me to those gracious words, "Having therefore boldness to enter into the holiest by the blood of Jesus,...let us draw near with a true heart in full assurance of faith...Let us hold fast the profession of our faith without wavering (for he is faithful that promised), and let us consider one another, to provoke unto love and to good works."

Saturday, June 3. I was so strongly assaulted by one of my old enemies that I had scarce strength to open my lips, or even to look up for help. But after I had prayed, faintly, as I could, the temptation vanished away.

Tue. 6. I had still more comfort, and peace, and joy; on which I fear I began to presume. For in the evening I received a letter from Oxford which threw me into much perplexity. It was asserted therein that no doubting could consist with the least degree of true faith; that whoever at any time felt any doubt or fear was not weak in faith, but had no faith at all; and that none hath any faith till the law of the Spirit of life has made him wholly free from the law of sin and death.

Begging of God to direct me, I opened my Testament on 1 Cor. 3, verse 1, etc., where St. Paul speaks of those whom he terms "babes in Christ," who were "not able to bear strong meat," nay (in a sense) "carnal;" to whom nevertheless he says, "Ye are God's building," "Ye are the temple of God." Surely, then these men had some degree of faith, though it is plain their faith was but weak.

After some hours spent in the Scripture and prayer I was much comforted. Yet I felt a kind of soreness in my heart, so that I found my wound was not fully healed. O God, save thou me, and all that are 'weak in the faith', from 'doubtful disputations'!

Wednesday, June 7. I determined, if God should permit, to retire for a short time into Germany. I had fully purposed before I left Georgia so to do, if it should please God to bring me back to Europe. And I now clearly saw the time was come. My weak mind could not bear to be thus sawn asunder. And I hoped the conversing with those holy men who were themselves *living witnesses of the full power of faith,* and yet able to bear with those that are weak, would be a means, under God, of so stablishing my soul, that I might "go on from faith to faith, and from strength to strength."

Living Proofs
July 1738

In June Wesley traveled to Germany to learn from the Moravian mother-church the nature of true faith and salvation. Wesley spent several days with Count Zinzendorf in early July where he says he "continually met what he sought for." The following two letters and journal excerpt offer insights into the kind of holiness Wesley was seeking at the time. The reader should take note how faith and assurance are linked to salvation from all sin. Sources: Letters: Telford; Journal: Works J 1:110.

To Brother Charles
July 7

Dear Brother,

I am now with the Count, at his uncle's the Count of Solms, five or six hours from Marienborn; and have stole an hour to let you know that hitherto God hath been very merciful to us in all things. The spirit of the Brethren is beyond our highest expectations. Young and old, they breathe nothing but faith and love at all times and in all places. I do not therefore concern myself with smaller points that touch not the essence of Christianity, but endeavor (God being my helper) to grow up in these after the glorious examples set before me; having already seen with my own eyes more than one hundred witnesses of that everlasting truth, "Every one that believeth hath peace with God and is freed from sin, and is in Christ a new creature."

See therefore, my brethren, that none of you receive the grace of God in vain! But be ye also living witnesses of the exceeding great and precious promises which are made unto every one of us through the blood of Jesus.

Adieu

To Brother Samuel
July 7

Dear Brother,

God has given me at length the desire of my heart. I am with a Church whose conversation is in heaven, in whom is the mind that was in Christ, and who so walk as He walked. As they have all one Lord and one faith, so they are all partakers of one Spirit, the spirit of meekness and love, which uniformly and continually animates all their conversation. Oh how high and holy a thing Christianity is! and how widely distant from that (I know not what) which is so called, though it neither purifies the heart nor renews the life after the image of our blessed Redeemer!

I grieve to think how that holy name by which we are called must be blasphemed among the heathen while they see discontented Christians, passionate Christians, resentful Christians, earthly-minded Christians--yea (to come to what we are apt to count small things), while they see Christians judging one another, ridiculing one another, speaking evil of one another, increasing instead of bearing one another's burdens. How bitterly would Julian have applied to these, 'See how these Christians love one another'! I know I myself, I doubt you sometimes, and my sister often, have been under this condemnation. Oh may God grant we may never more think to do Him service by breaking those commands which are the very life of His religion! But may we utterly put away all anger, and wrath, and malice, and bitterness, and evil-speaking...

Journal
July 8

I lodged with one of the brethren at Eckershausen, an English mile from Marienborne, where I usually spent the day, chiefly in conversing with those who could speak either Latin or English;

not being able, for want of more practice, to speak German readily. And here I continually met with what I sought for, viz., living proofs of the power of faith: Persons saved from inward as well as outward sin, by "the love of God shed abroad in their hearts;" and from all doubt and fear, by the abiding witness of "the Holy Ghost given unto them."

Christian David's Testimony
August, 1738

Christian David (1691-1747) was a carpenter by trade. Having been raised a Roman Catholic; he dabbled into Judaism before experiencing an evangelical conversion. David then became a revival preacher. He joined the Moravians in 1722. Wesley met with David for several days in mid-August and listened to him preach four times and give his testimony. His influence on Wesley's theological development becomes obvious upon a careful reading of his testimony below. Many of the key concepts and language found in Wesley's later explication on heart holiness were first expressed by David in this testimony. This shows that Wesley was first exposed to the idea of two works of grace from the German Moravians. He then adapted it to his own theological principles. Source: Works B 18:273-276, 279-28 (paragraphs numbered by editor).

1. When I was young I was much troubled at hearing some affirm that the Pope was antichrist. I read the Lutheran books writ against the Papists, and the popish books writ against the Lutherans. I easily saw that the Papists were in the wrong; but not that the Lutherans were in the right. I could not understand what they meant by being justified by faith, by faith alone, by faith without works. Neither did I like their talking so much of Christ. Then I began to think, How can Christ be the Son of God? But the more I reasoned with myself upon it, the more confused I was, till at last I loathed the very name of Christ. I could not bear to mention it. I hated the sound of it; and would never willingly have either read or heard it. In this temper I left Moravia, and wandered through many countries, seeking rest, but finding none.

2. In these wanderings I fell among some Jews. Their objections against the New Testament threw me into fresh doubts. At last I set myself to read over the Old Testament, and see if the prophecies therein contained were fulfilled. I was soon convinced they were. And thus much I gained, a fixed belief that Jesus was the Christ.

3. But soon after a new doubt arose: Are the New Testament prophecies fulfilled? This I next set myself to examine. I read them carefully over, and could not but see every event answered the prediction; so that the more I compared the one with the other, the more fully I was convinced that "all Scripture was given by inspiration of God."

Yet still my soul was not in peace. Nor indeed did I expect it till I should have openly renounced the errors of popery; which accordingly I did at Berlin. I now also led a very strict life. I read much, and prayed much. I did all I could to conquer sin; yet it profited not; I was still conquered by it. Neither found I any more rest among the Lutherans than I did before among the Papists.

4. At length, not knowing what to do, I listed myself a soldier. Now I thought I should have more time to pray, and read, having with me a New Testament and a hymn-book. But in one day both my books were stole. This almost broke my heart. Finding also in this way of life all the inconveniences which I thought to avoid by it, after six months I returned to my trade, and followed it two years. Removing then to Görlitz in Saxony, I fell into a dangerous illness. I could not stir hand nor foot for twenty weeks. Pastor Schwedler came to me every day. And from him it was that the gospel of Christ came first with power to my soul.

5. Here I found the peace I had long sought in vain; for I was assured my sins were forgiven. Not indeed all at once, but by degrees; not in one moment, nor in one hour. For I could not immediately believe that I was forgiven, because of the mistake I was then in concerning forgiveness. I saw not then that the first promise to the children of God is, "Sin shall no more reign over you;" but thought I was to *feel it in me* no more from the time it was forgiven. Therefore, although I had the mastery over it, yet I often feared it was not forgiven, because it still *stirred in me*, and at some times "thrust sore at me that I might fall." Because, though it did not *reign*, it did *remain* in me; and I was continually *tempted*, though not *overcome*. This at that time threw me into

many doubts; not understanding that the devil *tempts*, properly speaking, only those whom he perceives to be escaping from him. He need not tempt his own. For they "lie in the wicked one" (as St. John observes) and do his will with greediness. But those whom Christ is setting free he tempts day and night, to see if he can recover them to his kingdom. Neither saw I then that the "being justified" is widely different from the having the "full assurance of faith." I remembered not that our Lord told his apostles before his death, "Ye are clean;" whereas it was not till many days after it that they were fully assured, by the Holy Ghost then received, of their reconciliation to God through his blood. The difference between these fruits of the Spirit was as yet hid from me; so that I was hardly and slowly convinced I had the one, because I had not the other.

6. When I was recovered from my illness I resolved to return into Moravia, and preach Christ to my relations there. Thence I came back to Görlitz, where I continued five years, and there was a great awakening both in the town and country round about. In this space I made two more journeys into Moravia, where more and more came to hear me, many of whom promised to come to me, wherever I was, when a door should be opened for them.

After my return from my third journey Count Zinzendorf sent to Görlitz, the minister of Berthelsdorf being dead, for Mr. Rothe, who was in a gentleman's family there, to be minister of that place. Mr. Rothe told him of me, and he writ to me to come to him. And when I came said, "Let as many as will of your friends come hither; I will give them land to build on, and Christ will give the rest." I went immediately into Moravia and told them God had now found out a place for us. Ten of them followed me then; ten more the next year; one more in my following journey. The Papists were now alarmed, set a price upon my head, and leveled the house I had lodged in, even with the ground. I made however eleven journeys thither in all, and conducted as many as desired it to this place, the way to which was now so well known that many more came of themselves.

7. Eighteen years ago we built the first house. We chose to be near the great road rather than at Berthelsdorf (for the Count gave us our choice), hoping we might thereby find opportunities of instructing some that traveled by us. In two years we were increased to a hundred and fifty, when I contracted an intimate acquaintance with a Calvinist, who after some time brought me over to his opinions touching election and reprobation; and by me were most of our brethren likewise brought over to the same opinions. About this time we were in great straits, wherewith many were much dejected. I endeavoured to comfort them with the sense of God's love towards them. But they answered, "Nay, it may be he hath no love toward us; it may be we are not of the election, but God hated us from eternity, and therefore he has suffered all these things to come upon us." The Count, observing this, desired me to go to a neighbouring minister, Pastor Steinmetz, and talk with him fully on that head, "Whether Christ died for all." I did so, and by him God fully convinced me of that important truth. And not long after the Count desired we might all meet together, and consider these things thoroughly. We met accordingly at his house, and parted not for three days. We opened the Scriptures, and considered the account which is given therein of the whole economy of God with man, from the creation to the consummation of all things. And by the blessing of God we came all to one mind; particularly in that fundamental point that "he willeth all men to be saved, and to come to the knowledge of his truth."

8. In the meantime we found a great remissness of behaviour had crept in among us. And indeed the same was to be found in most of those round about us, whether Lutherans or Calvinists, so insisting on faith as to forget, at least in practice, both holiness and good works...

9. Observing this terrible abuse of preaching Christ *given for us*, we began to insist more than ever on Christ *living in us*. All our exhortations and preaching turned on this; we spoke, we writ, of

nothing else. Our constant inquiries were: "Is Christ formed in you? Have you a new heart? Is your soul renewed in the image of God? Is the whole body of sin destroyed in you? Are you fully assured, beyond all doubt or fear, that you are a child of God? In what manner and at what moment did you receive that full assurance?" If a man could not answer all these questions, we judged he had no true faith. Nor would we permit any to receive the Lord's Supper among us till he could.

10. In this persuasion we were when I went to Greenland five years ago. There I had a correspondence by letter with a Danish minister, Hans Egede, on the head of justification. And it pleased God to show me by him (though he was by no means a holy man, but openly guilty of gross sins) that we had now leaned too much to this hand, and were run into another extreme: that "*Christ in us*" and "*Christ for us*" ought indeed to be both insisted on, but first and principally "Christ for us," as being the ground of all. I now clearly saw we ought not to insist on anything we *feel*, any more than anything we *do*, as if it were necessary previous to justification or the remission of sins. I saw that least of all ought we so to insist on the full assurance of faith, or the destruction of the body of sin, and the extinction of all its motions, as to exclude those who had not attained this from the Lord's Table, or to deny that they had any faith at all. I plainly perceived this full assurance was a distinct gift from justifying faith, and often not given till long after it; and that justification does not imply that sin should not stir in us, but only that it should not *conquer*.

11. And now first it was that I had that full assurance of my own reconciliation to God through Christ. For many years I had had the forgiveness of my sins, and a measure of the peace of God; but I had not till now that witness of his Spirit which shuts out all doubt and fear. In all my trials I had always a confidence in Christ, who had done so great things for me. But it was a confidence mixed with fear: I was afraid *I had not done enough*. There was always something dark in my soul till now. But now the

clear light shined; and I saw that what I had hitherto so constantly insisted on, the *doing* so much and *feeling* so much, the long repentance and preparation for believing, the bitter sorrow for sin, and that deep contrition of heart which is found in some, were by no means essential to justification. Yea, that wherever the free grace of God is rightly preached, a sinner in the full career of his sins will probably receive it, and be justified by it, before one who insists on such previous preparation.

12. At my return to Herrnhut I found it difficult at first to make my brethren sensible of this, or to persuade them not to insist on the assurance of faith as a necessary qualification for receiving the Lord's Supper. But from the time they were convinced, which is now three years since, we have all chiefly insisted on Christ "given for us." This we urge as the principal thing, which if we rightly believe, Christ will surely be "formed in us." And this preaching we have always found to be accompanied with power, and to have the blessing of God following it. By this, believers receive a steady purpose of heart, and a more unshaken resolution to endure with a free and cheerful spirit whatsoever our Lord is pleased to lay upon them.

Falling Short
1738-1739

Throughout the remainder of the year Wesley continued to struggle with questions of assurance, faith, and personal holiness (or the lack thereof). These confessions reveal more than Wesley's struggles, they offer incisive insights his beliefs about perfection at the time. Wesley finally came to the understanding that he had genuine faith, but that his faith was not yet fully renewed. Along with Christian David's teachings, Wesley came to see there are degrees to saving faith. This opened the door for the idea of two works of grace within his theology. Source: Works B 19:16-19, 20, 21-22, 27-28, 29-31.

Journal

(October 14). An extract from this I wrote to a friend, concerning the state of those who are "weak in faith." His answer, which I received on *Saturday 14*, threw me into great perplexity, till after crying to God I took up a Bible, which opened on these words: "And Jabez called on the God of Israel, saying, O that thou wouldst bless me indeed and enlarge my coast! And that thine hand might be with me, and that thou wouldst keep me from evil, that it may not grieve me! And God granted him that which he requested."

This, however, with a sentence in the Evening Lesson, put me upon considering my own state more deeply. And what then occurred to me was as follows:

"Examine yourselves, whether ye be in the faith." Now the surest test whereby we can examine ourselves, whether we be indeed in the faith, is that given by St. Paul: "If any man be in Christ, he is a new creature. Old things are passed away. Behold all things are become new."

116

First, his judgments are new: his judgment of himself, of happiness, of holiness.

He judges himself to be altogether fallen short of the glorious image of God; to have no good thing abiding in him, but all that is corrupt and abominable; in a word, to be wholly earthly, sensual, and devilish—a motley mixture of beast and devil.

Thus, by the grace of God in Christ, I judge of myself. Therefore I am in this respect a new creature.

Again, his judgment concerning happiness is new. He would as soon expect to dig it out of the earth as to find it in riches, honour, pleasure (so called), or indeed in the enjoyment of any creature. He knows there can be no happiness on earth but in the enjoyment of God and in the foretaste of those "rivers of pleasure which flow at his right hand for evermore."

Thus, by the grace of God in Christ, I judge of happiness. Therefore I am in this respect a new creature.

Yet again, his judgment concerning holiness is new. He no longer judges it to be an outward thing, to consist either in doing no harm, in doing good, or in using the ordinances of God. He sees it is the life of God in the soul; the image of God fresh stamped on the heart; an entire renewal of the mind in every temper and thought, after the likeness of him that created it.

Thus, by the grace of God in Christ, I judge of holiness. Therefore I am in this respect a new creature.

Secondly, his designs are new. It is the design of his life not to heap up treasures upon earth, not to gain the praise of men, not to indulge the desires of the flesh, the desire of the eye, or the pride of life; but to regain the image of God, to have the life of God again planted in his soul, and to be renewed after his likeness, in righteousness and all true holiness.

This, by the grace of God in Christ, is the design of my life. Therefore I am in this respect a new creature.

Thirdly, his desires are new, and indeed the whole train of his passions and inclinations. They are no longer fixed on earthly things. They are now set on the things of heaven. His love and joy and hope, his sorrow and fear, have all respect to things above. They all point heavenward. Where his treasure is, there is his heart also.

I dare not say I am a new creature in this respect. For other desires often arise in my heart. But they do not reign. I put them all under my feet through Christ which strengtheneth me. Therefore I believe he is creating me anew in this also, and that he has begun, though not finished, his work.

Fourthly, his conversation is new. It is "always seasoned with salt," and fit to "minister grace to the hearers." So is mine, by the grace of God in Christ. Therefore in this respect I am a new creature.

Fifthly, his actions are new. The tenor of his life singly points at the glory of God. All his substance and time are devoted thereto. "Whether he eats or drinks, or whatever he does," it either springs from, or leads to, the love of God and man.

Such, by the grace of God in Christ, is the tenor of my life. Therefore in this respect I am a new creature.

But St. Paul tells us elsewhere that "the fruit of the Spirit is love, peace, joy, long-suffering, gentleness, meekness, temperance." Now although, by the grace of God in Christ, I find a measure of some of these in myself, viz. of peace, long-suffering, gentleness, meekness, temperance; yet others I find not. I cannot find in myself the love of God or of Christ. Hence my deadness and wanderings in public prayer. Hence it is that even in the

Holy Communion I have rarely any more than a cold attention. Hence when I hear of the highest instance of God's love, my heart is still senseless and unaffected. Yea, at this moment, I feel no more love to him than to one I had never heard of.

Again, I have not that "joy in the Holy Ghost;" no settled, lasting joy. Nor have I such a peace as excludes the possibility either of fear or doubt. When holy men have told me I had no faith, I have often doubted whether I had or no. And those doubts have made me very uneasy, till I was relieved by prayer and the Holy Scriptures.

Yet, upon the whole, although I have not yet that joy in the Holy Ghost, nor that love of God shed abroad in my heart, nor the full assurance of faith, nor the (proper) witness of the Spirit with my spirit that I am a child of God, much less am I, in the full and proper sense of the words, in Christ a new creature; I nevertheless trust that I have a measure of faith and am "accepted in the Beloved": I trust "the handwriting that was against me is blotted out," and that I am "reconciled to God through his Son."

(Sun. 29). In the evening, being troubled in what some said of "the kingdom of God within us," and doubtful of my own state, I called upon God and received this answer from his Word, "He himself also waited for the kingdom of God." "But should not I wait in silence and retirement?" was the thought that immediately struck into my mind. I opened my Testament again, on those words, "Seest thou not how faith wrought together with his works? And by works was faith made perfect?"

Finding the same doubts return on Tuesday, I consulted the oracles of God again and found much comfort from those words, "They which be of faith are blessed with faithful Abraham."

Thur. (November) 23. Returning from preaching at the Castle, I met once more with my old companion in affliction Charles Delamotte, who stayed with me till Monday. His last conversation with me was as follows:

> In this you are better than you was at Savannah. You know that you was then quite wrong. But you are not right yet. You know that you was then blind. But you do not see now.
>
> I doubt not but God will bring you to the right foundation. But I have no hope for you, while you are on your present foundation. It is as different from the true, as the right hand from the left. You have all to begin anew.
>
> I have observed all your words and actions, and I see you are of the same spirit still. You have a simplicity. But it is a simplicity of your own. It is not the simplicity of Christ. You think you do not trust in your own works. But you do trust in your own works. You do not yet believe in Christ.
>
> You have a present freedom from sin. But it is only a temporary suspension of it, not a deliverance from it. And you have a peace. But it is not a true peace. If death were to approach, you would find all your fears return.
>
> But I am forbid to say any more. My heart sinks in me like a stone.

I was troubled. I begged of God an answer of peace and opened on those words, "As many as walk according to this rule, peace be on them, and mercy, and upon the Israel of God." I was asking in the evening that God would fulfill all his promises in my soul, when I opened my Testament on those words, "My hour is not yet come."

Sat. (December) 16. One who had examined himself by the reflections wrote October 14 made the following observations on the state of his own soul:

Falling Short

I. 1. I judge thus of myself. But I feel it not. Therefore there is in me still the old heart of stone.

2. I judge thus of happiness. But I still hanker after creature happiness. My soul is almost continually running out after one creature or another and imagining how happy should I be in such or such a condition. I have more pleasure in eating and drinking, and in the company of those I love, than I have in God. I have a relish for earthly happiness. I have not a relish for heavenly. "I savour the things of men, not the things of God." Therefore there is in me still the carnal heart.

3. I judge thus of holiness. But I know it not. I know not (by experience) what the life of God means. Indeed I see neither myself, nor happiness, nor holiness, but by a natural light acquired in a natural way, by conversing, reading, and meditation. I have not spiritual light. I have not the supernatural light. I am not taught of God.

I speculatively know what light is, and I see the light of faith, just as that man sees the light of the sun, on whose closed eyes the sun shines. But I want the Holy Ghost to open my eyes, that I may see all things clearly.

Therefore the eyes of my understanding are not yet opened, but the old veil is still upon my heart.

II. "This is the design of my life." But a thousand little designs are daily stealing into my soul. This is my ultimate design; but intermediate designs are continually creeping in upon me, designs (though often disguised) of pleasing myself, of doing my own will; designs wherein I do not eye God, at least not him singly. Therefore my eye is not yet single, but I am still of a double heart.

III. Are my desires new? Not all. Some are new, some old. Not any properly; but partly new and partly old. My desires are like my designs. My great desire is to have "Christ formed in my heart by faith." But little desires are daily stealing into my soul. And so my great hopes and fears have respect to God. But a thousand little ones creep in between them.

Again, my desires, passions, and inclinations in general are mixed, having something of Christ and something of earth. I love you, for instance. But my love is only partly spiritual and partly natural. Something of my own cleaves to that which is of God. Nor can I divide the earthly part from the heavenly.

Thur. (January) 4. One who had had the form of godliness many years wrote the following reflections:

My friends affirm I am mad, because I said "I was not a Christian a year ago." I affirm, I am not a Christian now. Indeed, what I might have been I know not, had I been faithful to the grace then given, when, expecting nothing less, I received such a sense of the forgiveness of my sins as till then I never knew. But that I am not a Christian at this day I as assuredly know as that Jesus is the Christ.

For a Christian is one who has the fruits of the Spirit of Christ, which (to mention no more) are love, peace, joy. But these I have not. I have not any love of God. I do not love either the Father or the Son. Do you ask, How do I know whether I love God? I answer by another question, How do you know whether you love me? Why, as you know whether you are hot or cold. You feel this moment that you do or do not love me. And I feel this moment I do not love God; which therefore I know, because I feel it. There is no word more proper, more clear, or more strong.

And I know it also by St. John's plain rule, "If any man love the world, the love of the Father is not in him." For I love the world. I desire the things of the world, some or other of them, and have done all my life. I have always placed some part of my happiness in some or other of the things that are seen. Particularly in meat and drink, and in the company of those I loved. My desire, if not in a gross and lustful, yet in a more subtle and refined manner, has been almost continually running out towards this or that person. For many years I have been, yea, and still am, hankering after a happiness in loving and in being loved by one or another. And in these I have from time to time taken more pleasure than in God. Nay, I do so at this day. I often ask my heart, when I am in company with one that I love, "Do I take more delight in you or in God?" And cannot but answer, In you. For in truth I do not delight in God at all. Therefore I am so far from loving God with all my heart that whatever I love at all, I love more than God. So that all the love I have is flat idolatry.

Again, joy in the Holy Ghost I have not. I have now and then some starts of joy in God: but it is not that joy. For it is not abiding. Neither is it greater than I have had on some worldly occasions. So that I can in no wise be said to "rejoice evermore," much less to "rejoice with joy unspeakable and full of glory."

Yet again, I have not "the peace of God;" that peace, peculiarly so called. The peace I have may be easily accounted for on natural principles. I have health, strength, friends, a competent fortune, and a composed, cheerful temper. Who would not have a sort of peace in such circumstances? But I have none which can with any truth or propriety be called a peace which passeth all understanding.

From hence I conclude (and let all the "saints of the world" hear, that whereinsoever they boast they may be found even as I), though I have given, and do give, all my goods to feed the poor, I am not a Christian. Though I have endured hardship, though I have in all things denied myself and taken up my cross, I am not a Christian. My works are nothing, my sufferings are nothing; I have not the fruits of the Spirit of Christ. Though I have constantly used all the means of grace for twenty years, I am not a Christian. Yea, though I have all (other) faith, since I have not "that faith" which "purifieth the heart." Verily, verily I say unto you, I "must be born again." For except I, and you, be born again, we "cannot see the kingdom of God."

Degrees of Regeneration
January, 1739

This is Wesley's first journal comment following Aldersgate distinguishing between higher and lower degrees of regeneration. In the prior chapter we saw Wesley examining himself whether he was a new creation or not (cf. Oct. 14 & Dec. 16 comments). He denied his faith was fully renewed because he still lacked a single eye in his intentions and desires. Finally, on January 4 he claimed he was not a Christian because he was not a perfect one. Yet three weeks later he made a clear distinction between the new birth in a lower sense *and a* full sense. *Thus, Wesley is moving in the direction of formally embracing the idea of two works of grace. But the idea that regeneration comprehends the complete work of sanctification did persist for many years in Wesley's thought and writings. Source: Works J 1:172.*

Journal

I baptized John Smith (late an Anabaptist) and four other adults at Islington. Of the adults I have known baptized lately, one only was at that time born again, in the full sense of the word; that is, found a thorough, inward change, by the love of God filling her heart. Most of them were only born again in a lower sense; that is, received the remission of their sins. And some (as it has since too plainly appeared) neither in one sense nor the other.

The Kingdom Within
February, 1739

In early 1739 Wesley published An Abstract of the Life and Death of the Reverend Learned and Pious Mr. Thomas Halyburton. *In the preface Wesley spells out his sanctification views. Wesley's theme is the inward Kingdom of God, bringing happiness and holiness to the believer. The reader should take note how Wesley defines sin and its deliverance in this preface. Also, be attentive to how he supports his views on full salvation scripturally. What passages does he use? Over the next two years his scriptural arguments will change. Last, take note how salvation is received and why the blessing is so often intermittent. Source: Works J 14:211-214 (second edition).*

1. "The kingdom of God," saith our blessed Lord "is within you." It is no outward, no distant thing; "but a well of living water" in the soul, "springing up into ever-lasting life." It is "righteousness, and peace, and joy in the Holy Ghost." It is holiness and happiness.

2. The general manner wherein it pleases God to set it up in the heart is this: A sinner, being drawn by the love of the Father, enlightened by the Son, ("the true light which lighteth every man that cometh into the world,") and convinced of sin by the Holy Ghost; through the preventing grace which is given him freely, cometh weary and heavy laden, and casteth all his sins upon Him that is "mighty to save." He receiveth from Him true, living faith. Being justified by faith, he hath peace with God: He rejoices in hope of the glory of God, and knows that sin hath no more dominion over him. And the love of God is shed abroad in his heart, producing all holiness of heart and of conversation.

3. This work of God in the soul of man is so described in the following treatise, as I have not seen it in any other, either ancient or modern, in our own or any other language. So that I cannot but value it, next to the holy Scriptures, above any other human com-

position, excepting only the "Christian Pattern," and the small remains of Clemens Romanus, Polycarp, and Ignatius.

4. Yet this great servant of God at some times fell back from the glorious liberty he had received into the spirit of fear, and sin, and bondage. But why was it thus? because the hand of the Lord was shortened? No, verily; but because he did not abide in Christ; because he did not cleave to Him with all his heart; because he grieved the Holy Spirit, wherewith he was sealed, by some, perhaps undiscerned, unfaithfulness; who thereupon for a season departed from him, and left him weak and like another man.

5. But it may be said, "The Gospel covenant does not promise entire freedom from sin." What do you mean by the word "sin?" those numberless weaknesses and follies, sometimes (improperly) termed sins of infirmity? If you mean only this, we shall not put off these but with our bodies. But if you mean, "It does not promise entire freedom from sin, in its proper sense, or from committing sin," this is by no means true, unless the Scripture be false; for thus it is written: "Whosoever is born of God doth not commit sin;" (unless he lose the Spirit of adoption, if not finally, yet for a while, as did this child of God;) "for his seed remaineth in him, and he cannot sin, because he is born of God." He cannot sin so long as "he keepeth himself;" for then "that wicked one toucheth him not." (1 John 3:9; 5:18)

6. We see, then, how to judge of that other assertion, "that the mercy of God to his sons in Christ Jesus extends to all infirmities, follies, and sins; multiplied relapses not excepted." We grant, many of the children of God find mercy, notwithstanding multiplied relapses: But though it is possible a man may be a child of God who is not fully freed from sin, it does not follow, that freedom from sin is impossible; or, that it is not to be expected by all: For it is promised. It is describe by the Holy Ghost as the common privilege of all; and "God will be mindful" (O let us be so!)

127

"of his covenant and promise which He hath made to a thousand generations."

7. This caution is necessary to be remembered, that ye who are weak be not offended. Neither be ye offended, when ye hear the wisdom of the world pronounce all this mere enthusiasm: A hard word, which most of those who are fondest of it, no more understand than they do Arabic. Ask, in the spirit of meekness, him who calls it so, "Is the kingdom of God set up in your soul? Do you feel that peace of God which passeth all understanding? Do you rejoice with joy unspeakable and full of glory? Is the love of God shed abroad in your heart by the Holy Ghost which dwelleth in you? If not, you are no judge of these matters. You cannot discern the things of the Spirit of God. They are enthusiasm, madness, foolishness, to you; for they are spiritually discerned."

8. Ask such a one, (but with meekness and love,) "Are you taught of God? Do you know that he abideth in you? Have you the revelation of the Holy Ghost" (they are the words of our own Church) "inspiring into you the true meaning of Scripture? If you have not, with all your human science and worldly wisdom, you know nothing yet as you ought to know. Whatever you are in other respects, as to the things of God, you are an unlearned and ignorant man. And if you are unstable too, you will wrest these, as you do also the other scriptures, to your own destruction."

9. Be not then surprised, ye that wait for peace, and joy, and love, through faith in the blood of Jesus, that such judges as these are continually crying out, "Enthusiasm!" if you speak of the inward operations of the Holy Spirit. And as to you who have already peace with God, through our Lord Jesus Christ; who now feel his love shed abroad in your hearts, by the Holy Ghost which is given unto you; with whose spirit the Spirit of God beareth witness that ye are the sons of God, it is your part to confirm your love towards them, in all lowliness and meekness; (for who is it that maketh thee to differ? Or what hast thou, which thou hast not

received?) and to plead earnestly for them at the throne of grace, that the Day-star may appear in their hearts also, and the Sun of Righteousness at length arise upon them, with healing in his wings!

Key Doctrines Clarified
1739–1740

From the summer of 1739 through the early months of 1740 Wesley faced strong opposition to the Methodist revival and message. This opposition served as an opportunity to work out the interrelationship between the essential doctrines of his new gospel; specifically, justification, sanctification and the new birth. This process served to develop his own version of a gospel of two works of grace separate from the Moravians. Implicit in this process was the development of specific stages in the faith journey. Wesley's evangelical ordo salutis *is beginning to take shape.*

The first excerpt was Wesley's response to Henry Stebbing, a well-known champion of Anglican orthodoxy. Stebbing published a tract criticizing the Methodist message of the new birth. Pay close attention to how Wesley's theology of the new birth correlates to his doctrine of full sanctification.

The second extract involves a discussion with a serious clergyman *of the Church. Wesley now takes the important step to formally distinguish justification from sanctification, even though the latter is still treated as synonymous with the new birth.*

The last excerpt was Wesley's first written acknowledgment of the wilderness state, *which lies between justification and entire sanctification. Source: Works J 1:213-215, 224-225, 265.*

New Birth & Sanctification
Journal: July, 31, 1739

Having *A Caution against Religious Delusion* put into my hands about this time, I thought it my duty to write to the author of it, which I accordingly did, in the following terms:

Reverend Sir,

1. You charge me (for I am called a "Methodist," and consequently included within your charge) with "vain and confident

boastings, rash, uncharitable censures, damning all who do not feel what I feel;" "not allowing men to be in a salvable state unless they have experienced some sudden operation, which may be distinguished as the hand of God upon them, overpowering as it were the soul": with "denying men the use of God's creatures, which he hath appointed to be received with thanksgiving, and encouraging abstinence, prayer, and other religious exercises, to the neglect of the duties of our station." O sir, can you prove this charge upon me? The Lord shall judge in that day!

2. I do indeed go out into the highways and hedges to call poor sinners to Christ. But not "in a tumultuous manner," not "to the disturbance of the public peace" or "the prejudice of families." Neither herein do I break any law which I know, much less "set at naught all rule and authority." Nor can I be said to "intrude into the labours" of those who do not labour at all, but suffer thousands of those for whom Christ died to "perish for lack of knowledge."

3. They perish for want of knowing that we as well as the heathens are "alienated from the life of God;" that every one of us, by the corruption of our inmost nature, "is very far gone from original righteousness;" so far that "every person born into the world, deserveth God's wrath and damnation;" that we have by nature no power either to help ourselves, or even to call upon God to help us, all our tempers and works, in our natural state, being only evil continually. So that our coming to Christ, as well as theirs, "must infer a great and mighty change." It must infer, not only an outward change, from stealing, lying, and all corrupt communication; but a thorough change of heart, an inward renewal in the spirit of our mind. Accordingly "the old man" implies infinitely more than outward "evil conversation," even "an evil heart of unbelief," corrupted by pride and a thousand deceitful lusts. Of consequence the "new man" must imply infinitely more than outward "good conversation," even "a good heart," 'which after God is created in righteousness and true holiness;" a

heart full of that faith, which working by love, produces all holiness of conversation.

4. The change from the former of these states to the latter is what I call "the new birth." But, you say, I am "not content with this plain and easy notion of it, but fill myself and others with fantastical conceits" about it. Alas, sir, how can you prove this? And if you cannot prove it, what amends can you make, either to God or to me or to the world, for publicly asserting a gross falsehood?

5. Perhaps you say you "can prove this of Mr. Whitefield." What then? This is nothing to me. I am not accountable for his words. The Journal you quote I never saw till it was in print. But indeed you wrong him as much as me. First, where you represent him as judging the notions of the Quakers in general (concerning being led by the Spirit) to be right and good; whereas he speaks only of those particular men with whom he was then conversing. And again where you say he "supposes a person believing in Christ" to be without any "saving knowledge" of him. He supposes no such thing. "To believe in Christ" was the very thing he "supposed" wanting; as understanding that term "believing" to imply, not only an assent to the articles of our Creed, but also, "a true trust and confidence of the mercy of God through our Lord Jesus Christ."

6. Now this it is certain a man may want, although he can truly say, "I am chaste, I am sober, I am just in my dealings, I help my neighbour, and use the ordinances of God." "And however" such a man "may have behaved in these respects, he is not to think well of his own state till he experiences something within himself which he has not yet experienced," but "which he may be beforehand assured he shall," if the promises of God are true. That "something" is a living faith: "a sure trust and confidence in God, that by the merits of Christ his sins are forgiven, and he reconciled to the favour of God." And from this will spring many other things which till then he experienced not, as the love of God,

shed abroad in his heart, that peace of God which passeth all understanding, and joy in the Holy Ghost, joy though not unfelt, yet
unspeakable and full of glory.

7. These are some of those inward "fruits of the Spirit," which
must be felt, wheresoever they are. And without these I cannot
learn from Holy Writ that any man is "born of the Spirit." I beseech you, sir, by the mercies of God, that if as yet you "know
nothing of such inward feelings," if you do not "feel in yourself
these mighty workings of the Spirit of Christ," at least you would
not contradict and blaspheme. When the Holy Ghost hath fervently kindled your love towards God, you will know these to be
very sensible operations. As you "hear the wind, and feel it too,"
while it "strikes upon your bodily organs," you will know you are
under the guidance of God's Spirit the same way, namely, by
feeling it in your soul: by the present peace and joy and love
which you feel within, as well as by its outward and more distant
effects.

Justification, New Birth & Sanctification
Journal: September 13, 1739

A serious clergyman desired to know in what points we differed
from the Church of England. I answered: "To the best of my
knowledge, in none. The doctrines we preach are the doctrines of
the Church of England; indeed, the fundamental doctrines of the
Church, clearly laid down, both in her Prayers, Articles, and
Homilies."

He asked, "In what points, then, do you differ from the
other clergy of the Church of England?" I answered, "In none
from that part of the clergy who adhere to the doctrines of the
Church; but from that part of the clergy who dissent from the
Church (though they own it not) I differ in the points following:

First. They speak of justification either as the same thing as sanctification, or as something consequent upon it. I believe justification to be wholly distinct from sanctification and necessarily antecedent to it.

Secondly. They speak of our own holiness or good works as the cause of our justification, or that for the sake of which, on account of which, we are justified before God. I believe neither our own holiness nor good works are any part of the cause of our justification; but that the death and righteousness of Christ are the whole and sole cause of it, or that for the sake of which, on account of which, we are justified before God.

Thirdly. They speak of good works as a condition of justification, necessarily previous to it. I believe no good work can be previous to justification, nor, consequently, a condition of it; but that we are justified (being till that hour ungodly, and therefore incapable of doing any good work) by faith alone, faith without works, faith (though producing all, yet) including no good work.

Fourthly. They speak of sanctification (or holiness) as if it were an outward thing, as if it consisted chiefly, if not wholly, in these two points: (1) the doing no harm; (2) the doing good (as it is called), i.e., the using the means of grace, and helping our neighbour.

I believe it to be an inward thing, namely, "the life of God in the soul of man;" a "participation of the divine nature;" "the mind that was in Christ;" or "the renewal of our heart after the image of him that created us."

Lastly. They speak of the new birth as an outward thing, as if it were no more than baptism; or at most a change from outward wickedness to outward goodness; from a vicious to (what is called) a virtuous life. I believe it to be an inward thing; a change from inward wickedness to inward goodness; an entire change of our inmost nature from the image of the devil (wherein we are born) to the image of God; a change from the love of the creature to the love of the Creator, from earthly and sensual to heavenly and holy affections—in a word, a change from the tempers of the spirits of darkness to those of the angels of God as they are in heaven.

The Wilderness State
Journal: March 28, 1740

From these words, "Then was Jesus led by the Spirit into the wilderness, to be tempted of the devil," I took occasion to describe that wilderness state, that state of doubts, and fears, and strong temptation, which so many go through (though in different degrees) after they have received remission of sins.

A Second Work of Grace
1740

In the spring of 1740 the Wesley brothers released their second volume of Hymns and Sacred Poems. In the preface Wesley presented for the first time an explicit delineation of his gospel of two works of grace. The reader should carefully weigh how Wesley defines the believer's deliverance from sin in the most ideal terms. Many years later in his Plain Account *he will acknowledge that he went too far in this description.[5] Wesley then offers a fuller explication of the faith journey to perfect love. He now espouses three stages: forgiveness, full assurance, and a pure heart (cf. §9). This was a significant step in his* ordo salutis. *Though this preface was incorporated in* The Plain Account of Christian Perfection (1766), *I include it here because of its significant role in the development of Wesley's two-works gospel. Therefore it deserves a close reading. Source: Works J 14:323-327.*

1. "By grace," saith St. Paul, "ye are saved through faith." And it is indeed a great salvation which they have received, who truly "believe on the name of the Son of God." It is such as "eye hath not seen, nor ear heard, nor hath it entered into the heart of man to conceive," until God "hath revealed it by his Spirit," which alone showeth these "deep things of God."

2. "Of this salvation the Prophets inquired diligently, searching what manner of time the Spirit which was in them did signify, when it testified beforehand the sufferings of Christ, and the glory that should follow;" even that glorious liberty from the bondage of corruption, which should then be given to the children of God. Much more doth it behoove us, diligently to inquire after this "prize of our high calling;" and earnestly to "hope for the grace which is brought unto us by the revelation of Jesus Christ."

---

[5] See my *John Wesley's 'A Plain Account of Christian Perfection': The Annotated Edition,* 74.

136

3. Some faint description of this gracious gift of God is attempted in a few of the following verses. But the greater part of them relate to the way, rather than the end; either showing (so far as has fallen under our observation) the successive conquests of grace, and the gradual process of the work of God in the soul; or pointing out the chief hindrances in the way, at which many have stumbled and fallen.

4. This great gift of God, the salvation of our souls, which is begun on earth, but perfected in heaven, is no other than the image of God fresh stamped upon our hearts. It is a renewal in the spirit of our minds after the likeness of Him that created us. It is a salvation from sin, and doubt, and fear: From fear; for, "being justified freely," they who believe "have peace with God through Jesus Christ our Lord, and rejoice in hope of the glory of God": From doubt; for "the Spirit of God beareth witness with their spirit, that they are the children of God": And from sin; for being now "made free from sin, they are become the servants of righteousness."

5. God hath now "laid the axe to the root of the tree, purifying their hearts by faith, and cleansing all the thoughts of their hearts by the inspiration of his Holy Spirit." Having this hope, that they shall soon see God as he is, they "purify themselves even as He is pure;" and are "holy as he which hath called them is holy, in all manner of conversation." Not that they have "already attained" all they shall attain, either "are already," in this sense, "perfect." But they daily go on "from strength to strength: Beholding now as in a glass the glory of the Lord, they are changed into the same image, from glory to glory, as by the Spirit of the Lord."

6. And "where the Spirit of the Lord is, there is liberty;" such liberty from the law of sin and death as the children of this world "will not believe, though a man declare it unto them." The Son hath made them free, and they are free indeed: Insomuch that St. John lays it down as a first principle among true believers, "We

know that whosoever is born of God sinneth not; but he that is begotten of God keepeth himself, and that wicked one toucheth him not." And again: "Whosoever abideth in Him (in Christ) sinneth not." And yet again: "Whosoever is born of God, doth not commit sin. For his seed remaineth in him, and he cannot sin, because he is born of God."

7. The son hath made them free, who are thus born of God, from that great root of sin and bitterness, *pride*. They feel that All their sufficiency is of God; that it is he alone who is in all their thoughts, and "worketh in them both to will and to do of his good pleasure." They feel that it is not they who speak, but the Spirit of their Father which speaketh in them and that whatsoever is done by their hands, "the Father which is with them, he doeth the works." So that God is to them all in all, and they are as nothing in his sight. They are freed from *self-will*; as desiring nothing, no, not for one moment, (for perfect love casteth out all desire,) but the holy and perfect will of God: Not supplies in want; not ease in pain; not life or death, or any creature; but continually crying in their inmost soul, "Father, thy will be done."

They are freed from *evil thoughts*, so that they cannot enter into them; no, not for one instant. Aforetime, when an evil thought came in, they looked up, and is vanished away. But now it does not come in; there being no room for this in a soul which is full of God. They are freed from *wanderings* in prayer. Whensoever they pour out their hearts in a more immediate manner before God, they have no thought of anything past, or absent, or to come; but of God alone; to whom their whole souls flow in one even stream, and in whom they are swallowed up. In times past, they had wandering thoughts darted in; which yet fled away like smoke. But now that smoke does not rise at all, but they continually see Him which is invisible. They are freed from all *darkness*, having no fear, no doubt, either as to their state in general, or as to any particular action: For, their eye being single, their whole body is full of light. Whatsoever is needful, they are taught of God. They have an unction from the Holy One which abideth in them, and teacheth them every hour, what they shall do, and what they shall speak. Nor have they therefore any need to reason concerning it; for they see the way straight before them. The Lamb is their light, and they simply follow him, whithersoever he goeth.

Hence, also, they are, in one sense, freed from *temptations*; for though numberless temptations fly about them, yet they wound them not, they trouble them not, they have no place in them. At all times their soul is even and calm; their heart is steadfast and unmovable; their peace, flowing as a river, "passeth all understanding;" and they "rejoice with joy unspeakable and full of glory." For they are "sealed by the Spirit unto the day of redemption;" having the witness in themselves, that "there is laid up for them a crown of righteousness, which the Lord shall give them in that day;" and being fully persuaded, through the Holy Ghost, that "neither death nor life, nor things present, nor things to come, nor height, nor depth, nor any other creature, shall be able to separate them from the love of God, which is in Christ Jesus their Lord."

8. Not that every one is a child of the devil, (as some have rashly asserted, who know not what they speak, nor whereof they affirm,) till he is, in this *full sense*, born of God. On the contrary, whosoever he be, who hath a sure trust and confidence in God, that through the merits of Christ his sins are forgiven, and he reconciled to the favour of God; he is a child of God, and, if he abide in him, an heir of all the great and precious promises. Neither ought he in any wise to cast away his confidence, or to deny the faith he hath received, because it is weak, because hitherto it is only "as a grain of mustard-seed;" or because "it is tried with fire," so that his soul is "in heaviness through manifold temptations." For though "the heir, as long as he is a child, differeth nothing from a servant, yet is he lord of all." God doth not "despise the day of small things;" the day of fears, and doubts, and clouds, and darkness; but if there be first a willing mind, pressing toward the mark of the prize of our high calling, "it is accepted"

(for the present) "according to what a man hath, and not according to what he hath not."

9. Neither, therefore, dare we affirm (as some have done) that this full salvation is at once given to true believers. There is indeed, an instantaneous (as well as a gradual) work of God in the souls of his children; and there wants not, we know, a cloud of witnesses, who have received, in one moment, either a clear sense of the forgiveness of their sins, or the abiding witness of the Holy Spirit. But we do not know a single instance, in any place, of a person's receiving, in one and the same moment, remission of sins, the abiding witness of the Spirit, and a new, a clean heart.

10. Indeed, how God may work, we cannot tell; but the general manner wherein he does work, is this: Those who once trusted in themselves that they were righteous, who were rich and had need of nothing, are, by the Spirit of God, applying his word, convinced that they are poor and naked. All the things that they have done are brought to their remembrance, and set in array before them; so that they see the wrath of God hanging over their heads, and feel they deserve the damnation of hell. In their trouble they cry unto the Lord, and he shows he hath taken away their sins, and opens the kingdom of heaven in their hearts, even "righteousness, and peace, and joy in the Holy Ghost." Fear, and sorrow, and pain are fled away, and sin hath no more dominion over them. Knowing they are justified freely through faith in his blood, they have peace with God through Jesus Christ; they rejoice in hope of the glory of God; and the love of God is shed abroad in their hearts.

11. In this peace they remain for days, or weeks, or months, and commonly suppose they shall not know war any more, till some of their old enemies, their bosom sins, or the sin which did most easily beset them, (perhaps anger or desire,) assault them again, and thrust sore at them, that they may fall. Then arises fear, that they shall not endure to the end; and often doubt, whether God

has not forgotten them, or whether they did not deceive themselves, in thinking their sins were forgiven, and that they were children of God. Under these clouds, especially if they reason with the devil, or are received to doubtful disputations, they go mourning all the day long, even as a father mourneth for his only son whom he loveth.

But it is seldom long before their Lord answers for himself, sending them the Holy Ghost, to comfort them, to bear witness continually with their spirit, that they are the children of God. And then they are indeed meek, and gentle, and teachable, even as little children. Their stony heart was broken in pieces, before they received remission of sins: Yet it continued hard; but now it is melted down, it is soft, tender, and susceptible of any impression. And now first do they see the ground of their heart; which God would not before disclose unto them, lest the flesh should fail before him, and the spirit which he had made.

Now they see all the hidden abominations there; the depths of pride, and self, and hell: Yet, having the witness in themselves, Thou art "an heir of God, a joint heir with Christ;" thou shalt "inherit the new heavens and the new earth, wherein dwelleth righteousness;" their spirit rejoiceth in God their Saviour, even in the midst of this fiery trial, which continually heightens both the strong sense they then have of their inability to help themselves, and the inexpressible hunger they feel after a full renewal in his image, in righteousness, and all true holiness.

Then God is mindful of the desire of them that fear him: He remembers his holy covenant, and he giveth them a single eye and a clean heart. He stamps upon them his own image and superscription; he createth them anew in Christ Jesus; he cometh unto them with his Son and his blessed Spirit, and, fixing his abode in their souls, bringeth them into the "rest which remaineth for the people of God."

Stages of Growth to Perfection
1740

In the prior chapter we saw that Wesley delineated the faith journey in three stages: forgiveness, full assurance, and a pure heart. In his ensuing conflict with Moravian stillness he continued to develop these three stages by identifying them with the writings of the Apostle John and as degrees of faith. This involved further development in his perfection theology. Source: Works J 1:271, 275-276.

Journal

Mon. (May) 5. I expounded those words, "I write unto you, little children, because your sins are forgiven you," and described the state of those who have forgiveness of sins but have not yet a clean heart.

Sun. (June) 22. Finding there was no time to delay, without utterly destroying the cause of God, I began to execute what I had long designed, to strike at the root of the grand delusion. Accordingly, from those words of Jeremiah, "Stand ye in the way, ask for the old paths," I took occasion to give a plain account both of the work which God had begun among us and of the manner wherein the enemy had sown his tares among the good seed, to this effect:

> After we had wandered many years in the new path of salvation by faith and works, about two years ago it pleased God to show us the old way of salvation by faith only. And many soon tasted of this salvation, "being justified" freely, "having peace with God," "rejoicing in hope of the glory of God," and having his "love shed abroad in their hearts." These now ran the way of his commandments; they performed all their duty to God and man. They walked in all the ordinances of the Lord, and

through these means which he had appointed for that end, received daily grace to help in time of need, and went on "from faith to faith."

But eight or nine months ago certain men arose, speaking contrary to the doctrines we had received. They affirmed that we were all in a wrong way still! That we had no faith at all; that faith admits of no degrees, and consequently weak faith is no faith; that none is justified till he has a clean heart and is incapable of any doubt or fear.

They affirmed also that there is no commandment in the New Testament but to believe; that no other duty lies upon us; and that when a man does believe he is not bound or obliged to do anything which is commanded there: in particular, that he is not "subject to ordinances," that is (as they explained it), is not bound or obliged to pray, to communicate, to read or hear the Scriptures, but may or may not use any of these things (being in no bondage) according as he finds his heart free to it.

They farther affirmed that a believer cannot use any of these as a means of grace; that indeed there is no such thing as any means of grace, this expression having no foundation in Scripture; and that an unbeliever, or one who has not a clean heart, ought not to use them at all: ought not to pray, or search the Scriptures, or communicate, but to be still, i.e., leave off these works of the law. And then he will surely receive faith, which till he is still he cannot have.

All these assertions I propose to consider. The first was, that weak faith is no faith.

By "weak faith" I understand, (1) that which is mixed with fear, particularly of not enduring to the end; (2) that which is mixed with doubt whether we have not deceived ourselves and whether our sins be indeed forgiven; (3)

143

that which has not yet purified the heart, at least not from all its idols. And thus weak I find the faith of almost all believers to be within a short time after they have first "peace with God."

Yet that "weak faith" is faith appears,

> (1) From St. Paul, "Him that is weak in the faith, receive;"
> (2) From St. John, speaking of believers who were "little children," as well as of "young men" and "fathers;"
> (3) From our Lord's own words, "Why are ye fearful, O ye of little faith?" "O thou of little faith, wherefore didst thou doubt?" "I have prayed for thee (Peter) that thy faith fail thee not." Therefore he then had faith.

Yet so weak was that faith that not only doubt and fear, but gross sin in the same night prevailed over him.

> Nevertheless he was "clean, by the word" Christ had "spoken to him," i.e., justified, though it is plain he had not a clean heart.

> Therefore, there are degrees in faith, and weak faith may yet be true faith.

Christian Perfection
1741

This is the landmark sermon of Wesley's early middle period, and marks the maturation of his doctrinal development over the last three years. In the Plain Account *Wesley informs us he was prompted to write and publish this sermon by the bishop of London, Edmund Gibson.[6] Wesley recalls the bishop met with him in late 1740 to learn what he meant by perfection. Wesley answered "without any disguise or reserve." Gibson then told Wesley to "publish it to all the world."*

Wesley's purpose is to clarify what salvation from all sin entails. He opens by explaining what full salvation does not include. The qualifiers in section one will later coalesce into his doctrine of involuntary sin (next section). The reader will note how the stages of spiritual growth are based on 1 John 2:12-14. These stages become a permanent feature of Wesley's soteriology (ordo salutis). *The faith journey now involves degrees of deliverance from sin as* outward *and* inward. *Pay close attention to how Wesley defines sin, full salvation and links the latter to holy thoughts and tempers. The reader should also weigh the strength of Wesley's arguments for the believer's deliverance from sin. Finally, compare this sermon with the prior two landmark homilies,* The Circumcision of the Heart *and* Salvation By Faith. *What has changed? What remains the same? Source: Works J 6:1-19.*

> Not as though I had already attained,
> either were already perfect.
>
> Philippians 3:12

1. There is scarce any expression in holy writ, which has given more offence than this. The word perfect is what many cannot bear. The very sound of it is an abomination to them; and whosoever preaches perfection, (as the phrase is,) that is, asserts that it is attainable in this life, runs great hazard of being accounted by them worse than a heathen man or a publican.

---

[6] *A Plain Account of Christian Perfection: The Annotated Edition*, 54.

2. And hence some have advised, wholly to lay aside the use of those expressions; "because they have given so great offence." But are they not found in the oracles of God? If so, by what authority can any Messenger of God lay them aside, even though all men should be offended? We have not so learned Christ; neither may we thus give place to the devil. Whatsoever God hath spoken, that will we speak, whether men will hear, or whether they will forbear; knowing that then alone can any Minister of Christ be "pure from the blood of all men," when he hath "not shunned to declare unto them all the counsel of God."

3. We may not, therefore, lay these expressions aside, seeing they are the words of God and not of man. But we may and ought to explain the meaning of them; that those who are sincere of heart may not err to the right hand or left, from the mark of the prize of their high calling. And this is the more needful to be done, because, in the verse already repeated, the Apostle speaks of himself as not perfect: "Not," saith he, "as though I were already perfect." And yet immediately after, in the fifteenth verse, he speaks of himself, yea, and many others, as perfect: "Let us," saith he, "as many as be perfect, be thus minded."

4. In order, therefore, to remove the difficulty arising from this seeming contradiction, as well as to give light to them who are pressing forward to the mark, and that those who are lame be not turned out of the way, I shall endeavour to show,

First, In what sense Christians are not; and,
Secondly, In what sense they are, perfect.

I. 1. In the First place, I shall endeavour to show, in what sense Christians are not perfect. And both from experience and Scripture it appears, First, that they are not perfect in knowledge: They are not so perfect in this life as to be free from ignorance. They know, it may be, in common with other men, many things relating to the present world; and they know, with regard to the world to come, the general truths which God hath revealed. They know, likewise, (what the natural man receiveth not; for these things are spiritually discerned,) "what manner of love" it is, wherewith "the Father" hath loved them, "that they should be called the sons of God": They know the mighty working of his Spirit in their hearts; and the wisdom of his providence, directing all their paths, and causing all things to work together for their good. Yea, they know in every circumstance of life what the Lord requireth of them, and how to keep a conscience void of offence both toward God and toward man.

2. But innumerable are the things which they know not. Touching the Almighty himself, they cannot search him out to perfection. "Lo, these are but a part of his ways; but the thunder of his power, who can understand?" They cannot understand, I will not say, how "there are Three that bear record in heaven, the Father, the Son, and the Holy Spirit, and these Three are One;" or how the eternal Son of God "took upon himself the form of a servant;"—but not any one attribute, not any one circumstance, of the divine nature. Neither is it for them to know the times and seasons when God will work his great works upon the earth; no, not even those which he hath in part revealed by his servants and Prophets since the world began. Much less do they know when God, having "accomplished the number of his elect, will hasten his kingdom;" when "the heavens shall pass away with a great noise, and the elements shall melt with fervent heat."

3. They know not the reasons even of many of His present dispensations with the sons of men; but are constrained to rest here, Though "clouds and darkness are round about him, righteousness and judgment are the habitation of his seat." Yea, often with regard to his dealings with themselves, doth their Lord say unto them, "What I do, thou knowest not now; but thou shalt know hereafter." And how little do they know of what is ever before them, of even the visible works of his hands!—how "he spreadeth the north over the empty place, and hangeth the earth

upon nothing?" how he unites all the parts of this vast machine by a secret chain, which cannot be broken? So great is the ignorance, so very little the knowledge, of even the best of men!

4. No one, then, is so perfect in this life, as to be free from ignorance. Nor, Secondly, from mistake; which indeed is almost an unavoidable consequence of it; seeing those who "know but in part" are ever liable to err touching the things which they know not. It is true, the children of God do not mistake as to the things essential to salvation: They do not "put darkness for light, or light for darkness;" neither "seek death in the error of their life." For they are "taught of God;" and the way which he teaches them, the way of holiness, is so plain, that "the wayfaring man, though a fool, need not err therein." But in things unessential to salvation they do err, and that frequently. The best and wisest of men are frequently mistaken even with regard to facts; believing those things not to have been which really were, or those to have been done which were not. Or, suppose they are not mistaken as to the fact itself, they may be, with regard to its circumstances; believing them, or many of them, to have been quite different from what, in truth, they were. And hence cannot but arise many farther mistakes. Hence they may believe either past or present actions which were or are evil, to be good; and such as were or are good, to be evil. Hence also they may judge not according to truth with regard to the characters of men; and that, not only by supposing good men to be better, or wicked men to be worse, than they are, but by believing them to have been or to be good men, who were or are very wicked; or perhaps those to have been or to be wicked men, who were or are holy and unreprovable.

5. Nay, with regard to the Holy Scriptures themselves, as careful as they are to avoid it, the best of men are liable to mistake, and do mistake day by day; especially with respect to those parts thereof which less immediately relate to practice. Hence, even the children of God are not agreed as to the interpretation of many places in holy writ: Nor is their difference of opinion any proof

that they are not the children of God on either side; but it is a proof that we are no more to expect any living man to be infallible, than to be omniscient.

6. If it be objected to what has been observed under this and the preceding head, that St. John, speaking to his brethren in the faith, says, "Ye have an unction from the Holy One, and ye know all things:" (1 John 2:20) The answer is plain: "Ye know all things that are needful for your souls' health." That the Apostle never designed to extend this farther, that he could not speak it in an absolute sense, is clear, First, from hence;—that otherwise he would describe the disciple as "above his Master;" seeing Christ himself, as man, knew not all things: "Of that hour," saith he, "knoweth no man; no, not the Son, but the Father only." It is clear, Secondly, from the Apostle's own words that follow: "These things have I written unto you concerning them that deceive you;" as well as from his frequently repeated caution, "Let no man deceive you;" which had been altogether needless, had not those very persons who had that unction from the Holy One been liable, not to ignorance only, but to mistake also.

7. Even Christians, therefore, are not so perfect as to be free either from ignorance or error: We may, Thirdly, add, nor from infirmities.—Only let us take care to understand this word aright: Only let us not give that soft title to known sins, as the manner of some is. So, one man tells us, "Every man has his infirmity, and mine is drunkenness": Another has the infirmity of uncleanness; another that of taking God's holy name in vain; and yet another has the infirmity of calling his brother, "Thou fool," or returning "railing for railing." It is plain that all you who thus speak, if ye repent not, shall, with your infirmities, go quick into hell! But I mean hereby, not only those which are properly termed bodily infirmities, but all those inward or outward imperfections which are not of a moral nature. Such are the weakness or slowness of understanding, dullness or confusedness of apprehension, incoherency of thought, irregular quickness or heaviness of imagina-

tion. Such (to mention no more of this kind) is the want of a ready or retentive memory. Such, in another kind, are those which are commonly, in some measure, consequent upon these; namely, slowness of speech, impropriety of language, ungracefulness of pronunciation; to which one might add a thousand nameless defects, either in conversation or behaviour. These are the infirmities which are found in the best of men, in a larger or smaller proportion. And from these none can hope to be perfectly freed, till the spirit returns to God that gave it.

8. Nor can we expect, till then, to be wholly free from temptation. Such perfection belongeth not to this life. It is true, there are those who, being given up to work all uncleanness with greediness, scarce perceive the temptations which they resist not; and so seem to be without temptation. There are also many whom the wise enemy of souls, seeing to be fast asleep in the dead form of godliness, will not tempt to gross sin, lest they should awake before they drop into everlasting burnings. I know there are also children of God who, being now justified freely, having found redemption in the blood of Christ, for the present feel no temptation. God hath said to their enemies, "Touch not mine anointed, and do my children no harm." And for this season, it may be for weeks or months, he causeth them to ride on high places, he beareth them as on eagles' wings, above all the fiery darts of the wicked one. But this state will not last always; as we may learn from that single consideration, that the Son of God himself, in the days of his flesh, was tempted even to the end of his life. Therefore, so let his servant expect to be; for "it is enough that he be as his Master."

9. Christian perfection, therefore, does not imply (as some men seem to have imagined) an exemption either from ignorance, or mistake, or infirmities, or temptations. Indeed, it is only another term for holiness. They are two names for the same thing. Thus, every one that is holy is, in the Scripture sense, perfect. Yet we may, Lastly, observe, that neither in this respect is there any ab-

solute perfection on earth. There is no perfection of degrees, as it is termed; none which does not admit of a continual increase. So that how much soever any man has attained, or in how high a degree soever he is perfect, he hath still need to "grow in grace," and daily to advance in the knowledge and love of God his Saviour.

II. 1. In what sense, then, are Christians perfect? This is what I shall endeavour, in the Second place, to show. But it should be premised, that there are several stages in Christian life, as in natural;—some of the children of God being but new-born babes; others having attained to more maturity. And accordingly St. John, in his First Epistle, (2:12-14) applies himself severally to those he terms little children, those he styles young men, and those whom he entitles fathers. "I write Unto you, little children," saith the Apostle, "because your sins are forgiven you": Because thus far you have attained, being "justified freely," you "have peace with God through Jesus Christ." "I write unto you, young men, because ye have overcome the wicked one;" or, (as he afterwards addeth) "because ye are strong, and the word of God abideth in you." Ye have quenched the fiery darts of the wicked one, the doubts and fears wherewith he disturbed your first peace; and the witness of God, that your sins are forgiven, now abideth in your heart. "I write unto you, fathers, because ye have known Him that is from the beginning." Ye have known both the Father, and the Son, and the Spirit of Christ, in your inmost soul Ye are "perfect men," being grown up to "the measure of the stature of the fullness of Christ."

2. It is of these chiefly I speak in the latter part of this discourse: For these only are perfect Christians. But even babes in Christ are in such a sense perfect, or born of God, (an expression taken also in divers senses,) as, First, not to commit sin. If any doubt of this privilege of the sons of God, the question is not to be decided by abstract reasonings, which may be drawn out into an endless length, and leave the point just as it was before. Neither is it to be

determined by the experience of this or that particular person. Many may suppose they do not commit sin, when they do; but this proves nothing either way. To the law and to the testimony we appeal. "Let God be true, and every man a liar." By His word will we abide, and that alone. Hereby we ought to be judged.

3. Now the word of God plainly declares, that even those who are justified, who are born again in the lowest sense, "do not continue in sin;" that they cannot "live any longer therein;" (Rom 6:1, 2) that they are "planted together in the likeness of the death" of Christ; (v 5) that their "old man is crucified with him," the body of sin being destroyed, so that henceforth they do not serve sin; that, being dead with Christ, they are free from sin; (vv 6, 7) that they are "dead unto sin, and alive unto God;" (v 11) that "sin hath no more dominion over them," who are "not under the law, but under grace;" but that these, "being free from sin, are become the servants of righteousness." (vv 14, 18)

4. The very least which can be implied in these words, is, that the persons spoken of therein, namely, all real Christians, or believers in Christ, are made free from outward sin. And the same freedom, which St. Paul here expresses in such variety of phrases, St. Peter expresses in that one: (1 Peter 4:1, 2) "He that hath suffered in the flesh, hath ceased from sin, that he no longer should live to the desires of men, but to the will of God." For this ceasing from sin, if it be interpreted in the lowest sense, as regarding only the outward behaviour, must denote the ceasing from the outward act, from any outward transgression of the law.

5. But most express are the well known words of St. John, in the third chapter of his First Epistle, verse 8, &c.: "He that committeth sin is of the devil; for the devil sinneth from the beginning. For this purpose the Son of God was manifested, that he might destroy the works of the devil. Whosoever is born of God doth not commit sin; for his seed remaineth in him: And he cannot sin because he is born of God." And those in the fifth: (v 18) "We

know that whosoever is born of God sinneth not; but he that is begotten of God keepeth himself, and that wicked one toucheth him not."

6. Indeed it is said, this means only, He sinneth not willfully; or he doth not commit sin habitually; or, not as other men do; or, not as he did before. But by whom is this said? by St. John? No: There is no such word in the text; nor in the whole chapter; nor in all his Epistle; nor in any part of his writings whatsoever. Why then, the best way to answer a bold assertion, is, simply to deny it. And if any man can prove it from the word of God, let him bring forth his strong reasons.

7. And a sort of reason there is, which has been frequently brought to support these strange assertions, drawn from the examples recorded in the word of God: "What!" say they, "did not Abraham himself commit sin, prevaricating, and denying his wife? Did not Moses commit sin, when he provoked God at the waters of strife? Nay, to produce one for all, did not even David, 'the man after God's own heart,' commit sin, in the matter of Uriah the Hittite; even murder and adultery?" It is most sure he did. All this is true. But what is it you would infer from hence? It may be granted, First, that David, in the general course of his life, was one of the holiest men among the Jews; and, Secondly, that the holiest men among the Jews did sometimes commit sin. But if you would hence infer, that all Christians do and must commit sin as long as they live; this consequence we utterly deny: It will never follow from those premises.

8. Those who argue thus, seem never to have considered that declaration of our Lord: (Matt 11:11) "Verily I say unto you, Among them that are born of women there hath not risen a greater than John the Baptist: Notwithstanding he that is least in the kingdom of heaven is greater than he." I fear, indeed, there are some who have imagined "the kingdom of heaven," here, to mean the kingdom of glory; as if the Son of God had just discovered to us, that

the least glorified saint in heaven is greater than any man upon earth! To mention this is sufficiently to refute it. There can, therefore, no doubt be made, but "the kingdom of heaven," here, (as in the following verse, where it is said to be taken by force,) or, "the kingdom of God," as St. Luke expresses it, is that kingdom of God on earth whereunto all true believers in Christ, all real Christians, belong. In these words, then, our Lord declares two things: First, that before his coming in the flesh, among all the children of men there had not been one greater than John the Baptist; whence it evidently follows, that neither Abraham, David, nor any Jew, was greater than John. Our Lord, Secondly, declares, that he which is least in the kingdom of God (in that kingdom which he came to set up on earth, and which the violent now began to take by force) is greater than he:—Not a greater Prophet, as some have interpreted the word; for this is palpably false in fact; but greater in the grace of God, and the knowledge of our Lord Jesus Christ. Therefore we cannot measure the privileges of real Christians by those formerly given to the Jews. Their "ministration," (or dispensation,) we allow, "was glorious;" but ours "exceeds in glory." So that whosoever would bring down the Christian dispensation to the Jewish standard, whosoever gleans up the examples of weakness, recorded in the Law and the Prophets. And thence infers that they who have "put on Christ" are endued with no greater strength, doth greatly err, neither "knowing the Scriptures, nor the power of God."

9. "But are there not assertions in Scripture which prove the same thing, if it cannot be inferred from those examples? Does not the Scripture say expressly, 'Even a just man sinneth seven times a day?'" I answer, No: The Scripture says no such thing. There is no such text in all the Bible. That which seems to be intended is the sixteenth verse of the twenty-fourth chapter of the Proverbs; the words of which are these: "A just man falleth seven times, and riseth up again." But this is quite another thing. For, First, the words "a day," are not in the text. So that if a just man fall seven times in his life, it is as much as is affirmed here. Secondly, here

is no mention of falling into sin at all; what is here mentioned is, falling into temporal affliction. This plainly appears from the verse before, the words of which are these: "Lay not wait, O wicked man, against the dwelling of the righteous; spoil not his resting-place." It follows, "For a just man falleth seven times, and riseth up again; but the wicked shall fall into mischief." As if he had said, "God will deliver him out of his trouble; but when thou fallest, there shall be none to deliver thee."

10. "But, however, in other places," continue the objectors, "Solomon does assert plainly, 'There is no man that sinneth not;' (1 Kgs 8:46; 2 Ch 6:36) yea, 'There is not a just man upon earth that doeth good, and sinneth not' (Ecc 7:20)." I answer, Without doubt, thus it was in the days of Solomon. Yea, thus it was from Adam to Moses, from Moses to Solomon, and from Solomon to Christ. There was then no man that sinned not. Even from the day that sin entered into the world, there was not a just man upon earth that did good and sinned not, until the Son of God was manifested to take away our sins. It is unquestionably true, that "the heir, as long as he is a child, differeth nothing from a servant." And that even so they (all the holy men of old, who were under the Jewish dispensation) were, during that infant state of the Church, "in bondage under the elements of the world." "But when the fullness of the time was come, God sent forth his Son, made under the law, to redeem them that were under the law, that they might receive the adoption of sons;"—that they might receive that "grace which is now made manifest by the appearing of our Saviour Jesus Christ; who hath abolished death, and brought life and immortality to light through the Gospel." (2 Tim 1:10) Now, therefore, they "are no more servants, but sons." So that, whatsoever was the case of those under the law, we may safely affirm with St. John, that, since the gospel was given, "he that is born of God sinneth not."

11. It is of great importance to observe, and that more carefully than is commonly done, the wide difference there is between the

Jewish and the Christian dispensation; and that ground of it which the same Apostle assigns in the seventh chapter of his Gospel. (vv 38, &c.) After he had there related those words of our blessed Lord, "He that believeth on me, as the Scripture hath said, out of his belly shall flow rivers of living water," he immediately subjoins, "This spake he of the Spirit, ou emellon lambanein oi pisteuontes eis auton, *which they who should believe on him were afterwards to receive.* For the Holy Ghost was not yet given, because that Jesus was not yet glorified." Now, the Apostle cannot mean here, (as some have taught,) that the miracle-working power of the Holy Ghost was not yet given. For this was given; our Lord had given it to all the Apostles, when he first sent them forth to preach the gospel. He then gave them power over unclean spirits to cast them out; power to heal the sick; yea, to raise the dead. But the Holy Ghost was not yet given in his sanctifying graces, as he was after Jesus was glorified. It was then when "he ascended up on high, and led captivity captive," that he "received" those "gifts for men, yea, even for the rebellious, that the Lord God might dwell among them." And when the day of Pentecost was fully come, then first it was, that they who "waited for the promise of the Father" were made more than conquerors over sin by the Holy Ghost given unto them.

12. That this great salvation from sin was not given till Jesus was glorified, St. Peter also plainly testifies; where, speaking of his brethren in the flesh, as now "receiving the end of their faith, the salvation of their souls," he adds, (1 Pet 1:9.10, &c.,) "Of which salvation the Prophets have inquired and searched diligently, who prophesied of the grace," that is, the gracious dispensation, "that should come unto you: Searching what, or what manner of time the Spirit of Christ which was in them did signify, when it testified beforehand the sufferings of Christ, and the glory," the glorious salvation, "that should follow. Unto whom it was revealed, that not unto themselves, but unto us they did minister the things which are now reported unto you by them that have preached the Gospel unto you with the Holy Ghost sent down from heaven;"

viz., at the day of Pentecost, and so unto all generations, into the hearts of all true believers On this ground, even "the grace which was brought unto them by the revelation of Jesus Christ," the Apostle might well build that strong exhortation, "Wherefore girding up the loins of your mind, as he which hath called you is holy, so be ye holy in all manner of conversation."

13. Those who have duly considered these things must allow, that the privileges of Christians are in no wise to be measured by what the Old Testament records concerning those who were under the Jewish dispensation; seeing the fullness of time is now come; the Holy Ghost is now given; the great salvation of God is brought unto men, by the revelation of Jesus Christ. The kingdom of heaven is now set up on earth; concerning which the Spirit of God declared of old, (so far is David from being the pattern or standard of Christian perfection,) "He that is feeble among them at that day shall be as David; and the house of David shall be as God, as the angel of the Lord before them." (Zec 12:8)

14. If, therefore, you would prove that the Apostle's words, "He that is born of God sinneth not," are not to be understood according to their plain, natural, obvious meaning, it is from the New Testament you are to bring your proofs, else you will fight as one that beateth the air. And the first of these which is usually brought is taken from the examples recorded in the New Testament. "The Apostles themselves," it is said, "committed sin; nay, the greatest of them, Peter and Paul: St. Paul, by his sharp contention with Barnabas; and St. Peter, by his dissimulation at Antioch." Well: Suppose both Peter and Paul did then commit sin; what is it you would infer from hence? that all the other Apostles committed sin sometimes? There is no shadow of proof in this. Or would you thence infer, that all the other Christians of the apostolic age committed sin? Worse and worse: This is such an inference as, one would imagine, a man in his senses could never have thought of. Or will you argue thus: "If two of the Apostles did once commit sin, then all other Christians, in all ages, do and

will commit sin as long as they live?" Alas, my brother! a child of common understanding would be ashamed of such reasoning as this. Least of all can you with any colour of argument infer, that any man must commit sin at all. No: God forbid we should thus speak! No necessity of sinning was laid upon them. The grace of God was surely sufficient for them. And it is sufficient for us at this day. With the temptation which fell on them, there was a way to escape; as there is to every soul of man in every temptation. So that whosoever is tempted to any sin, need not yield; for no man is tempted above that he is able to bear.

15. "But St. Paul besought the Lord thrice, and yet he could not escape from his temptation." Let us consider his own words literally translated: "There was given to me a thorn to the flesh, an angel" (or messenger) "of Satan, to buffet me. Touching this, I besought the Lord thrice, that it" (or he) "might depart from me. And he said unto me, My grace is sufficient for thee: For my strength is made perfect in weakness. Most gladly therefore will I rather glory in" these "my weaknesses, that the strength of Christ may rest upon me. Therefore I take pleasure in weaknesses;—for when I am weak, then am I strong."

16. As this scripture is one of the strong-holds of the patrons of sin, it may be proper to weigh it thoroughly. Let it be observed, then, First, it does by no means appear that this thorn, whatsoever it was, occasioned St. Paul to commit sin; much less laid him under any necessity of doing so. Therefore, from hence it can never be proved that any Christian must commit sin. Secondly, the ancient Fathers inform us, it was bodily pain:—a violent headache, saith Tertullian; (De Pudic.;) to which both Chrysostom and St. Jerome agree. St. Cyprian1 expresses it, a little more generally in those terms

"Many and grievous torments of the flesh and of the body." Thirdly, to this exactly agree the Apostle's own words:—"A thorn to the flesh, to smite, beat, or buffet me." "My strength is made perfect in weakness":—Which same word occurs no less than four times in these two verses only. But, Fourthly, whatsoever it was, it could not be either inward or outward sin. It could no more be inward stirrings, than outward expressions, of pride, anger, or lust. This is manifest, beyond all possible exception, from the words that immediately follow: "Most gladly will I glory in" these "my weaknesses, that the strength of Christ may rest upon me." What! did he glory in pride, in anger, in lust? Was it through these weaknesses, that the strength of Christ rested upon him? He goes on: "Therefore I take pleasure in weaknesses; for when I am weak, then am I strong;" that is, when I am weak in body, then am I strong in spirit. But will any man dare to say, "When I am weak by pride or lust, then am I strong in spirit?" I call you all to record this day, who find the strength of Christ resting upon you, can you glory in anger, or pride, or lust? Can you take pleasure in these infirmities? Do these weaknesses make you strong? Would you not leap into hell, were it possible, to escape them? Even by yourselves, then, judge, whether the Apostle could glory and take pleasure in them?

Let it be, Lastly, observed, that this thorn was given to St. Paul above fourteen years before he wrote this Epistle; which itself was wrote several years before he finished his course. So that he had, after this, a long course to run, many battles to fight, many victories to gain, and great increase to receive in all the gifts of God, and the knowledge of Jesus Christ. Therefore, from any spiritual weakness (if such had been) which he at that time felt, we could by no means infer that he was never made strong; that Paul the aged, the father in Christ, still laboured under the same weaknesses; that he was in no higher state till the day of his death. From all which it appears, that this instance of St. Paul is quite foreign to the question, and does in nowise clash with the assertion of St. John, "He that is born of God sinneth not."

17. "But does not St. James directly contradict this? His words are, 'In many things we offend all': (3:2) And is not offending the same as committing sin?" In this place, I allow it is: I allow the persons here spoken of did commit sin; yea, that they all

159

committed many sins. But who are the persons here spoken of? Why, those many masters or teachers, whom God had not sent; (probably the same vain men who taught that faith without works, which is so sharply reproved in the preceding chapter;) not the Apostle himself, nor any real Christian. That in the word we (used by a figure of speech common in all other, as well as the inspired, writings) the Apostle could not possibly include himself or any other true believer, appears evidently, First, from the same word in the ninth verse:—"Therewith," saith he, "bless we God, and therewith curse we men. Out of the same mouth proceedeth blessing and cursing." True; but not out of the mouth of the Apostle, nor of any one who is in Christ a new creature. Secondly, from the verse immediately preceding the text, and manifestly connected with it: "My brethren, be not many masters," (or teachers,) "knowing that we shall receive the greater condemnation;" "For in many things we offend all." We! Who? Not the Apostles, nor true believers; but they who knew they should receive the greater condemnation, because of those many offences. But this could not be spoke of the Apostle himself, or of any who trod in his steps; seeing "there is no condemnation to them who walk not after the flesh, but after the Spirit." Nay, Thirdly, the very verse itself proves, that "we offend all," cannot be spoken either of all men, or of all Christians: For in it there immediately follows the mention of a man who offends not, as the we first mentioned did; from whom, therefore, he is professedly contradistinguished, and pronounced a perfect man.

18. So clearly does St. James explain himself, and fix the meaning of his own words. Yet, lest any one should still remain in doubt, St. John, writing many years after St. James, puts the matter entirely out of dispute, by the express declarations above recited. But here a fresh difficulty may arise: How shall we reconcile St. John with himself? In one place be declares, "Whosoever is born of God doth not commit sin;" and again, "We know that he which is born of God sinneth not." And yet in another he saith, "If we say that we have no sin, we deceive ourselves, and the

truth is not in us;" and again, "If we say that we have not sinned, we make him a liar, and his word is not in us."

19. As great a difficulty as this may at first appear, it vanishes away, if we observe, First, that the tenth verse fixes the sense of the eighth: "If we say we have no sin," in the former, being explained by, "If we say we have not sinned," in the latter verse. Secondly, that the point under present consideration is not whether we have or have not sinned heretofore; and neither of these verses asserts that we do sin, or commit sin now. Thirdly, that the ninth verse explains both the eighth and tenth: "If we confess our sins, he is faithful and just to forgive us our sins, and to cleanse us from all unrighteousness." As if he had said, "I have before affirmed, 'The blood of Jesus Christ cleanseth us from all sin;' but let no man say, I need it not; I have no sin to be cleansed from. If we say that we have no sin, that we have not sinned, we deceive ourselves and make God a liar. But, "If we confess our sins, he is faithful and just,' not only 'to forgive our sins,' but also 'to cleanse us from all unrighteousness;' that we may 'go and sin no more.'"

20. St. John, therefore, is well consistent with himself, as well as with the other holy writers; as will yet more evidently appear, if we place all his assertions touching this matter in one view. He declares, First, the blood of Jesus Christ cleanseth us from all sin. Secondly, no man can say, I have not sinned, I have no sin to be cleansed from. Thirdly, but God is ready both to forgive our past sins, and to save us from them for the time to come. Fourthly, "These things write I unto you," saith the Apostle, "that you may not sin. But if any man" should "sin," or have sinned, (as the word might be rendered,) he need not continue in sin; seeing "we have an Advocate with the Father, Jesus Christ the righteous." Thus far all is clear. But lest any doubt should remain in a point of so vast importance the Apostle resumes this subject in the third chapter, and largely explains his own meaning: "Little children," saith he, "let no man deceive you" (As though I had given any

161

encouragement to those that continue in sin). "He that doeth righteousness is righteous, even as He is righteous. He that committeth sin is of the devil; for the devil sinneth from the beginning. For this purpose the Son of God was manifested, that he might destroy the works of the devil. Whosoever is born of God doth not commit sin: For his seed remaineth in him; and he cannot sin, because he is born of God. In this the children of God are manifest, and the children of the devil" (vv 7-10). Here the point, which till then might possibly have admitted of some doubt in weak minds, is purposely settled by the last of the inspired writers, and decided in the clearest manner. In conformity, therefore, both to the doctrine of St. John, and to the whole tenor of the New Testament, we fix this conclusion: A Christian is so far perfect, as not to commit sin.

21. This is the glorious privilege of every Christian; yea, though he be but a babe in Christ. But it is only of those who are strong in the Lord, "and have overcome the wicked one," or rather of those who "have known him that is from the beginning," that it can be affirmed they are in such a sense perfect, as, Secondly, to be freed from evil thoughts and evil tempers. First, from evil or sinful thoughts. But here let it be observed, that thoughts concerning evil are not always evil thoughts; that a thought concerning sin, and a sinful thought, are widely different. A man, for instance, may think of a murder which another has committed; and yet this is no evil or sinful thought. So our blessed Lord himself doubtless thought of, or understood, the thing spoken by the devil, when he said, "All these things will I give thee, if thou wilt fall down and worship me." Yet had he no evil or sinful thought; nor indeed was capable of having any. And even hence it follows, that neither have real Christians: For "every one that is perfect is as his Master." (Lk 6:40) Therefore, if He was free from evil or sinful thoughts, so are they likewise.

22. And, indeed, whence should evil thoughts proceed, in the servant who is as his Master? "Out of the heart of man" (if at all)

"proceed evil thoughts." (Mark 7:21) If, therefore, his heart be no longer evil, then evil thoughts can no longer proceed out of it. If the tree were corrupt, so would be the fruit: But the tree is good; the fruit, therefore, is good also; (Matt. xii. 33;) our Lord himself bearing witness, "Every good tree bringeth forth good fruit. A good tree cannot bring forth evil fruit," as "a corrupt tree cannot bring forth good fruit." (Matt 7:17, 18)

23. The same happy privilege of real Christians, St. Paul asserts from his own experience. "The weapons of our warfare," saith he, "are not carnal, but mighty through God to the pulling down of strong-holds; casting down imaginations," (or reasonings rather, for so the word logismous signifies; all the reasonings of pride and unbelief against the declarations, promises, or gifts of God,) "and every high thing that exalteth itself against the knowledge of God, and bringing into captivity every thought to the obedience of Christ." (2 Cor 10:4, &c.)

24. And as Christians indeed are freed from evil thoughts, so are they, Secondly, from evil tempers. This is evident from the above-mentioned declaration of our Lord himself: "The disciple is not above his Master; but every one that is perfect shall be as his Master." He had been delivering, just before, some of the sub-limest doctrines of Christianity, and some of the most grievous to flesh and blood. "I say unto you, Love your enemies, do good to them which hate you;—and unto him that smiteth thee on the one cheek, offer also the other." Now these he well knew the world would not receive; and therefore immediately adds, "Can the blind lead the blind? Will they not both fall into the ditch?" As if he had said, "Do not confer with flesh and blood touching these things, with men void of spiritual discernment, the eyes of whose understanding God hath not opened, lest they and you perish to-gether." In the next verse he removes the two grand objections with which these wise fools meet us at every turn: "These things are too grievous to be borne;" or, "They are too high to be at-tained;"—saying, "'The disciple is not above his Master;' there-

fore, if I have suffered, be content to tread in my steps. And doubt ye not then, but I will fulfill my word: 'For every one that is perfect, shall be as his Master.'" But his Master was free from all sinful tempers. So, therefore, is his disciple, even every real Christian.

25. Every one of these can say, with St. Paul, "I am crucified with Christ: Nevertheless I live; yet not I, but Christ liveth in me"—Words that manifestly describe a deliverance from inward as well as from outward sin. This is expressed both negatively, I live not; (my evil nature, the body of sin, is destroyed;) and positively, Christ liveth in me; and, therefore, all that is holy, and just, and good. Indeed, both these, Christ liveth in me, and I live not, are inseparably connected; for "what communion hath light with darkness, or Christ with Belial?"

26. He, therefore, who liveth in true believers, hath "purified their hearts by faith;" insomuch that every one that hath Christ in him the hope of glory, "purifieth himself, even as He is pure." (1 John 3:3) He is purified from *pride*; for Christ was lowly of heart. He is pure from *self-will* or *desire*; for Christ desired only to do the will of his Father, and to finish his work. And he is pure from *anger*, in the common sense of the word; for Christ was meek and gentle, patient and longsuffering. I say, in the common sense of the word; for all anger is not evil. We read of our Lord himself, (Mark 3:5) that he once "looked round with anger." But with what kind of anger? The next word shows, sullupoumenos, being, at the same time, "grieved for the hardness of their hearts." So then he was angry at the sin, and in the same moment grieved for the sinners; angry or displeased at the offence, but sorry for the offenders. With anger, yea, hatred, he looked upon the thing; with grief and love upon the persons. Go, thou that art perfect, and do likewise. Be thus angry, and thou sinnest not; feeling a displacency at every offence against God, but only love and tender compassion to the offender.

164

27. Thus doth Jesus "save his people from their sins." And not only from outward sins, but also from the sins of their hearts; from evil thoughts, and from evil tempers.—"True," say some, "we shall thus be saved from our sins; but not till death; not in this world." But how are we to reconcile this with the express words of St. John?—"Herein is our love made perfect, that we may have boldness in the day of judgment. Because as he is, so are we in this world." The Apostle here, beyond all contradiction, speaks of himself and other living Christians, of whom (as though he had foreseen this very evasion, and set himself to overturn it from the foundation) he flatly affirms, that not only at or after death, but in this world, they are as their Master. (1 Jn 4:17)

28. Exactly agreeable to this are his words in the first chapter of this Epistle, (v 5, &c.) "God is light, and in him is no darkness at all. If we walk in the light, we have fellowship one with another, and the blood of Jesus Christ his Son cleanseth us from all sin." And again: "If we confess our sins, he is faithful and just to forgive us our sins, and to cleanse us from all unrighteousness." Now, it is evident, the Apostle here also speaks of a deliverance wrought in this world. For he saith not, the blood of Christ will cleanse at the hour of death, or in the day of judgment, but, it "cleanseth," at the time present, "us," living Christians, "from all sin." And it is equally evident that if any sin remain, we are not cleansed from all sin. If any unrighteousness remains in the soul, it is not cleansed from all unrighteousness. Neither let any sinner against his own soul say, that this relates to justification only, or the cleansing us from the guilt of sin; First, because this is confounding together what the Apostle clearly distinguishes, who mentions first, to forgive us our sins, and then to cleanse us from all unrighteousness. Secondly, because this is asserting justification by works, in the strongest sense possible; it is making all inward as well as outward holiness necessarily previous to justification. For if the cleansing here spoken of is no other than the cleansing us from the guilt of sin, then we are not cleansed from guilt, that is, are not justified, unless on condition of "walking in

the light, as he is in the light." It remains, then, that Christians are saved in this world from all sin, from all unrighteousness; that they are now in such a sense perfect, as not to commit sin, and to be freed from evil thoughts and evil tempers.

29. Thus hath the Lord fulfilled the things he spake by his holy Prophets, which have been since the world began;—by Moses in particular, saying, (Dt 30:6) I "will circumcise thine heart, and the heart of thy seed, to love the Lord thy God with all thy heart, and with all thy soul;"—by David, crying out, "Create in me a clean heart, and renew a right spirit within me;"—and most remarkably by Ezekiel, in those words: "Then will I sprinkle clean water upon you, and ye shall be clean: From all your filthiness, and from all your idols, will I cleanse you. A new heart also will I give you, and a new spirit will I put within you;—and cause you to walk in my statutes, and ye shall keep my judgments, and do them.—Ye shall be my people, and I will be your God. I will also save you from all your uncleannesses.—Thus saith the Lord God, In the day that I shall have cleansed you from all your iniquities, the Heathen shall know that I the Lord build the ruined places;—I the Lord have spoken it, and I will do it." (Eze 36:25 &c.)

30. "Having therefore these promises, dearly beloved," both in the Law and in the Prophets, and having the prophetic word confirmed unto us in the Gospel, by our blessed Lord and his Apostles; "let us cleanse ourselves from all filthiness of flesh and spirit, perfecting holiness in the fear of God." "Let us fear, lest" so many "promises being made us of entering into his rest," which he that hath entered into, has ceased from his own works, "any of us should come short of it." "This one thing let us do, forgetting those things which are behind, and reaching forth unto those things which are before, let us press toward the mark, for the prize of the high calling of God in Christ Jesus;" crying unto him day and night, till we also are "delivered from the bondage of corruption, into the glorious liberty of the sons of God!"

Biblical Promises of Perfection
1747

Wesley often said he was a "man of one book." There is no doubt he believed the sacred scriptures taught the perfection of Christians in their love to God and neighbor. He therefore appealed to Holy Scripture for support, specifically its promises, prayers, commands and examples. The following questions and answers are from the 1747 conference minutes. Source: Works J 8:294-296

Q. Is there any clear scripture promise of this; that God will save us from all sin?
A. There is: "He shall redeem Israel from all his sins." (Ps 130:8) This is more largely expressed in the prophecy of Ezekiel: "Then will I sprinkle clean water upon you, and ye shall be clean: From all your filthiness, and from all your idols, will I cleanse you. I will also save you from all your uncleannesses" (36:25, 29). No promise can be more clear. And to this the Apostle plainly refers in that exhortation: "Having these promises, let us cleanse ourselves from all filthiness of flesh and spirit, perfecting holiness in the fear of God" (2 Cor 7:1). Equally clear and express is that ancient promise: "The Lord thy God will circumcise thine heart, and the heart of thy seed, to love the Lord thy God with all thy heart and with all thy soul" (Dt 30:6).

Q. But does any assertion answerable to this occur in the New Testament?
A. There does, and that laid down in the plainest terms. So St. John: "For this purpose the Son of God was manifested, that he might destroy the works of the devil" (1 Jn 3:8); the works of the devil, without any limitation or restriction: But all sin is the work of the devil. Parallel to which is that assertion of St. Paul: "Christ loved the Church, and gave himself for it; that he might present it to himself a glorious Church, not having spot, or wrinkle, or any such thing; but that it should be holy and without blemish" (Eph 5:25, 27). And to the same effect is his assertion in the eighth of

167

the Romans: "God sent his Son—that the righteousness of the law might be fulfilled in us, walking not after the flesh, but after the Spirit" (8:3, 4).

Q. Does the New Testament afford any farther ground for expecting to be saved from all sin?
A. Undoubtedly it does, both in those prayers and commands which are equivalent to the strongest assertions.

Q. What prayers do you mean?
A. Prayers for entire sanctification; which, were there no such thing, would be mere mockery of God. Such, in particular, are, (1.) "Deliver us from evil," or rather, "from the evil one." Now, when this is done, when we are delivered from all evil, there can be no sin remaining. (2.) "Neither pray I for these alone, but for them also which shall believe on me through their word; that they all may be one; as thou, Father, art in me, and I in thee, that they also may be one in us: I in them, and thou in me, that they may be made perfect in one" (Jn 17:20, 21, 23). (3.) "I bow my knees unto the Father of our Lord Jesus Christ—that he would grant you—that ye, being rooted and grounded in love, may be able to comprehend, with all saints, what is the breadth, and length, and depth, and height; and to know the love of Christ, which passeth knowledge, that ye might be filled with all the fullness of God" (Eph 3:14, 16-19). (4.) "The very God of peace sanctify you wholly; and I pray God your whole spirit and soul and body be preserved blameless unto the coming of our Lord Jesus Christ" (1 Th 5:23).

Q. What command is there to the same effect?
A. (1.) "Be ye perfect, even as your Father which is in heaven is perfect" (Matt 5:48). (2.) "Thou shalt love the Lord thy God with all thy heart, and with all thy soul, and with all thy mind" (Matt 22:37). But if the love of God fill all the heart, there can be no sin there.

Q. But how does it appear that this is to be done before the article of death?

A. First. From the very nature of a command, which is not given to the dead, but to the living. Therefore, "Thou shalt love God with all thy heart," cannot mean, Thou shalt do this when thou diest, but while thou livest.

Secondly. From express texts of Scripture: (1.) "The grace of God that bringeth salvation hath appeared to all men, teaching us that, having renounced (arnesamenoi) ungodliness and worldly lusts, we should live soberly, righteously, and godly, in this present world; looking for—the glorious appearing of our Saviour Jesus Christ; who gave himself for us, that he might redeem us from all iniquity, and purify unto himself a peculiar people, zealous of good works" (Tit 2:11-14). (2.) "He hath raised up an horn of salvation for us, to perform the mercy promised to our fathers; the oath which he sware to our father Abraham, that he would grant unto us, that we, being delivered out of the hand of our enemies, should serve him without fear, in holiness and righteousness before him, all the days of our life" (Lk 1:69-75).

Q. Is there any example in Scripture of persons who had attained to this?

A. Yes. St. John, and all those of whom he says in his First Epistle, "Herein is our love made perfect, that we may have confidence in the day of judgment: Because as he is, so are we in this world" (4:17).

Q. But why are there not more examples of this kind recorded in the New Testament?

A. It does not become us to be peremptory in this matter. One reason might possibly be, because the Apostles wrote to the Church while it was in a state of infancy. Therefore they might mention such persons the more sparingly, lest they should give strong meat to babes.

Biblical Expositions
1755

In the mid-fifties Wesley spent a couple years writing his commentary on the New Testament. The following excerpts illustrate how he interpreted key passages regarding heart holiness. Source: Explanatory Notes Upon the New Testament.

Matthew 5:1-12

And seeing the multitudes, he went up into a mountain: and when he was set, his disciples came unto him: [2] And he opened his mouth, and taught them, saying, [3] Blessed *are* the poor in spirit: for theirs is the kingdom of heaven. [4] Blessed *are* they that mourn: for they shall be comforted. [5] Blessed *are* the meek: for they shall inherit the earth. [6] Blessed *are* they which do hunger and thirst after righteousness: for they shall be filled. [7] Blessed *are* the merciful: for they shall obtain mercy. [8] Blessed *are* the pure in heart: for they shall see God. [9] Blessed *are* the peacemakers: for they shall be called the children of God. [10] Blessed *are* they which are persecuted for righteousness' sake: for theirs is the kingdom of heaven. [11] Blessed are ye, when *men* shall revile you, and persecute *you,* and shall say all manner of evil against you falsely, for my sake. [12] Rejoice, and be exceeding glad: for great *is* your reward in heaven: for so persecuted they the prophets which were before you.

3. *The poor in spirit* — They who are unfeignedly penitent, they who are truly convinced of sin; who see and feel the state they are in by nature, being deeply sensible of their sinfulness, guiltiness, helplessness. *For theirs is the kingdom of heaven* — The present inward kingdom: righteousness, and peace, and joy in the Holy Ghost, as well as the eternal kingdom, if they endure to the end. Luke 6:20.

170

4. *They that mourn* — Either for their own sins, or for other men's, and are steadily and habitually serious. *They shall be comforted* — More solidly and deeply even in this world, and eternally in heaven.

5. *Happy are the meek* — They that hold all their passions and affections evenly balanced. *They shall inherit the earth* — They shall have all things really necessary for life and godliness. They shall enjoy whatever portion God hath given them here, and shall hereafter possess the new earth, wherein dwelleth righteousness.

6. *They that hunger and thirst after righteousness* — After the holiness here described. They shall be satisfied with it.

7. *The merciful* — The tender-hearted: they who love all men as themselves: *They shall obtain mercy* — Whatever mercy therefore we desire from God, the same let us show to our brethren. He will repay us a thousand fold, the love we bear to any for his sake.

8. *The pure in heart* — The sanctified: they who love God with all their hearts. *They shall see God* — In all things here; hereafter in glory.

9. *The peace makers* — They that out of love to God and man do all possible good to all men. Peace in the Scripture sense implies all blessings temporal and eternal. *They shall be called the children of God* — Shall be acknowledged such by God and man. One would imagine a person of this amiable temper and behavior would be the darling of mankind. But our Lord well knew it would not be so, as long as Satan was the prince of this world. He therefore warns them before of the treatment all were to expect, who were determined thus to tread in his steps, by immediately subjoining, Happy are they who are persecuted for righteousness' sake. Through this whole discourse we cannot but observe the most exact method which can possibly be conceived. Every paragraph, every sentence, is closely connected both with that which precedes, and that which follows it. And is not this the pattern for every Christian preacher? If any then are able to follow it without any premeditation, well: if not, let them not dare to preach with-

out it. No rhapsody, no incoherency, whether the things spoken be true or false, comes of the Spirit of Christ.

10. *For righteousness' sake* — That is, because they have, or follow after, the righteousness here described. He that is truly a righteous man, he that mourns, and he that is pure in heart, yea, all that will live godly in Christ Jesus, shall suffer persecution, 2 Timothy 3:12. The world will always say, Away with such fellows from the earth. They are made to reprove our thoughts. They are grievous to us even to behold. Their lives are not like other men's; their ways are of another fashion.

11. *Revile* — When present: *say all evil* — When you are absent.

12. *Your reward* — Even over and above the happiness that naturally and directly results from holiness.

Matthew 5:48

> Be ye therefore perfect, even as your Father which is in heaven is perfect.

Therefore ye shall be perfect; as your Father who is in heaven is perfect — So the original runs, referring to all that holiness which is described in the foregoing verses, which our Lord in the beginning of the chapter recommends as happiness, and in the close of it as perfection. And how wise and gracious is this, to sum up, and, as it were, seal all his commandments with a promise! Even the proper promise of the Gospel! That he will put those laws in our minds, and write them in our hearts! He well knew how ready our unbelief would be to cry out, this is impossible! And therefore stakes upon it all the power, truth, and faithfulness of him to whom all things are possible.

Biblical Expositions

Matthew 6:22-23

> The light of the body is the eye: if therefore thine eye be single, thy whole body shall be full of light. [23] But if thine eye be evil, thy whole body shall be full of darkness. If therefore the light that is in thee be darkness, how great *is* that darkness!

22. *The eye is the lamp of the body* — And what the eye is to the body, the intention is to the soul. We may observe with what exact propriety our Lord places purity of intention between worldly desires and worldly cares, either of which directly tend to destroy. *If thine eye be single* — Singly fixed on God and heaven, thy whole soul will be full of holiness and happiness. *If thine eye be evil* — Not single, aiming at any thing else.

Romans 6:1-14

> What shall we say then? Shall we continue in sin, that grace may abound? [2] God forbid. How shall we, that are dead to sin, live any longer therein? [3] Know ye not, that so many of us as were baptized into Jesus Christ were baptized into his death? [4] Therefore we are buried with him by baptism into death: that like as Christ was raised up from the dead by the glory of the Father, even so we also should walk in newness of life. [5] For if we have been planted together in the likeness of his death, we shall be also *in the likeness* of *his* resurrection: [6] Knowing this, that our old man is crucified with *him,* that the body of sin might be destroyed, that henceforth we should not serve sin. [7] For he that is dead is freed from sin. [8] Now if we be dead with Christ, we believe that we shall also live with him: [9] Knowing that Christ being raised from the dead dieth no more; death hath no more dominion over him. [10] For in that he died, he died unto sin once: but in that he liveth, he liveth unto God. [11] Likewise reckon ye also

173

yourselves to be dead indeed unto sin, but alive unto God through Jesus Christ our Lord. [12] Let not sin therefore reign in your mortal body, that ye should obey it in the lusts thereof. [13] Neither yield ye your members *as* instruments of unrighteousness unto sin: but yield yourselves unto God, as those that are alive from the dead, and your members *as* instruments of righteousness unto God. [14] For sin shall not have dominion over you: for ye are not under the law, but under grace.

1. The apostle here sets himself more fully to vindicate his doctrine from the consequence above suggested, Romans 3:7, 8. He had then only in strong terms denied and renounced it: here he removes the very foundation thereof.

2. *Dead to sin* — Freed both from the guilt and from the power of it.

3. *As many as have been baptized into Jesus Christ have been baptized into his death* — In baptism we, through faith, are ingrafted into Christ; and we draw new spiritual life from this new root, through his Spirit, who fashions us like unto him, and particularly with regard to his death and resurrection.

4. *We are buried with him* — Alluding to the ancient manner of baptizing by immersion. *That as Christ was raised from the dead by the glory* — Glorious power. Of the Father, so we also, by the same power, should rise again; and as he lives a new life in heaven, so we should walk in newness of life. This, says the apostle, our very baptism represents to us.

5. *For* — Surely these two must go together; so that if we are indeed made conformable to his death, we shall also know the power of his resurrection.

6. *Our old man* — Coeval with our being, and as old as the fall; our evil nature; a strong and beautiful expression for that entire depravity and corruption which by nature spreads itself over the whole man, leaving no part uninfected. This in a believer is crucified with Christ, mortified, gradually killed, by virtue of our union with him. *That the body of sin* — All evil tempers, words, and

actions, which are the "members" of the "old man," Colossians 3:5, might be destroyed.

7. *For he that is dead* — With Christ. Is freed from the guilt of past, and from the power of present, sin, as dead men from the commands of their former masters.

8. *Dead with Christ* — Conformed to his death, by dying to sin.

10. *He died to sin* — To atone for and abolish it. *He liveth unto God* — A glorious eternal life, such as we shall live also.

12. *Let not sin reign even in your mortal body* — It must be subject to death, but it need not be subject to sin.

13. *Neither present your members to sin* — To corrupt nature, a mere tyrant. *But to God* — Your lawful King.

14. *Sin shall not have dominion over you* — It has neither right nor power. *For ye are not under the law* — A dispensation of terror and bondage, which only shows sin, without enabling you to conquer it. *But under grace*— Under the merciful dispensation of the gospel, which brings complete victory over it to every one who is under the powerful influences of the Spirit of Christ.

2 Corinthians 7:1

> Having therefore these promises, dearly beloved, let us cleanse ourselves from all filthiness of the flesh and spirit, perfecting holiness in the fear of God.

1. *Let us cleanse ourselves* — This is the latter part of the exhortation, which was proposed, 2 Corinthians 6:1, and resumed, 2 Corinthians 6:14. *From all pollution of the flesh* — All outward sin. *And of the spirit*— All inward. Yet let us not rest in negative religion, *but perfect holiness*— Carrying it to the height in all its branches, and enduring to the end in the loving fear of God, the sure foundation of all holiness.

Galatians 5:13-17

> For, brethren, ye have been called unto liberty; only
> *use* not liberty for an occasion to the flesh, but by love
> serve one another. [14] For all the law is fulfilled in one
> word, *even* in this; Thou shalt love thy neighbour as thy-
> self. [15] But if ye bite and devour one another, take heed
> that ye be not consumed one of another. [16] *This* I say
> then, Walk in the Spirit, and ye shall not fulfil the lust of
> the flesh. [17] For the flesh lusteth against the Spirit, and
> the Spirit against the flesh: and these are contrary the
> one to the other: so that ye cannot do the things that ye
> would.

13. *Ye have been called to liberty* — From sin and misery, as well
as from the ceremonial law. *Only use not liberty for an occasion
to the flesh* — Take not occasion from hence to gratify corrupt
nature. *But by love serve one another* — And hereby show that
Christ has made you free.

14. *For all the law is fulfilled in this, Thou shalt love thy
neighbor as thyself* — inasmuch as none can do this without loving God, 1 John 4:12; and the love of God and man includes all
perfection. Leviticus 19:18.

15. *But if* — On the contrary, in consequence of the divisions
which those troublers have occasioned among you, ye bite one
another by evil speaking. *And devour one another* — By railing
and clamor. *Take heed ye be not consumed one of another* — By
bitterness, strife, and contention, our health and strength, both of
body and soul, are consumed, as well as our substance and reputation.

16. *I say then* — He now explains what he proposed, Galatians
5:13. *Walk by the Spirit* — Follow his guidance in all things. *And
fulfil not* — In anything. *The desire of the flesh* — Of corrupt nature.

17. *For the flesh desireth against the Spirit* — Nature desires
what is quite contrary to the Spirit of God. *But the Spirit against
the flesh-* — But the Holy Spirit on his part opposes your evil na-

ture. *These are contrary to each other* — The flesh and the Spirit; there can be no agreement between them. *That ye may not do the things which ye would-* — That, being thus strengthened by the Spirit, ye may not fulfill the desire of the flesh, as otherwise ye would do.

Philippians 3:12-15

> [12] Not as though I had already attained, either were already perfect: but I follow after, if that I may apprehend that for which also I am apprehended of Christ Jesus. [13] Brethren, I count not myself to have apprehended: but *this* one thing *I do,* forgetting those things which are behind, and reaching forth unto those things which are before, [14] I press toward the mark for the prize of the high calling of God in Christ Jesus. [15] Let us therefore, as many as be perfect, be thus minded: and if in any thing ye be otherwise minded, God shall reveal even this unto you.

12. *Not that I have already attained* — The prize. He here enters on a new set of metaphors, taken from a race. But observe how, in the utmost fervor, he retains his sobriety of spirit. *Or am already perfected* — There is a difference between one that is perfect, and one that is perfected. The one is fitted for the race, Philippians 3:15; the other, ready to receive the prize. But I pursue, *if I may apprehend that* — Perfect holiness, preparatory to glory. For, *in order to which I was apprehended by Christ Jesus* — A pearing to me in the way, Acts 26:14. The speaking conditionally both here and in the preceding verse, implies no uncertainty, but only the difficulty of attaining.
13. *I do not account myself to have apprehended this already; to be already possessed of perfect holiness.*
14. *Forgetting the things that are behind* — Even that part of the race which is already run. *And reaching forth unto* — Literally, *stretched out over the things that are before* — Pursuing with the

whole bent and vigor of my soul, perfect holiness and eternal glory. *In Christ Jesus* — The author and finisher of every good thing.

15. *Let us, as many as are perfect* — Fit for the race, strong in faith; so it means here. *Be thus minded* — Apply wholly to this one thing. *And if in anything ye* — Who are not perfect, who are weak in faith. *Be otherwise minded* — Pursuing other things. God, if ye desire it, *shall reveal even this unto you* — Will convince you of it.

1 Thessalonians 5:16-18

Rejoice evermore. [17] Pray without ceasing. [18] In every thing give thanks: for this is the will of God in Christ Jesus concerning you.

Rejoice evermore — In uninterrupted happiness in God. *Pray without ceasing* — Which is the fruit of always rejoicing in the Lord. *In everything give thanks* — Which is the fruit of both the former. This is Christian perfection. Farther than this we cannot go; and we need not stop short of it. Our Lord has purchased joy, as well as righteousness, for us. It is the very design of the gospel that, being saved from guilt, we should be happy in the love of Christ. Prayer may be said to be the breath of our spiritual life. He that lives cannot possibly cease breathing. So much as we really enjoy of the presence of God, so much prayer and praise do we offer up without ceasing; else our rejoicing is but delusion. Thanksgiving is inseparable from true prayer: it is almost essentially connected with it. He that always prays is ever giving praise, whether in ease or pain, both for prosperity and for the greatest adversity. He blesses God for all things, looks on them as coming from him, and receives them only for his sake; not choosing nor refusing, liking nor disliking, anything, but only as it is agreeable or disagreeable to his perfect will.

1 Thessalonians 5:23-24

> And the very God of peace sanctify you wholly; and *I pray God* your whole spirit and soul and body be preserved blameless unto the coming of our Lord Jesus Christ. [24] Faithful *is* he that calleth you, who also will do *it.*

And may the God of peace sanctify you — By the peace he works in you, which is a great means of sanctification. *Wholly* — The word signifies wholly and perfectly; every part and all that concerns you; all that is of or about you. And may the whole of you, *the spirit and the soul and the body* — Just before he said you; now he denominates them from their spiritual state. *The spirit* — Galatians 6:8; wishing that it may be preserved whole and entire: then from their natural state, the soul and the body; (for these two make up the whole nature of man, Matthew 10:28) wishing it may be preserved blameless till the coming of Christ. To explain this a little further: of the three here mentioned, only the two last are the natural constituent parts of man. The first is adventitious, and the supernatural gift of God, to be found in Christians only. That man cannot possibly consist of three parts, appears hence: The soul is either matter or not matter: there is no medium. But if it is matter, it is part of the body: if not matter, it coincides with the Spirit.

1 John 1:5-10

> This then is the message which we have heard of him, and declare unto you, that God is light, and in him is no darkness at all. [6] If we say that we have fellowship with him, and walk in darkness, we lie, and do not the truth: [7] But if we walk in the light, as he is in the light, we have fellowship one with another, and the blood of Jesus Christ his Son cleanseth us from all sin. [8] If we say that we have no sin, we deceive ourselves, and the truth is not in us. [9] If we confess our sins, he is faithful and just to

forgive us *our* sins, and to cleanse us from all unrighteousness. [10] If we say that we have not sinned, we make
him a liar, and his word is not in us.

5. And this is the sum of the message which we have heard of him
— The Son of God. *That God is light* — The light of wisdom,
love, holiness, glory. What light is to the natural eye, that God is
to the spiritual eye. *And in him is no darkness at all* — No contrary principle. He is pure, unmixed light.
6. *If we say* — Either with our tongue, or in our heart, if we endeavor to persuade either ourselves or others. We have fellowship
with him, while we walk, either inwardly or outwardly, *in darkness* — In sin of any kind. *We do not the truth* — Our actions
prove, that the truth is not in us.
7. *But if we walk in the light* — In all holiness. As God is (a
deeper word than walk, and more worthy of God) in the light,
then we may truly say, *we have fellowship one with another* —
We who have seen, and you who have not seen, do alike enjoy
that fellowship with God. The imitation of God being the only
sure proof of our having fellowship with him. *And the blood of
Jesus Christ his Son* — With the grace purchased thereby. *Cleanseth us from all sin* — Both original and actual, taking away all
the guilt and all the power.
8. *If we say* — Any child of man, before his blood has cleansed
us. *We have no sin* — To be cleansed from, instead of confessing
our sins,1 John 1:9, *the truth is not in us* — Neither in our mouth
nor in our heart.
9. *But if with a penitent and believing heart, we confess our sins,
he is faithful* — Because he had promised this blessing, by the
unanimous voice of all his prophets. *Just* — Surely then he will
punish: no; for this very reason he will pardon. This may seem
strange; but upon the evangelical principle of atonement and redemption, it is undoubtedly true; because, when the debt is paid,
or the purchase made, it is the part of equity to cancel the bond,
and consign over the purchased possession. *Both to forgive us
our sins* — To take away all the guilt of them. *And to cleanse us*

from all unrighteousness — To purify our souls from every kind and every degree of it.

10. *Yet still we are to retain, even to our lives' end, a deep sense of our past sins. Still if we say, we have not sinned, we make him a liar* — Who saith, all have sinned. *And his word is not in us* — We do not receive it; we give it no place in our hearts.

1 John 3:4-9

> Whosoever committeth sin transgresseth also the law: for sin is the transgression of the law. [5] And ye know that he was manifested to take away our sins; and in him is no sin. [6] Whosoever abideth in him sinneth not: whosoever sinneth hath not seen him, neither known him. [7] Little children, let no man deceive you: he that doeth righteousness is righteous, even as he is righteous. [8] He that committeth sin is of the devil; for the devil sinneth from the beginning. For this purpose the Son of God was manifested, that he might destroy the works of the devil. [9] Whosoever is born of God doth not commit sin; for his seed remaineth in him: and he cannot sin, because he is born of God.

4. *Whosoever committeth sin* — Thereby transgresseth the holy, just, and good law of God, and so sets his authority at nought; for this is implied in the very nature of sin.

5. *And ye know that he* — Christ. *Was manifested* — That he came into the world for this very purpose. *To take away our sins* — To destroy them all, root and branch, and leave none remaining. *And in him is no sin* — So that he could not suffer on his own account, but to make us as himself.

6. *Whosoever abideth in communion with him, by loving faith, sinneth not* — While he so abideth. *Whosoever sinneth certainly seeth him not* — The loving eye of his soul is not then fixed upon God; *neither doth he then experimentally know him* — Whatever he did in time past.

181

7. *Let no one deceive you* — Let none persuade you that any man is righteous but he that uniformly practices righteousness; he alone is righteous, after the example of his Lord.

8. *He that committeth sin is a child of the devil; for the devil sinneth from the beginning* — That is, was the first sinner in the universe, and has continued to sin ever since. *The Son of God was manifested to destroy the works of the devil* — All sin. And will he not perform this in all that trust in him?

9. *Whosoever is born of God* — By living faith, whereby God is continually breathing spiritual life into his soul, and his soul is continually breathing out love and prayer to God, doth not commit sin. For the divine seed of loving faith abideth in him; and, so long as it doth, he cannot sin, *because he is born of God* — Is inwardly and universally changed.

Section Four

The Middle Period

Part Two

1756 – 1767

Questions to Consider for
John Wesley's Middle Period

1. In this section Wesley begins to emphasize the instantaneous reception of perfecting grace. In the *Plain Account* he claims to have taught this truth beginning in 1740. Do you agree? Or, was Wesley's earlier teaching on the reception of perfecting grace less clear?

2. How does Wesley's doctrine of involuntary sin (mistakes and infirmities) now shape his views on Christian perfection? Can it now be said that *all* sin is removed in the gift of perfect love? Is Wesley consistent?

3. What were Thomas Maxfield's views on perfection? How do they differ from Wesley's?

4. Once again, note how Wesley defines perfection in this section. What are the essential ideas? What has changed? What remains constant?

5. In this section Wesley spends much energy articulating a clearer message on how Christian perfection is attained. What, if anything, has changed over time regarding the conditions and means of perfection?

6. What role does repentance, the means of grace, and good works play in attaining full salvation? Has Wesley's views changed at all from prior periods, including his early middle period?

Letter to William Dodd
1756

William Dodd (1729-1777) was a distinguished Anglican lecturer, preacher, chaplain, author and editor of the Christian Magazine. *He was later convicted of forgery and executed. Dodd had sent a letter to Wesley on the subject of Christian perfection in January, 1756, and had received a courteous response (Works J 11:448). He then sent another letter with Wesley's response below. Wesley repeats several of his core convictions regarding holiness, perfection and salvation from sin. Again, take note how sin is defined, specifically outward sin, and the arguments against the necessity of continued sinning. Dodd remained a critic of Wesley's perfection views and section IV of* On Sin in Believers *was a response to several of Dodd's arguments (Works B 1:328 note l). Source: Works J 11:450-454.*

March 12, 1756

Reverend Sir,

1. You and I may the more easily bear with each other, because we are both of us rapid writers, and therefore the more liable to mistake. I will thank you for showing me any mistake I am in; being not so tenacious of my opinions now, as I was twenty or thirty years ago. Indeed, I am not fond of any opinion as such. I read the Bible with what attention I can, and regulate all my opinions thereby, to the best of my understanding. But I am always willing to receive more light; particularly with regard to any less common opinions, because the explaining and defending of them takes up much time, which I can ill spare from other employments. Whoever, therefore, will give me more light with regard to Christian perfection, will do me a singular favour. The opinion I have concerning it at present, I espouse merely because I think it is scriptural. If therefore I am convinced it is not scriptural, I shall willingly relinquish it.

2. I have no particular fondness for the term. It seldom occurs either in my preaching or writings. It is my opponents who thrust it upon me continually, and ask me what I mean by it. So did Bishop Gibson, till by his advice I publicly declared what I did not mean by it, and what I did. This I supposed might be best done in the form of a sermon, having a text prefixed, wherein that term occurred. But that text is there used only as an occasion or introduction to the subject. I do not build any doctrine thereupon, nor undertake critically to explain it.[7]

3. What is the meaning of the term perfection is another question; but that it is a scriptural term is undeniable. Therefore, none ought to object to the use of the term, whatever they may do to this or that explication of it. I am very willing to consider whatever you have to object to what is advanced under the first head of that sermon. But I still think that perfection is only another term for holiness, or the image of God in man. "God made man perfect," I think is just the same as, "He made him holy," or 'in his own image;" and you are the first person I ever read of or spoke with, who made any doubt of it. Now this perfection does certainly admit of degrees. Therefore, I readily allow the propriety of that distinction, perfection of kinds, and perfection of degrees. Nor do I remember one writer, ancient or modern, who excepts against it.

4. In the sermon of *Salvation by Faith,* I say, "He that is born of God sinneth not," (a proposition explained at large in another sermon, and everywhere either explicitly or virtually connected with, "while he keepeth himself,") 'by any sinful desire; any unholy desire he stifleth in the birth." (Assuredly he does, "while he keepeth himself.") "Nor doth he sin by infirmities; for his infirmities have no concurrence of his will; and without this they are not properly sins." Taking the words as they lie in connexion thus, (and taken otherwise they are not my words but yours,) I

---

[7] In this paragraph Wesley is referring to the sermon *Christian Perfection.*

must still aver, they speak both my own experience, and that of many hundred children of God whom I personally know. And all this, with abundantly more than this, is contained in that single expression, "the loving God with all our heart, and serving him with all our strength." Nor did I ever say or mean any more by perfection, than thus loving and serving God. But I dare not say less than this; for it might be attended with worse consequences than you seem to be aware of. If there be a mistake, it is far more dangerous on the one side than on the other. If I set the mark too high, I drive men into needless fears; if you set it too low, you drive them into hell-fire.

5. We agree, that true "Christianity implies a destruction of the kingdom of sin, and a renewal of the soul in righteousness; which even babes in Christ do in a measure experience, though not in so large a measure as young men and fathers." But here we divide. I believe even babes in Christ, "while they keep themselves, do not commit sin." By sin, I mean, outward sin; and the word commit, I take in its plain, literal meaning. And this I think is fully proved by all the texts cited Sermon III., from the sixth chapter to the Romans. Nor do I conceive there is any material difference between committing sin, and continuing therein. I tell my neighbour here, "William, you are a child of the devil, for you commit sin; you was drunk yesterday." "No, Sir," says the man, "I do not live or continue in sin" (which Mr. Dodd says is the true meaning of the text); "I am not drunk continually, but only now and then, once in a fortnight, or once in a month." Now, Sir, how shall I deal with this man? Shall I tell him he is in the way to heaven or hell? I think he is in the high road to destruction; and that if I tell him otherwise his blood will be upon my head. And all that you say of living, continuing in, serving sin, as different from committing it, and of its not reigning, not having dominion, over him who still frequently commits it, is making so many loopholes whereby any impenitent sinner may escape from all the terrors of the Lord. I dare not therefore give up the plain, literal meaning either of St. Paul's or St. Peter's words.

6. As to those of St. John, cited Sermon V., I do not think you have proved they are not to be taken literally. In every single act of obedience, as well as in a continued course of it, *poiei dikaiosunen*: And in either an act or a course of sin *poiei amartian*. Therefore, that I may give no countenance to any kind or degree of sin, I still interpret these words by those in the fifth chapter, and believe, "he that is born of God" (while he keepeth himself) "sinneth not;" doth not commit outward sin.

7. But "it is absolutely necessary," as you observe, "to add sometimes explanatory words to those of the sacred penmen." It is so; to add words explanatory of their sense, but not subversive of it. The words added to this text, "Ye know all things," are such; and you yourself allow them so to be. But I do not allow the words willfully and habitually to be such. These do not explain, but overthrow, the text. That the first Fathers thus explained it, I deny; as also that I ever spoke lightly of them.

8. You proceed: "You allow in another sermon, in evident contradiction to yourself, that the true children of God could, and did, commit sin." This is no contradiction to anything I ever advanced. I everywhere allow that a child of God can and will commit sin, if he does not keep himself. "But this," you say, "is nothing to the present argument." Yes, it is the whole thing. If they keep themselves, they do not; otherwise, they can and do commit sin. I say nothing contrary to this in either sermon. But "hence," you say, "we conclude that he who is born of God, may possibly commit sin:" An idle conclusion as ever was formed; for who ever denied it? I flatly affirm it in both the sermons, and in the very paragraph now before us. The only conclusion which I deny is, that "all Christians do and will commit sin, as long as they live." Now this you yourself (though you seem to start at it) maintain from the beginning of your Letter to the end; namely, that all Christians do sin, and cannot but sin, more or less, to their lives' end. Therefore I do not "artfully put this conclusion;" but it is your own conclusion, from your own premises. Indeed were I

artfully to put in anything in expounding the word of God, I must be an arrant knave. But I do not; my conscience bears me witness, that I speak the very truth, so far as I know it, in simplicity and godly sincerity.

9. I think that all this time you are directly pleading for looseness of manners, and that everything you advance naturally tends thereto. This is my grand objection to that doctrine of the necessity of sinning: Not only that it is false, but that it is directly subversive of all holiness. The doctrine of the Gnostics was, not that a child of God does not commit sin, that is, act the things which are forbidden in Scripture, but that they are not sin in him, that he is a child of God still; so they contend, not for sinless, but sinful, perfection; just as different from what I contend for, as heaven is from hell. What the Donatists were, I do not know; but I suspect they were the real Christians of that age; and were therefore served by St. Augustine and his warm adherents, as the Methodists are now by their zealous adversaries. It is extremely easy to blacken; and could I give myself leave, I could paint the consequences of your doctrine, in at least as dark and odious colours as you could paint mine.

10. The passage of St. Peter, mentioned Sermon XII., I still think proves all which I brought it to prove.

"But you allow that Paul and Barnabas did commit sin. And these were, without all controversy, fathers in Christ." That is not without controversy, that either Barnabas when he left Paul, or Peter when he dissembled at Antioch, was at that time a father in Christ in St. John's sense; though by office undoubtedly they were. Their example, therefore, only proves what no one denies, namely, that if a believer keeps not himself, he may commit sin. Would the conclusions here drawn "be made only by a very weak opponent?" Then you are a weak opponent; for you make them all, either from these or other premises: For you believe and maintain, (1.) That all the other Apostles committed sin sometimes. (2.) That all the other Christians of the apostolic age sometimes committed sin. (3.) That all other Christians, in all ages, do and will commit sin as long as they live. And, (4.) That every man must commit sin, cannot help it, as long as he is in the body. You cannot deny one of these propositions, if you understand your own premises.

I am, Rev. Sir,

Your affectionate brother

Perfection in an Instant
1757-58

Beginning in 1757 we see a change in Wesley's correspondence. For starters, he became more involved in counseling seekers of heart holiness (mostly women). Second, he began to emphasize the instantaneous reception of perfecting grace. Though he later denied any change in this regard,[8] the reader can decide for themselves by comparing Wesley's writings in this section with what he wrote earlier. Source: Telford.

To Miss Furly
June 11, 1757

You have reason to praise God for what he has done, and to expect all that he has promised. Indeed, if it were required that you should work this in yourself, your impotence might be a bar to your expectations; and so might your unworthiness, if God required any merit of yours, in order to his working in you. But what impotence in you can be a bar to the almighty power of God? And what unworthiness can hinder the free love of God? his love in and through Christ Jesus? So that all the promises lie fair before you. The land flowing with milk and honey, the Canaan of his perfect love, is open. Believe, and enter in!

It is an observation of one of the ancients, that it is far easier not to desire praise, than not to be pleased with it. A bare conviction that it is, generally speaking, deadly poison, may prevent our desiring it; but nothing less than humble love filling the heart, will prevent our being pleased with it: For the sense of honour is as natural to man as the sense of tasting or feeling. But when that which is spiritual is fully come, this which is corruptly natural shall be done away.

---

[8] *The Plain Account of Christian Perfection: The Annotated Edition,* 11-16, 78, 111-112.

Whatever enemies you have, it is enough that you have a Friend who is mightier than them all. O let Him reign in your heart alone! Do not spare to speak with all freedom to,

Dear Miss Furly,

Your affectionate brother and servant

September 6, 1757

Why you should be afraid, on account of anything you said to me, I do not know. Certainly if you had said what- ever was in your heart, it might have been a means of lessening your burden, and not of increasing it. I believe you have often a desire, and almost a resolution, of saying a great deal to me; but when you come to write or speak, your heart fails. Why should it? Why should you repress yourself? I should not despise but love you for your openness. It is the fruit and the proof of an honest heart. I know you are weak; I know a little of your particular weaknesses. But so much the more am I concerned for you, as a tender, sickly flower. Away then with this reserve: It answers no end, but to trouble and embarrass you: Tell me, freely and plainly, any diffi- culty you meet with; any enemy against whom you want help. Use me as a friend; as I hope you will use sister Crosby; and you will find it a blessing to your soul. It will again bring the promise of holiness near; which indeed always seems to be far off, when we give way to any known sin; when we anyway grieve the Spirit of God. There may be some rare cases wherein God has deter- mined not to bestow his perfect love till a little before death; but this I believe is uncommon: He does not usually put off the ful- filling of his promises. Seek, and you shall find; seek earnestly, and you shall find speedily. Lift up the hands that hang down; deny yourself; take up your cross, whether that of meeting your class, or any other. Fight on, and victory is at hand!

I am, dear Miss Furly,

Your affectionate servant.

Perfection in an Instant

To Sarah Moore
November, 22, 1758

My Dear Sister,
   Praise God for what he hath already done. Let those give thanks whom the Lord hath redeemed and delivered from the hand of the enemy; but you know a greater deliverance at hand. What have you to do but to fight your way through the world, the flesh, and the devil? It is good though a painful fight. Unless you yield, you cannot but conquer. It is true you will first conquer by little and little. For

> *More of this life and more we have*
> *As the old Adam dies.*

But there is also an instantaneous conquest: in a moment sin shall be no more. You are gradually dying for a long time. But you will die in a moment. O hasten to the happy time! Pray, strive, hope for it!
   I am—

Your affectionate brother

Thoughts on Christian Perfection
1759

By the late fifties erroneous notions about perfection were begin-
ning to pop up among some of the Methodist preachers, especially the
younger ones, and in the societies. With the winds of revival in the air,
renewed interest in perfection was captivating many. So at the annual
conference Wesley felt the need to explain himself once more on the
subject. He later published the questions and answers under the title
Thoughts on Christian Perfection. *The following excerpts address fur-*
ther developments in Wesley's doctrine of sin by delineating sin as vol-
untary and involuntary. As we will see, this distinction will profoundly
shape Wesley's mature theology in several ways. He also explains the
believer's continued reliance on Christ's atonement and heavenly in-
tercession, and responds to several concerns regarding attainment of
the blessing. Note how perfection involves both instantaneous gift and
gradual growth. The tract was later incorporated in the Plain Account.
Source: Outler, John Wesley *New York: Oxford University Press,*
1964, 284-287, 293-295.

Q.1 What is Christian Perfection?
A. The loving God with all our heart, mind, soul and strength.
This implies that no wrong temper, none contrary to love, remains in the soul and that all the thoughts, words and action are
governed by pure love.

Q.2 But do you affirm that this perfection excludes all infirmities,
ignorance and mistake?
A. I continually affirm the contrary, and always have done so.
The sermon "Christian Perfection" was published eighteen years
ago. And therein I expressly declare "Christians are not so perfect
in *this life* as to be free from ignorance..."

Q.3 "But is not this scheme contradictory to itself? How can
every thought, word and work be governed by pure love and the
man be subject at the same time to ignorance and mistake? This

194

we think is not Christian perfection but imperfection, and is not a pin different from Calvinism."

A. So one of my correspondence writes. But I see no argument therein. I see nothing contradictory here. "A man may be filled with pure love and still liable to mistake." Indeed, I expect not to be free from actual mistakes till this mortal puts on immortality (cf. 1 Cor 15:54). I believe this to be a natural consequence of the soul's dwelling in flesh and blood. For we cannot now think at all but by the mediation of those organs which have suffered equally with the rest of our frame. And hence we cannot avoid sometimes thinking wrong till "this corruptible shall have put on incorruption."

But we may carry this thought further. A mistake in judgment may possibly occasion a mistake in practice. For instance: the mistake arising from prejudice of education in M. De Renty concerning the nature of mortification occasioned that practical mistake, his wearing an iron girdle. And a thousand such instances there may be, even in those who are in the highest state of grace. Yet where every word and action springs from love, such a mistake is not properly a sin. However, it cannot bear the rigour of God's justice, but needs the atoning blood.

Q.4 What was the judgment of all our brethren who met at Bristol in August, 1758, on this head?
A. It was expressed in these words:

1. Every one may mistake as long as he lives.
2. A mistake in opinion may occasion a mistake in practice.
3. Every such mistake is a transgression of the perfect law.
4. Therefore every such mistake, were it not for the blood of atonement, would expose to eternal damnation.
5. It follows that the most perfect have continual need of the merits of Christ, even for their actual transgressions, and may well say for themselves, as well as their brethren, "Forgive us our trespasses" (Matt 6:12).

This easily accounts for what otherwise might seem to be utterly unaccountable: namely, that they who are not offended when we speak of the highest degree of love, yet will not hear of "living without sin." The reason is, they know all men are liable to mistake, and that in practice as well as in judgment. But they do not know, or do not observe, that this is not sin if love is the sole principle of action.

Q.5 But still, if they live without sin, does not this exclude the necessity of a mediator? At least, is it not plain that they stand no longer in need of Christ in his priestly office?
A. Far from it. None feel their need of Christ like these; none so entirely depend upon him. For Christ does not give life to the soul separate from, but in and with, himself. Hence his words are equally true of all men, in whatever state of grace they are: "As the branch cannot bear fruit of itself, except it abide in the vine, no more can ye except ye abide in me...without," or separate from, "me, ye can do nothing" (Jn 15:4-5).
In every state, we need Christ in the following respects:

1. Whatever grace we receive, it is a free gift from him.
2. We receive it as his purchase merely in consideration of the price he paid.
3. We have this grace not from Christ but in him. For our perfection is not like that of a tree, which flourishes by the sap derived from its own root, but like that of a branch, which, united to the vine, bears fruit, but severed from it, is "dried up and withered" (Jn 15:16).
4. All our blessings, temporal, spiritual and eternal, depend on his intercession for us; which is one great branch of his priestly office, of which, therefore, we have always equal need.
5. The best of men still need Christ in his priestly office to atone for their omissions, their shortcomings (as some, not improperly, speak), their mistakes in judgment and practice, and their defects of various kinds. For these are

all deviations from the perfect law and consequently need an atonement. Yet that they are not properly sins, we apprehend, may appear from the words of St. Paul, "He that loveth hath fulfilled the law; for love is the fulfilling of the law." Now mistakes and whatever infirmities necessarily flow from the corruptible state of the body are no way contrary to love nor therefore, in the Scripture sense, "sins."

The truth is, in a state of perfection every desire is in subjection to the obedience of Christ. The will is entirely subject to the will of God and the affections wholly fixed on him. Now what motive can remain sufficient to induce such a person to a transgression of the law? Surely none that can induce him to do any that is formally evil, although he may, through human infirmity, speak or do what is materially so and, as such, condemned by the perfect law. And the soul that any way deviates from this would, without an atonement, be lost forever. Yet these deviations are not properly sins. But if any will call them so, they may.

Q.6 I am not yet clear on this head. Will you answer me a few questions?[9]

1&2. Is there any thing besides sin that would expose to eternal damnation? Is there any thing besides sin that needs the atoning blood?
A. Not only sin properly so called (that is, a voluntary transgression of a known law) but sin improperly so called (that is, an involuntary transgression of a divine law, known or unknown) needs the atoning blood, and without this would expose to eternal damnation.

---

[9] The editor combined Wesley's answers to the questions. In the original *Thoughts* the two were in separate paragraph sections.

3. Is there no such perfection in this life as absolutely excludes all sin?

A. I believe there is no such perfection in this life as excludes these involuntary transgressions, which I apprehend to be naturally consequent on the ignorance and mistakes inseparable from mortality.

4. If we do not allow this, do we not contradict ourselves in talking of sinless perfection?

A. "Sinless perfection" is a phrase I never use lest it should *seem* to contradict myself.

5. Can a person be filled with the love of God and yet be liable to sin, to transgress the perfect law?

A. I believe a person filled with the love of God is still liable to these involuntary transgressions.

6. How can we call such a transgression of the perfect law, as without the blood of atonement would expose us to eternal damnation, any other than sin?

A. Such transgressions you may call sins if you please. I do not for the reason above mentioned.

I would only add that man, in his original state, was not liable to these transgressions. He knew every law of God in every possible case, and was able to obey it. Therefore any transgression must have exposed him to eternal damnation: and so would it every one of his posterity, but that the law of love, by virtue of the atoning blood, now stands in the room of the law of fire.

Q. 26 When may a person judge himself to have attained this (perfection)?

A. When, after having been fully convinced of inbred sin, by a far deeper and clearer conviction than that he experienced before justification and after having experienced a gradual mortification of it, he experiences a total death to sin and an entire renewal in the love and image of God, so as to rejoice evermore, to pray without ceasing and in everything to give thanks (1 Th 5:16-18). Not that the feeling all love and no sin is a sufficient proof. Several have experienced this for a time and yet were afterwards convinced that their souls not entirely renewed and that sin was only laid asleep, not destroyed. None, therefore, ought to believe that the work is done till there is added the testimony of the Spirit, witnessing his entire sanctification as clearly as his justification.

Q. 27 But whence is it that some imagine they are thus sanctified when in reality they are not?
A. It is hence: They do not judge by all the preceding marks but either by part of them or by others that are inconclusive. But I know no instance of any person duly attending to them all and yet deceived in this matter. I believe there can be none in the world. If a man be deeply and fully convinced after justification of inbred sin; if he then experiences a gradual mortification of it and afterward an entire renewal in the image of God; if to this change, immensely greater than that wrought when he was justified, there be added a clear, direct witness of that renewal—I judge it as impossible this man should be deceived herein as that God should lie. And if one whom I know to be a man of veracity testify these things to me, without some sufficient reason I ought not to reject his testimony.

Q. 28 Is this death to sin and renewal in love gradual or instantaneous?
A. A man may be "dying" for some time, yet he does not, properly speaking, "die" till the instant the soul is separated from the body. And in that instant he lives the life of eternity. In like manner, he may be "dying to sin" for some time; yet he is not "dead to sin" till sin is separated from his soul. And in that instant he lives the full life of love. And as the change undergone when the

body dies is of a different kind and infinitely greater than any we had known before, yea, such as till then it is impossible to conceive, so the change wrought when the soul dies to sin is of a different kind and infinitely greater than any before, and than any can conceive till he experiences it. Yet he stills "grows in grace in the knowledge of Christ" (2 Pet 3:18), in the love and image of God, and will do so not only till death, but to all eternity.

Q. 29 How are we to wait for this change?
A. Not in careless indifference or indolent inactivity, but in vigorous and universal obedience; in a zealous keeping of all the commandments; in watchfulness and painfulness; in denying ourselves and taking up our cross daily; as well as in earnest prayer and fasting and a close attendance on all the ordinances of God. And if any man dream of attaining it any other way, he deceiveth his own soul. It is true we receive it by simple faith; but God does not, will not, give that faith unless we seek it with all diligence in the way which he hath ordained. This consideration may satisfy those who inquire why so few have received the blessing. Inquire how many are seeking it in this way and you have a sufficient answer.

Prayer especially is wanting. Who continues instant therein? Who wrestles with God for this very thing? So, "ye have not because ye ask not" or because ye ask amiss—namely, "that you may be renewed before you die." Before you die? Will that content you? Nay, but ask that it may be done now, today, while it is called today (Heb 3:13). Do not call this "setting God a time." Certainly, *today* is his time, as well as to-morrow. Make haste, man, make haste! Let

Thy soul break out in strong desire
The perfect bliss to prove;
Thy longing heart be all on fire
To be dissolved in love!

Wandering Thoughts
1760

In the sermon Christian Perfection (1741) *Wesley defined perfection as holy thoughts and tempers. He now tackles the question as to which thoughts are sinful and which are holy. The following excerpt is from section three of the sermon. Source: Works J 6:27-30.*

Bringing into captivity every thought
to the obedience of Christ.

2 Corinthians 10:5

1. What kind of wandering thoughts are sinful, and what not, is the third thing to be inquired into. And, First, all those thoughts which wander from God, which leave him no room in our minds, are undoubtedly sinful. For all these imply practical Atheism; and by these we are without God in the world. And so much more are all those which are contrary to God, which imply opposition or enmity to him. Such are all murmuring, discontented thoughts, which say, in effect, "We will not have thee to rule over us;"—all unbelieving thoughts, whether with regard to his being, his attributes, or his providence. I mean, his particular providence over all things, as well as all persons, in the universe; that without which "not a sparrow falls to the ground,' by which "the hairs of our head are all numbered;" for as to a general providence, (vulgarly so called,) contradistinguished from a particular, it is only a decent, well-sounding word, which means just nothing.

2. Again: All thoughts which spring from sinful tempers, are undoubtedly sinful. Such, for instance, are those that spring from a revengeful temper, from pride, or lust, or vanity. "An evil tree cannot bring forth good fruit:" Therefore if the tree be evil, so must the fruit be also.

3. And so must those be which either produce or feed any sinful temper; those which either give rise to pride or vanity, to anger or

201

love of the world, or confirm and increase these or any other unholy temper, passion, or affection. For not only whatever flows
from evil is evil; but also whatever leads to it; whatever tends to
alienate the soul from God, and to make or keep it earthly, sensual, and devilish.

4. Hence, even those thoughts which are occasioned by weakness
or disease, by the natural mechanism of the body, or by the laws
of vital union, however innocent they may be in themselves, do
nevertheless become sinful, when they either produce or cherish
and increase in us any sinful temper; suppose the desire of the
flesh, the desire of the eye, or the pride of life. In like manner, the
wandering thoughts which are occasioned by the words or actions
of other men, if they cause or feed any wrong disposition, then
commence sinful. And the same we may observe of those which
are suggested or injected by the devil. When they minister to any
earthly or devilish temper, (which they do, whenever we give
place to them, and thereby make them our own,) then they are
equally sinful with the tempers to which they minister.

5. But, abstracting from these cases, wandering thoughts, in the
latter sense of the word, that is, thoughts wherein our understanding wanders from the point it has in view, are no more sin- ful
than the motion of the blood in our veins, or of the spirits in our
brain. If they arise from an infirm constitution, or from some ac-
cidental weakness or distemper, they are as innocent as it is to
have a weak constitution or a distempered body. And surely no
one doubts but a bad state of nerves, a fever of any kind, and either a transient or a lasting delirium, may consist with perfect in-
nocence. And if they should arise in a soul which is united to a
healthful body, either from the natural union between the body
and soul, or from any of ten thousand changes which may occur
in those organs of the body that minister to thought;—in any of
these cases they are as perfectly innocent as the causes from
which they spring. And so they are when they spring from the
casual, involuntary associations of our ideas.

6. If our thoughts wander from the point we had in view, by means of other men variously affecting our senses, they are equally innocent still: For it is no more a sin to understand what I see and hear, and in many cases cannot help seeing, hearing, and understanding, than it is to have eyes and ears. "But if the devil injects wandering thoughts, are not those thoughts evil?" They are troublesome, and in that sense evil; but they are not sinful. I do not know that he spoke to our Lord with an audible voice; perhaps he spoke to his heart only, when he said, "All these things will I give thee, if thou wilt fall down and worship me." But whether he spoke inwardly or outwardly, our Lord doubtless understood what he said. He had therefore a thought correspondent to those words. But was it a sinful thought? We know it was not. In him was no sin, either in action, or word, or thought. Nor is there any sin in a thousand thoughts of the same kind, which Satan may inject into any of our Lord's followers.

7. It follows that none of these wandering thoughts (what ever unwary persons have affirmed, thereby grieving whom the Lord had not grieved) are inconsistent with perfect love. Indeed, if they were, then not only sharp pain, but sleep itself, would be inconsistent with it:—Sharp pain; for whenever this supervenes, whatever we were before thinking of, it will interrupt our thinking, and of course draw our thoughts into another channel:—Yea, and sleep itself; as it is a state of insensibility and stupidity; and such as is generally mixed with thoughts wandering over the earth, loose, wild, and incoherent. Yet certainly these are consistent with perfect love: So then are all wandering thoughts of this kind.

Clarifying Perfection
1760-62

The great perfection revival of the early sixties swept many Methodists into a profession of the experience. But it also left others perplexed and confused, with many unanswered questions. In the following letters Wesley seeks to remove the confusion. Source: Telford.

To Miss March
June 27, 1760

A day or two ago I was quite surprised to find among my papers a letter of yours, which I apprehend I have not answered.

Every one, though born of God in an instant, yea, and sanctified in an instant, yet undoubtedly grows by slow degrees, both after the former and the latter change. But it does not follow from thence that there must be a considerable tract of time between the one and the other. A year or a month is the same with God as a thousand. If He wills, to do is present with him. Much less is there any necessity for much suffering: God can do his work by pleasure as well as by pain. It is therefore undoubtedly our duty to pray and look for full salvation every day, every hour, every moment, without waiting till we have either done or suffered more. Why should not this be the accepted time?

Certainly your friend will suffer loss, if he does not allow himself time every day for private prayer. Nothing will supply the want of this. Praying with others is quite another thing. Besides, it may expose us to great danger; it may turn prayer into an abomination to God; for

> *Guilty we speak, if subtle from within*
> *Blows on our words the self-admiring sin!*

O make the best of every hour!

Clarifying Perfection

To Elizabeth Hardy
December 26, 1761.

Dear Sister,

The path of controversy is a rough path. But it seems smoother while I am walking with you: So that I could follow you through all its windings; only my time will not permit.

The plain fact is this: I know many who love God with all their heart, mind, soul, and strength. He is their one desire, their one delight, and they are continually happy in him. They love their neighbour as themselves. They feel as sincere, fervent, constant a desire for the happiness of every man, good or bad, friend or enemy, as for their own. They "rejoice evermore, pray without ceasing, and in everything give thanks." Their souls are continually streaming up to God in holy joy, prayer, and praise. This is plain, sound, scriptural experience: And of this we have more and more living witnesses.

But these souls dwell in a shattered, corruptible body, and are so pressed down thereby, that they cannot exert their love as they would, by always thinking, speaking, and acting precisely right. For want of better bodily organs, they sometimes inevitably think, speak, or act wrong. Yet I think they need the advocacy of Christ, even for these involuntary defects; although they do not imply a defect of love, but of understanding. However that be, I cannot doubt the fact. They are all love; yet they cannot walk as they desire. "But are they all love while they grieve the Holy Spirit?" No, surely; they are then fallen from their steadfastness; and this they may do even after they are sealed. So that, even to such, strong cautions are needful. After the heart is cleansed from pride, anger, and desire, it may suffer them to re-enter: Therefore I have long thought some expressions in the Hymns are abundantly too strong; as I cannot perceive any state mentioned in Scripture from which we may not (in a measure, at least) fall.

Persons who talked of being emptied before they were filled, were, for some time, a great stumbling-block to me too; but I have since considered it thus: The great point in question is, Can we be saved from all sin, or not? Now, it may please God to act in that uncommon manner, purposely to clear this point: To satisfy those persons that they are saved from all sin, before he goes on in his work.

Forgive me, dear Miss Hardy, that I do but just touch upon the heads of your letter. Indeed, this defect does not spring from the want of love, but only from want of time. I should not wonder if your soul was one of the next that was filled with pure love. Receive it freely, thou poor bruised reed! It is able to make thee stand.

I am—

Your affectionate friend and brother

To Dorothy Furly
September 15, 1762

My Dear Sister,

Whereunto you have attained, hold fast. But expect that greater things are at hand; although our friend talks as if you were not to expect them till the article of death.

Certainly sanctification (in the proper sense) is "an instantaneous deliverance from all sin;" and includes "an instantaneous power then given, always to cleave to God." Yet this sanctification (at least, in the lower degrees) does not include a power never to think an useless thought, nor ever speak an useless word. I myself believe that such a perfection is inconsistent with living in a corruptible body: For this makes it impossible "always to think right." While we breathe, we shall, more or less, mistake. If, therefore, Christian perfection implies this, we must not expect it till after death.

I want you to be all love. This is the perfection I believe and teach. And this perfection is consistent with a thousand nervous disorders, which that high-strained perfection is not. Indeed, my judgment is, that (in this case particularly) to overdo, is to undo; and that to set perfection too high, (so high as no man that we ever heard or read of attained,) is the most effectual (because un-suspected) way of driving it out of the world.

Take care you are not hurt by anything in the "Short Hymns," contrary to the doctrines you have long received. Peace be with your spirit! I am—

Your affectionate brother

To Samuel Furly
September 15, 1762

Dear Sir,

Spectatum satis, ac donatum jam rude quæris,
Mæcenas, iterum antiquo me includere ludo?
Non eadem est ætas, non mens.[10]

I have entirely lost my taste for controversy. I have lost my readiness in disputing; and I take this to be a providential dis-charge from it. All I can now do with a clear conscience is, not to enter into a formal controversy about the new birth, or justifica-tion by faith, any more than Christian perfection, but simply to declare my judgment; and to explain myself as clearly as I can upon any difficulty that may arise concerning it.

So far I can go with you, but no farther. I still say, and with-out any self-contradiction, I know no persons living who are so deeply conscious of their needing Christ both as Prophet, Priest, and King, as those who believe themselves, and whom I believe, to be cleansed from all sin; I mean, from all pride, anger, evil de-sire, idolatry, and unbelief. These very persons feel more than ever their own ignorance, littleness of grace, coming short of the

---

[10] This quotation from Horace is thus translated by Francis:

Wherefore, Mæcenas, would you thus engage
Your bard, dismiss'd with honour from the stage,
Again to venture in the lists of fame,
His youth, his genius, now no more the same?

full mind that was in Christ, and walking less accurately than they might have done after their Divine Pattern; are more convinced of the insufficiency of all they are, have, or do, to bear the eye of God without a Mediator; are more penetrated with the sense of the want of Him than ever they were before.

If Mr. Maxfield or you say, "that coming short is sin," be it so; I contend not. But still I say, "These are they whom I believe to be scripturally perfect. And yet these never felt their want of Christ so deeply and strongly as they do now." If in saying this I have "fully given up the point," what would you have more? Is it not enough that I leave you to "boast your superior power against the little, weak shifts of baffled error?" "Canst thou not be content," as the Quaker said, "to lay J. W. on his back, but thou must tread his guts out?"

Here are persons exceeding holy and happy; rejoicing evermore, praying always, and in everything giving thanks; feeling the love of God and man every moment; feeling no pride, or other evil temper. If these are not perfect, that scriptural word has no meaning. Stop! you must not cavil at that word: You are not wiser than the Holy Ghost. But if you are not, see that you teach perfection too. "But are they not sinners?" Explain the term one way, and I say, Yes; another, and I say, No. "Are they cleansed from all sin?" I believe they are; meaning from all sinful tempers. "But have they then need of Christ?" I believe they have, in the sense, and for the reasons above mentioned. Now, be this true or false, it is no contradiction; it is consistent with itself; and, I think, consistent with right reason, and the whole oracles of God.

O let you and I go on to perfection! God grant we may so run as to attain!

I am,

Your affectionate friend and brother

Perfection Distorted
1762

In the heat of revival many came to believe they were not only per-
fected in love, but were as perfect as the angels. This led to schism
within the societies, and stirred criticism toward Wesley from outsid-
ers. The main ringleaders behind the schism were long-time "son in the
gospel" Thomas Maxfield, and a fairly new recruit George Bell. Both
leaders espoused extreme views. They claimed victory over physical
death and temptation, and that the charismatic gifts had been restored
in their ministries. Finally, in December Bell prophesied the world
would end on February 28, 1763. Both accused Wesley of changing his
views on the subject. On the opposite side, many felt Wesley was too
slow in responding to the schism. But in November he finally took the
time to confront Maxfield regarding some of his errors.

This letter offers important insights into Wesley's present under-
standing of perfection and the kind of sin he believed was removed in
the blessing. The letter further explains why he found it necessary to
stress a clear doctrine of involuntary sin to his people. Simply stated,
Maxfield and Bell collapsed the eschatological tension by claiming the
new age had fully arrived. Source: Telford.

To Thomas Maxfield
November 2, 1762

Without any preface or ceremony, which is needless between
you and me, I will simply and plainly tell what I dislike in your
doctrine, spirit, or outward behaviour. When I say yours, I include brother Bell and Owen, and those who are most closely
connected with them.

(1). I like your doctrine of perfection, or pure love—love excluding sin. Your insisting that it is merely by faith; that consequently
it is instantaneous (though preceded and followed by a gradual
work), and that it may be now, at this instant.

209

But I dislike your supposing man may be as perfect "as an angel," that he can be absolutely perfect; that he can be infallible, or above being tempted; or that the moment he is pure in heart he cannot fall from it.

I dislike the saying, "This was not known or taught among us till within two or three years." I grant, You did not know it. You have over and over denied instantaneous sanctification to me. But I have known and taught it (and so has my brother, as our writings show) above these twenty years.

I dislike your directly or indirectly depreciating justification: saying, a justified person is not "in Christ," is not "born of God," is not "a new creature," has not a "new heart," is not "sanctified," not a "temple of the Holy Ghost;" or that he "cannot please God," or cannot "grow in grace."

I dislike your saying that one saved from sin needs nothing more than "looking to Jesus," needs not to hear or think of anything else—"Believe, believe" is enough—that he needs no self-examination, no times of private prayer; needs not mind little, or outward things; and that he cannot be taught by any person who is not in the same state.

I dislike your affirming that justified persons in general persecute them that are saved from sin; that they have persecuted you on this account; and that for two years past you have been more persecuted by "the two brothers" than ever you was by the world in all your life.

(2). As to your spirit, I like your confidence in God and your zeal for the salvation of souls.

But I dislike something which has the appearance of pride, of overvaluing yourselves and undervaluing others; particularly the preachers, thinking not only that they are blind, and that they are not sent of God, but even that they are dead, dead to God, and walking in the way to hell; that "they are going one way," you another; that "they have no life in" them! Your speaking of yourselves as though you were the only men who knew and taught the gospel; and as if not only all the clergy but all the Methodists be-sides, were in utter darkness.

I dislike something that has the appearance of enthusiasm: overvaluing feelings and inward impressions; mistaking the mere work of imagination for the voice of the Spirit; expecting the end without the means, and undervaluing reason, knowledge, and wisdom, in general.

I dislike something that has the appearance of antinomianism: not magnifying the law and making it honourable; not enough valuing tenderness of conscience, and exact watchfulness in order thereto; using faith rather as contradistinguished from holiness than as productive of it.

But what I most of all dislike is your littleness of love to your brethren, to your own society: your want of union of heart with them, and 'bowels of mercies' toward them; your want of meek-ness, gentleness, long-suffering, your "impatience of contradic-tion;" your counting every man your enemy that reproves or ad-monishes you in love; your bigotry and narrowness of spirit, lov-ing in a manner only those that love you; your censoriousness, proneness to think hardly of all who do not exactly agree with you: in one word, your divisive spirit. Indeed I do not believe that any of you either design or desire a separation. But you do not enough fear, abhor, and detest it, shuddering at the very thought. And all the preceding tempers tend to it, and gradually prepare you for it. Observe, I tell you before! God grant you may imme-diately and affectionately take the warning!

(3). As to your outward behaviour, I like the general tenor of your life, devoted to God, and spent in doing good.

But I dislike your slighting any, the very least rules of the bands or society; and your doing anything that tends to hinder others from exactly observing them. Therefore

I dislike your appointing such meetings as hinder others from attending either the public preaching or their class or band; or any other meeting which the rules of the society or their office re-quires them to attend.

I dislike your spending so much time in several meetings, as many that attend can ill spare from their other duties of their calling, unless they omit either the preaching, or their class or band. This naturally tends to dissolve our society, by cutting the sinews of it.

As to your more public meetings, I like the praying fervently and largely for all the blessings of God. And I know much good has been done hereby, and hope much more will be done.

But I dislike several things therein: (i) the singing or speaking or praying of several at once; (ii) the praying to the Son of God only, or more than to the Father; (iii) the using improper expressions in prayer: sometimes too bold, if not irreverent, sometimes too pompous and magnificent, extolling yourselves rather than God, and telling him what you are, not what you want; (iv) using poor, flat, bald hymns; (v) the never kneeling at prayer; (vi) your using postures or gestures highly indecent; (vii) your screaming, even so as to make the words unintelligible; (viii) your affirming people will be justified or sanctified just now; (ix) the affirming they are, when they are not; (x) the bidding them say, I believe; (xi) the bitterly condemning any that oppose, calling them wolves, etc., and pronouncing them hypocrites or not justified.

Read this calmly and impartially before the Lord in prayer. So shall the evil cease and the good remain. And you will then be more than ever united to,

Your affectionate brother

On Sin in Believers
1763

This is an important sermon in the Wesley corpus. The perfection revival and ensuing schism led some to deny the reality of sin in those who believe in Christ. This was rank antinomianism. Wesley here presents his most thorough argument that sin does remain in believers until they are perfected in love. Even then involuntary transgressions continue until this mortal body is laid aside. This sermon introduces into Wesley's theology the three-fold definition of sin as guilt, power and being. The reader should pay careful attention how Wesley defines and nuances his doctrine of sin in this homily. Source: Works J 5:144-156.

> If any man be in Christ, he is a new creature.
>
> 2 Corinthians 5:17

I. 1. Is there then sin in him that is in Christ? Does sin remain in one that believes in him? Is there any sin in them that are born of God, or are they wholly delivered from it? Let no one imagine this to be a question of mere curiosity; or that it is of little importance whether it be determined one way or the other. Rather it is a point of the utmost moment to every serious Christian; the resolving of which very nearly concerns both his present and eternal happiness.

2. And yet I do not know that ever it was controverted in the primitive Church. Indeed there was no room for disputing concerning it, as all Christians were agreed. And so far as I have ever observed, the whole body of ancient Christians, who have left us anything in writing, declare with one voice, that even believers in Christ, till they are "strong in the Lord and in the power of his might," have need to "wrestle with flesh and blood," with an evil nature, as well as "with principalities and powers."

3. And herein our own Church (as indeed in most points) exactly copies after the primitive; declaring in her Ninth Article, "Origi-

nal sin is the corruption of the nature of every man, whereby man is in his own nature inclined to evil, so that the flesh lusteth contrary to the Spirit. And this infection of nature doth remain, yea, in them that are regenerated; whereby the lust of the flesh, called in Greek phronema sarkos, is not subject to the law of God. And although there is no condemnation for them that believe, yet this lust hath of itself the nature of sin."

4. The same testimony is given by all other Churches; not only by the Greek and Romish Church, but by every Reformed Church in Europe, of whatever denomination. Indeed some of these seem to carry the thing too far; so describing the corruption of heart in a believer, as scarce to allow that he has dominion over it, but rather is in bondage thereto; and, by this means, they leave hardly any distinction between a believer and an unbeliever.

5. To avoid this extreme, many well-meaning men, particularly those under the direction of the late Count Zinzendorf, ran into another; affirming, that "all true believers are not only saved from the dominion of sin, but from the being of inward as well as outward sin, so that it no longer remains in them:" And from them, about twenty years ago, many of our countrymen imbibed the same opinion, that even the corruption of nature is no more, in those who believe in Christ.

6. It is true that, when the Germans were pressed upon this head, they soon allowed, (many of them at least,) that "sin did still remain in the flesh, but not in the heart of a believer;" and, after a time, when the absurdity of this was shown, they fairly gave up the point; allowing that sin did still remain, though not reign, in him that is born of God.

7. But the English, who had received it from them, (some directly, some at second or third hand,) were not so easily prevailed upon to part with a favourite opinion: And even when the gener-

ality of them were convinced it was utterly indefensible, a few could not be persuaded to give it up, but maintain it to this day.

II. 1. For the sake of these who really fear God, and desire to know "the truth as it is in Jesus," it may not be amiss to consider the point with calmness and impartiality. In doing this, I use indifferently the words, regenerate, justified, or believers; since, though they have not precisely the same meaning, (the First implying an inward, actual change, the Second a relative one, and the Third the means whereby both the one and the other are wrought,) yet they come to one and the same thing; as every one that believes, is both justified and born of God.

2. By sin, I here understand inward sin; any sinful temper, passion, or affection; such as pride, self-will, love of the world, in any kind or degree; such as lust, anger, peevishness; any disposition contrary to the mind which was in Christ.

3. The question is not concerning outward sin; whether a child of God commit sin or no. We all agree and earnestly maintain, "He that committeth sin is of the devil." We agree, "Whosoever is born of God doth not commit sin." Neither do we now inquire whether inward sin will always remain in the children of God; whether sin will continue in the soul as long as it continues in the body: Nor yet do we inquire whether a justified person may relapse either into inward or outward sin; but simply this, Is a justified or regenerate man freed from all sin as soon as he is justified? Is there then no sin in his heart?—nor ever after, unless he fall from grace?

4. We allow that the state of a justified person is inexpressibly great and glorious. He is born again, "not of blood, nor of the flesh, nor of the will of man, but of God." He is a child of God, a member of Christ, an heir of the kingdom of heaven. "The peace of God, which passeth all understanding, keepeth his heart and mind in Christ Jesus." His very body is a "temple of the Holy

Ghost," and an "habitation of God through the Spirit." He is "created anew in Christ Jesus:" He is washed, he is sanctified. His heart is purified by faith; he is cleansed "from the corruption that is in the world;" "the love of God is shed abroad in his heart by the Holy Ghost which is given unto him." And so long as he "walketh in love," (which he may always do,) he worships God in spirit and in truth. He keepeth the commandments of God, and doeth those things that are pleasing in his sight; so exercising himself as to "have a conscience void of offence, toward God and toward men:" And he has power both over outward and inward sin, even from the moment he is justified.

III. 1. "But was he not then freed from all sin, so that there is no sin in his heart?" I cannot say this; I cannot believe it; because St. Paul says the contrary. He is speaking to believers, and describing the state of believers in general, when he says, "The flesh lusteth against the Spirit, and the Spirit against the flesh: These are contrary the one to the other." (Gal 5:17) Nothing can be more express. The Apostle here directly affirms that the flesh, evil nature, opposes the Spirit, even in believers; that even in the regenerate there are two principles, "contrary the one to the other."

2. Again: When he writes to the believers at Corinth, to those who were sanctified in Christ Jesus, (1 Cor 1:2) he says, "I, brethren, could not speak unto you, as unto spiritual, but as unto carnal, as unto babes in Christ. Ye are yet carnal: For whereas there is among you envying and strife, are ye not carnal?" (3:1-3.) Now here the Apostle speaks unto those who were unquestionably believers, whom, in the same breath, he styles his brethren in Christ, as being still, in a measure, carnal. He affirms, there was envying, (an evil temper,) occasioning strife among them, and yet does not give the least intimation that they had lost their faith. Nay, he manifestly declares they had not; for then they would not have been babes in Christ. And (what is most remarkable of all) he speaks of being carnal, and babes in Christ, as one and the

same thing; plainly showing that every believer is (in a degree) carnal, while he is only a babe in Christ.

3. Indeed this grand point, that there are two contrary principles in believers, nature and grace, the flesh and the Spirit, runs through all the Epistles of St. Paul, yea, through all the Holy Scriptures; almost all the directions and exhortations therein are founded on this supposition; pointing at wrong tempers or practices in those who are, notwithstanding, acknowledged by the inspired writers to be believers. And they are continually exhorted to fight with and conquer these, by the power of the faith which was in them.

4. And who can doubt, but there was faith in the angel of the church of Ephesus, when our Lord said to
him, "I know thy works, and thy labour, and thy patience: Thou hast patience, and for my name's sake hast laboured, and hast not fainted?" (Rev 2:2, 3, 4.) But was there, meantime, no sin in his heart? Yea, or Christ would not have added, "Nevertheless, I have somewhat against thee, because thou hast left thy first love." This was real sin which God saw in his heart; of which, accordingly, he is exhorted to repent: And yet we have no authority to say, that even then he had no faith.

5. Nay, the angel of the church at Pergamos, also, is exhorted to repent, which implies sin, though our Lord expressly says, "Thou hast not denied my faith." (vv 13,16.) And to the angel of the church in Sardis, he says, "Strengthen the things which remain, that are ready to die." The good which remained was ready to die; but was not actually dead. (3:2) So there was still a spark of faith even in him; which he is accordingly commanded to hold fast (v 3).

6. Once more: When the Apostle exhorts believers to "cleanse themselves from all filthiness of flesh and spirit," (2 Cor 7:1) he

plainly teaches, that those believers were not yet cleansed there-from.

Will you answer, "He that abstains from all appearance of evil, does ipso facto cleanse himself from all filthiness?" Not in anywise. For instance: A man reviles me: I feel resentment, which is filthiness of spirit; yet I say not a word. Here I "abstain from all appearance of evil;" but this does not cleanse me from that filthiness of spirit, as I experience to my sorrow.

7. And as this position, "There is no sin in a believer, no carnal mind, no bent to backsliding," is thus contrary to the word of God, so it is to the experience of his children. These continually feel an heart bent to backsliding; a natural tendency to evil; a proneness to depart from God, and cleave to the things of earth. They are daily sensible of sin remaining in their heart, pride, self-will, unbelief; and of sin cleaving to all they speak and do, even their best actions and holiest duties. Yet at the same time they "know that they are of God;" they cannot doubt of it for a moment. They feel his Spirit clearly "witnessing with their spirit, that they are the children of God." They "rejoice in God through Christ Jesus, by whom they have now received the atonement." So that they are equally assured, that sin is in them, and that "Christ is in them the hope of glory."

8. "But can Christ be in the same heart where sin is?" Undoubtedly he can; otherwise it never could be saved therefrom. Where the sickness is, there is the Physician:

> *Carrying on his work within,*
> *Striving till he cast out sin.*

Christ indeed cannot reign, where sin reigns; neither will he dwell where any sin is allowed. But he is and dwells in the heart of every believer, who is fighting against all sin; although it be not yet purified, according to the purification of the sanctuary.

9. It has been observed before, that the opposite doctrine, that there is no sin in believers, is quite new in the church of Christ; that it was never heard of for seventeen hundred years; never till it was discovered by Count Zinzendorf. I do not remember to have seen the least intimation of it, either in any ancient or modern writer; unless perhaps in some of the wild, ranting Antinomians. And these likewise say and unsay, acknowledging there is sin in their flesh, although no sin in their heart. But whatever doctrine is new must be wrong; for the old religion is the only true one; and no doctrine can be right, unless it is the very same "which was from the beginning."

10. One argument more against this new, unscriptural doctrine may be drawn from the dreadful consequences of it. One says, "I felt anger to-day." Must I reply, "Then you have no faith?" Another says, "I know what you advise is good, but my will is quite averse to it." Must I tell him, "Then you are an unbeliever, under the wrath and the curse of God?" What will be the natural consequence of this? Why, if he believe what I say, his soul will not only be grieved and wounded, but perhaps utterly destroyed; inasmuch as he will "cast away" that "confidence which hath great recompence of reward:" And having cast away his shield, how shall he "quench the fiery darts of the wicked one?" How shall he overcome the world?—seeing "this is the victory that overcometh the world, even our faith." He stands disarmed in the midst of his enemies, open to all their assaults. What wonder, then, if he be utterly overthrown; if they take him captive at their will; yea, if he fall from one wickedness to another, and never see good any more? I cannot, therefore, by any means receive this assertion, that there is no sin in a believer from the moment he is justified; First, because it is contrary to the whole tenor of Scripture;—Secondly, because it is contrary to the experience of the children of God;—Thirdly, because it is absolutely new, never heard of in the world till yesterday;—and, Lastly, because it is naturally attended with the most fatal consequences; not only grieving those

whom God hath not grieved, but perhaps dragging them into everlasting perdition.

IV. 1. However, let us give a fair hearing to the chief arguments of those who endeavour to support it. And it is, First, from Scripture they attempt to prove that there is no sin in a believer. They argue thus: "The Scripture says, Every believer is born of God, is clean, is holy, is sanctified, is pure in heart, has a new heart, is a temple of the Holy Ghost. Now, as 'that which is born of the flesh is flesh,' is altogether evil, so 'that which is born of the Spirit is spirit,' is altogether good. Again: A man cannot be clean, sanctified, holy, and at the same time unclean, unsanctified, unholy. He cannot be pure and impure, or have a new and an old heart together. Neither can his soul be unholy, while it is a temple of the Holy Ghost."

I have put this objection as strong as possible, that its full weight may appear. Let us now examine it, part by part. And, 1. "That which is born of the Spirit is spirit, is altogether good." I allow the text, but not the comment. For the text affirms this, and no more, that every man who is "born of the Spirit," is a spiritual man. He is so: But so he may be, and yet not be altogether spiritual. The Christians at Corinth were spiritual men; else they had been no Christians at all; and yet they were not altogether spiritual: They were still, in part, carnal.—"But they were fallen from grace." St. Paul says, No. They were even then babes in Christ. 2. "But a man cannot be clean, sanctified, holy, and at the same time unclean, unsanctified, unholy." Indeed he may. So the Corinthians were. "Ye are washed," says the Apostle, "ye are sanctified;" namely, cleansed from "fornication, idolatry, drunkenness," and all other outward sin; (1 Cor 6:9, 10, 11) and yet at the same time, in another sense of the word, they were unsanctified; they were not washed, not inwardly cleansed from envy, evil surmising, partiality.—"But sure, they had not a new heart and an old heart together." It is most sure they had; for, at that very time, their hearts were truly, yet not entirely, renewed. Their carnal mind was nailed to the cross; yet it was not wholly destroyed.—

"But could they be unholy while they were 'temples of the Holy Ghost?'" Yes; that they were temples of the Holy Ghost, is certain; (1 Cor 6:19) and it is equally certain, they were, in some degree, carnal, that is, unholy.

2. "However, there is one scripture more which will put the matter out of question: "If any man be" a believer "in Christ, he is a new creature. Old things are passed away; behold, all things are become new" (2 Cor 5:17). Now certainly a man cannot be a new creature and an old creature at once." Yes, he may: He may be partly renewed, which was the very case with those at Corinth. They were doubtless "renewed in the spirit of their mind," or they could not have been so much as "babes in Christ;" yet they had not the whole mind which was in Christ, for they envied one another. "But it is said expressly, 'Old things are passed away: All things are become new.'" But we must not so interpret the Apostle's words, as to make him contradict himself. And if we will make him consistent with himself, the plain meaning of the words is this: His old judgment concerning justification, holiness, happiness, indeed concerning the things of God in general, is now passed away; so are his old desires, designs, affections, tempers, and conversation. All these are undeniably become new, greatly changed from what they were; and yet, though they are new, they are not wholly new. Still he feels, to his sorrow and shame, remains of the old man, too manifest taints of his former tempers and affections, though they cannot gain any advantage over him, as long as he watches unto prayer.

3. This whole argument, "If he is clean, he is clean;" "If he is holy, he is holy;" (and twenty more expressions of the same kind may easily be heaped together) is really no better than playing upon words: It is the fallacy of arguing from a particular to a general; of inferring a general conclusion from particular premises. Propose the sentence entire, and it runs thus: "If he is holy at all, he is holy altogether." That does not follow: Every babe in Christ is holy, and yet not altogether so. He is saved from sin; yet

not entirely: It remains, though it does not reign. If you think it does not remain, (in babes at least, whatever be the case with young men or fathers,) you certainly have not considered the height, and depth, and length, and breadth of the law of God; (even the law of love, laid down by St. Paul in the thirteenth of Corinthians;) and that every anomia, disconformity to, or deviation from, this law is sin. Now, is there no disconformity to this in the heart or life of a believer? What may be in an adult Christian, is another question; but what a stranger must he be to human nature, who can possibly imagine, that this is the case with every babe in Christ!

4. "But believers walk after the Spirit, (Rom 8:1) and the Spirit of God dwells in them; consequently, they are delivered from the *guilt*, the *power*, or, in one word, the *being* of sin."

These are coupled together, as if they were the same thing. But they are not the same thing. The *guilt* is one thing, the *power* another, and the *being* yet another. That believers are delivered from the *guilt* and *power* of sin we allow; that they are delivered from the *being* of it we deny. Nor does it in any wise follow from these texts. A man may have the Spirit of God dwelling in him, and may "walk after the Spirit," though he still feels "the flesh lusting against the Spirit."

5. "But 'the church is the body of Christ;' (Col 1:24) this implies, that its members are washed from all filthiness; otherwise it will follow, that Christ and Belial are incorporated with each other."

Nay, it will not follow from hence, "Those who are the mystical body of Christ, still feel the flesh lusting against the Spirit," that Christ has any fellowship with the devil; or with that sin which he enables them to resist and overcome.

6. "But are not Christians 'come to the heavenly Jerusalem,' where 'nothing defiled can enter?'" (Heb 12:22) Yes; "and to an innumerable company of angels, and to the spirits of just men made perfect:" That is,

On Sin in Believers

Earth and heaven all agree;
All is one great family.

And they are likewise holy and undefiled, while they "walk after the Spirit;" although sensible there is another principle in them, and that "these are contrary to each other."

7. "But Christians are reconciled to God. Now this could not be, if any of the carnal mind remained; for this is enmity against God: Consequently, no reconciliation can be effected, but by its total destruction."

We are "reconciled to God through the blood of the cross:" And in that moment the phronema sarkos, the corruption of nature, which is enmity with God, is put under our feet; the flesh has no more dominion over us. But it still exists; and it is still in its nature enmity with God, lusting against his Spirit.

8. "But 'they that are Christ's have crucified the flesh, with its affections and lusts.'" (Gal 5:24) They have so; yet it remains in them still, and often struggles to break from the cross. "Nay, but they have 'put off the old man with his deeds.'" (Col 3:9) They have; and, in the sense above described, "old things are passed away; all things are become new." A hundred texts may be cited to the same effect; and they will all admit of the same answer.— "But, to say all in one word, 'Christ gave himself for the Church, that it might be holy, and without blemish.'" (Eph 5:25, 27) And so it will be in the end: But it never was yet, from the beginning to this day.

9. "But let experience speak: All who are justified do at that time find an absolute freedom from all sin." That I doubt: But, if they do, do they find it ever after? Else you gain nothing.—"If they do not, it is their own fault." That remains to be proved.

10. "But in the very nature of things, can a man have pride in him; and not be proud; anger, and yet not be angry?"

223

A man may have pride in him, may think of himself in some particulars above what he ought to think, (and so be proud in that particular,) and yet not be a proud man in his general character. He may have anger in him, yea, and a strong propensity to furious anger, without giving way to it.—"But can anger and pride be in that heart, where only meekness and humility are felt?" No: But some pride and anger may be in that heart, where there is much humility and meekness.

"It avails not to say, These tempers are there, but they do not reign: For sin cannot, in any kind or degree, exist where it does not reign; for guilt and power are essential properties of sin. Therefore, where one of them is, all must be."

Strange indeed! "Sin cannot, in any kind or degree, exist where it does not reign?" Absolutely contrary this to all experience, all Scripture, all common sense. Resentment of an affront is sin; it is anomia, disconformity to the law of love. This has existed in me a thousand times. Yet it did not, and does not reign.— "But guilt and power are essential properties of sin; therefore, where one is, all must be." No: In the instance before us, if the resentment I feel is not yielded to, even for a moment, there is no guilt at all, no condemnation from God upon that account. And in this case, it has no power: Though it "lusteth against the Spirit," it cannot prevail. Here, therefore, as in ten thousand instances, there is sin without either guilt or power.

11. "But the supposing sin in a believer is pregnant with every thing frightful and discouraging. It implies the contending with a power that has the possession of our strength; maintains his usurpation of our hearts; and there prosecutes the war in defiance of our Redeemer." Not so: The supposing sin is in us, does not imply that it has the possession of our strength; no more than a man crucified has the possession of those that crucify him. As little does it imply, that "sin maintains its usurpation of our hearts." The usurper is dethroned. He remains indeed where he once reigned; but remains in chains. So that he does, in some sense, "prosecute the war," yet he grows weaker and weaker; while the

believer goes on from strength to strength, conquering and to conquer.

12. "I am not satisfied yet: He that has sin in him, is a slave to sin. Therefore, you suppose a man to be justified, while he is a slave to sin. Now, if you allow men may be justified while they have pride, anger, or unbelief in them; nay, if you aver, these are (at least for a time) in all that are justified; what wonder that we have so many proud, angry, unbelieving believers?"
I do not suppose any man who is justified is a slave to sin. Yet I do suppose sin remains (at least for a time) in all that are justified.

But, "if sin remains in a believer, he is a sinful man: If pride, for instance, then he is proud; if self-will, then he is self-willed; if unbelief, then he is an unbeliever; consequently, no believer at all. How then does he differ from unbelievers, from unregenerate men?" This is still mere playing upon words. It means no more than, if there is sin, pride, self-will in him, then—there is sin, pride, self-will. And this nobody can deny. In that sense then he is proud, or self-willed. But he is not proud or self-willed in the same sense that unbelievers are; that is, governed by pride or self-will. Herein he differs from unregenerate men. They obey sin; he does not. Flesh is in them both: But they "walk after the flesh;" he "walks after the Spirit."

"But how can unbelief be in a believer?" That word has two meanings. It means either no faith, or little faith; either the absence of faith or the weakness of it. In the former sense, unbelief is not in a believer; in the latter, it is in all babes. Their faith is commonly mixed with doubt or fear; that is, in the latter sense, with unbelief. "Why are ye fearful," says our Lord, "O ye of little faith?" Again: "O thou of little faith, wherefore didst thou doubt?" You see here was unbelief in believers; little faith and much unbelief.

13. "But this doctrine, that sin remains in a believer; that a man may be in the favour of God, while he has sin in his heart; cer-

tainly tends to encourage men in sin." Understand the proposition right, and no such consequence follows. A man may be in God's favour though he feel sin; but not if he yields to it. Having sin does not forfeit the favour of God; giving way to sin does. Though the flesh in you "lust against the Spirit," you may still be a child of God; but if you "walk after the flesh," you are a child of the devil. Now this doctrine does not encourage to obey sin, but to resist it with all our might.

V. 1. The sum of all is this: There are in every person, even after he is justified, two contrary principles, nature and grace, termed by St. Paul, the flesh and the Spirit. Hence, although even babes in Christ are sanctified, yet it is only in part. In a degree, according to the measure of their faith, they are spiritual; yet, in a degree they are carnal. Accordingly, believers are continually exhorted to watch against the flesh, as well as the world and the devil. And to this agrees the constant experience of the children of God. While they feel this witness in themselves, they feel a will not wholly resigned to the will of God. They know they are in him; and yet find an heart ready to depart from him, a proneness to evil in many instances, and a backwardness to that which is good. The contrary doctrine is wholly new; never heard of in the church of Christ, from the time of his coming into the world, till the time of Count Zinzendorf; and it is attended with the most fatal consequences. It cuts off all watching against our evil nature, against the Delilah which we are told is gone, though she is still lying in our bosom. It tears away the shield of weak believers, deprives them of their faith, and so leaves them exposed to all the assaults of the world, the flesh, and the devil.

2. Let us, therefore, hold fast the sound doctrine "once delivered to the saints," and delivered down by them, with the written word, to all succeeding generations: That, although we are renewed, cleansed, purified, sanctified, the moment we truly believe in Christ, yet we are not then renewed, cleansed, purified altogether; but the flesh, the evil nature, still remains, (though

subdued,) and wars against the Spirit. So much the more let us use all diligence in "fighting the good fight of faith." So much the more earnestly let us "watch and pray" against the enemy within. The more carefully let us take to ourselves, and "put on, the whole armour of God;" that, although "we wrestle" both "with flesh and blood, and with principalities, and powers, and wicked spirits in high places," we "may be able to withstand in the evil day, and having done all, to stand."

The Scripture Way of Salvation
1765

This is the landmark sermon of Wesley's later middle period. It is often regarded as his best explication of perfection as a second work of grace. Using the same text as in Salvation By Faith, *and following the same general outline, Wesley here diverges from that sermon in several ways. Thus, this homily reflects development in his holiness views. One of the constants is Wesley's emphasis on present salvation. But carefully note the distinctions made between* Christ for us *and* Christ in us. *Weigh thoughtfully the relationship between repentance, good works, and faith in attaining perfect love. Finally, reflect on what has changed (if any) from his views expressed twenty-four years earlier in his last landmark sermon on holiness,* Christian Perfection. *Source: Works J 6:43-54.*

Ye are saved through faith.

Ephesians 2:8

1. Nothing can be more intricate, complex, and hard to be understood than religion, as it has been often described. And this is not only true concerning the religion of the Heathens, even many of the wisest of them, but concerning the religion of those also who were, in some sense, Christians; yea, and men of great name in the Christian world; men who seemed to be pillars thereof. Yet how easy to be understood, how plain and simple a thing is the genuine religion of Jesus Christ; provided only that we take it in its native form, just as it is described in the oracles of God! It is exactly suited, by the wise Creator and Governor of the world, to the weak understanding and narrow capacity of man in his present state. How observable is this, both with regard to the end it proposes, and the means to attain that end! The end is, in one word, salvation; the means to attain it, faith.

2. It is easily discerned, that these two little words, I mean faith and salvation, include the substance of all the Bible, the marrow, as it were, of the whole Scripture. So much the more should we

take all possible care to avoid all mistake concerning them, and to form a true and accurate judgment concerning both the one and the other.

3. Let us then seriously inquire,

I. What is salvation?
II. What is that faith whereby we are saved? And,
III. How we are saved by it?

I. 1. And, First, let us inquire, What is salvation? The salvation which is here spoken of is not what is frequently understood by that word, the going to heaven, eternal happiness. It is not the soul's going to paradise, termed by our Lord, "Abraham's bosom." It is not a blessing which lies on the other side death; or, as we usually speak, in the oilier world. The very words of the text itself put this beyond all question: "Ye are saved." It is not something at a distance: It is a present thing; a blessing which, through the free mercy of God, ye are now in possession of. Nay, the words may be rendered, and that with equal propriety, "Ye have been saved:" So that the salvation which is here spoken of might be extended to the entire work of God, from the first dawning of grace in the soul, till it is consummated in glory.

2. If we take this in its utmost extent, it will include all that is wrought in the soul by what is frequently termed natural conscience, but more properly, preventing grace;—all the drawings of the Father; the desires after God, which, if we yield to them, increase more and more;—all that light wherewith the Son of God "enlighteneth every one that cometh into the world;" showing every man "to do justly, to love mercy, and to walk humbly with his God;"—all the convictions which his Spirit, from time to time, works in every child of man; although, it is true, the generality of men stifle them as soon as possible, and after a while forget, or at least deny, that they ever had them at all.

3. But we are at present concerned only with that salvation which the Apostle is directly speaking of. And this consists of two general parts, justification and sanctification.

Justification is another word for pardon. It is the forgiveness of all our sins; and, what is necessarily implied therein, our acceptance with God. The price whereby this hath been procured for us, (commonly termed the meritorious cause of our justification,) is the blood and righteousness of Christ; or, to express it a little more clearly, all that Christ hath done and suffered for us, till he "poured out his soul for the transgressors."

The immediate effects of justification are, the peace of God, a "peace that passeth all understanding," and a "rejoicing in hope of the glory of God" "with joy unspeakable and full of glory."

4. And at the same time that we are justified, yea, in that very moment, sanctification begins. In that instant we are born again, born from above, born of the Spirit: There is a real as well as a relative change. We are inwardly renewed by the power of God. We feel "the love of God shed abroad in our heart by the Holy Ghost which is given unto us;" producing love to all mankind, and more especially to the children of God; expelling the love of the world, the love of pleasure, of ease, of honour, of money, together with pride, anger, self-will, and every other evil temper; in a word, changing the earthly,

5. How naturally do those who experience such a change imagine that all sin is gone; that it is utterly rooted out of their heart, and has no more any place therein! How easily do they draw that inference, "I feel no sin; therefore, I have none: It does not stir; therefore, it does not exist: It has no motion; therefore, it has no being!"

6. But it is seldom long before they are undeceived, finding sin was only suspended, not destroyed. Temptations return, and sin revives; showing it was but stunned before, not dead. They now feel two principles in themselves, plainly contrary to each other;

"the flesh lusting against the Spirit;" nature opposing the grace of God. They cannot deny, that, although they still feel power to believe in Christ, and to love God; and although his "Spirit" still "witnesses with their spirits, that they are children of God;" yet they feel in themselves sometimes pride or self-will, sometimes anger or unbelief. They find one or more of these frequently stirring in their heart, though not conquering; yea, perhaps, "thrusting sore at them that they may fall;" but the Lord is their help.

7. How exactly did Macarius, fourteen hundred years ago, describe the present experience of the children of God! "The unskilful," or unexperienced, "when grace operates, presently imagine they have no more sin. Whereas they that have discretion cannot deny, that even we who have the grace of God may be molested again.—For we have often had instances of some among the brethren, who have experienced such grace as to affirm that they had no sin in them; and yet, after all, when they thought themselves entirely freed from it, the corruption that lurked within was stirred up anew, and they were well nigh burned up."

8. From the time of our being born again, the gradual work of sanctification takes place. We are enabled "by the Spirit" to "mortify the deeds of the body," of our evil nature; and as we are more and more dead to sin, we are more and more alive to God. We go on from grace to grace, while we are careful to "abstain from all appearance of evil," and are "zealous of good works," as we have opportunity, doing good to all men; while we walk in all His ordinances blameless, therein worshiping Him in spirit and in truth; while we take up our cross, and deny ourselves every pleasure that does not lead us to God.

9. It is thus that we wait for entire sanctification; for a full salvation from all our sins, from pride, self-will, anger, unbelief; or, as the Apostle expresses it, "go on unto perfection." But what is perfection? The word has various senses: Here it means perfect love. It is love excluding sin; love filling the heart, taking up the whole

231

capacity of the soul. It is love "rejoicing evermore, praying without ceasing, in every thing giving thanks."

II. But what is that faith through which we are saved? This is the Second point to be considered.

1. Faith, in general, is defined by the Apostle, pragmaton elegchos ou blepomenon--An evidence, A divine evidence and conviction (the word means both) of things not seen; not visible, not perceivable either by sight, or by any other of the external senses. It implies both a supernatural evidence of God, and of the things of God; a kind of spiritual light exhibited to the soul, and a supernatural sight or perception thereof. Accordingly, the Scripture speaks of God's giving sometimes light, sometimes a power of discerning it. So St. Paul: "God, who commanded light to shine out of darkness, hath shined in our hearts, to give us the light of the knowledge of the glory of God in the face of Jesus Christ." And else where the same Apostle speaks of "the eyes of" our "understanding being opened." By this two-fold operation of the Holy Spirit, having the eyes of our soul both opened and enlightened we see the things which the natural "eye hath not seen, neither the ear heard." We have a prospect of the invisible things of God; we see the spiritual world, which is all round about us, and yet no more discerned by our natural faculties than if it had no being: And we see the eternal world; piercing through the veil which hangs between time and eternity. Clouds and darkness then rest upon it no more, but we already see the glory which shall be revealed.

2. Taking the word in a more particular sense, faith is a divine evidence and conviction, not only that "God was in Christ, reconciling the world unto himself," but also that Christ loved me, and gave himself for me. It is by this faith (whether we term it the essence, or rather a property thereof) that we receive Christ; that we receive him in all his offices, as our Prophet, Priest, and King.

It is by this that he is "made of God unto us wisdom, and righteousness, and sanctification, and redemption."

3. "But is this the faith of assurance, or faith of adherence?" The Scripture mentions no such distinction. The Apostle says, "There is one faith, and one hope of our calling;" one Christian, saving faith; "as there is one Lord," in whom we believe, and "one God and Father of us all." And it is certain, this faith necessarily implies an assurance (which is here only another word for evidence, it being hard to tell the difference between them) that Christ loved me, and gave himself for me. For "he that believeth" with the true living faith, "hath the witness in himself:" "The Spirit witnesseth with his spirit, that he is a child of God." "Because he is a son, God hath sent forth the Spirit of his Son into his heart, crying, Abba, Father;" giving him an assurance that he is so, and a childlike confidence in him. But let it be observed, that, in the very nature of the thing, the assurance goes before the confidence. For a man cannot have a childlike confidence in God till he knows he is a child of God. Therefore confidence, trust, reliance, adherence, or whatever else it be called, is not the first, as some have supposed, but the second branch or act of faith.

4. It is by this faith we are saved, justified and sanctified; taking that word in its highest sense. But how are we justified and sanctified by faith? This is our Third head of inquiry. And this being the main point in question, and a point of no ordinary importance, it will not be improper to give it a more distinct and particular consideration.

III. 1. And, First, how are we justified by faith? In what sense is this to be understood? I answer, Faith is the condition, and the only condition, of justification. It is the condition: None is justified but he that believes: Without faith no man is justified. And it is the only condition: This alone is sufficient for justification. Every one that believes is justified, whatever else he has or has not. In other words: No man is justified till he believes; every man, when he believes, is justified.

2. "But does not God command us to repent also? Yea, and to 'bring forth fruits meet for repentance?'—to cease, for instance, from doing evil; and learn to do well? And is not both the one and the other of the utmost necessity, insomuch that if we willingly neglect either, we cannot reasonably expect to be justified at all? But if this be so, how can it be said that faith is the only condition of justification?"

God does undoubtedly command us both to repent, and to bring forth fruits meet for repentance; which if we willingly neglect, we cannot reasonably expect to be justified at all: Therefore both repentance, and fruits meet for repentance, are, in some sense, necessary to justification. But they are not necessary in the same sense with faith, nor in the same degree. Not in the same degree; for those fruits are only necessary conditionally; if there be time and opportunity for them. Otherwise a man may be justified without them, as was the thief upon the cross; (if we may call him so; for a late writer has discovered that he was no thief, but a very honest and respectable person!) but he cannot be justified without faith; this is impossible. Likewise, let a man have ever so much repentance, or ever so many of the fruits meet for repentance, yet all this does not at all avail; he is not justified till he believes. But the moment he believes, with or without those fruits, yea, with more or less repentance, he is justified.—Not in the same sense; for repentance and its fruits are only remotely necessary; necessary in order to faith; whereas faith is immediately and directly necessary to justification. It remains, that faith is the only condition, which is immediately and proximately necessary to justification.

3. "But do you believe we are sanctified by faith? We know you believe that we are justified by faith; but do not you believe, and accordingly teach, that we are sanctified by our works?" So it has been roundly and vehemently affirmed for these five-and-twenty

years: But I have constantly declared just the contrary; and that in all manner of ways. I have continually testified in private and in public, that we are sanctified as well as justified by faith. And indeed the one of those great truths does exceedingly illustrate the other. Exactly as we are justified by faith, so are we sanctified by faith. Faith is the condition, and the only condition, of sancti-fication, exactly as it is of justification. It is the condition: None is sanctified but he that believes; without faith no man is sancti-fied. And it is the only condition: This alone is sufficient for sanctification. Every one that believes is sanctified, whatever else he has or has not. In other words, no man is sanctified till he be-lieves: Every man when he believes is sanctified.

4. "But is there not a repentance consequent upon, as well as a repentance previous to, justification? And is it not incumbent on all that are justified to be 'zealous of good works?' Yea, are not these so necessary, that if a man willingly neglect them he cannot reasonably expect that he shall ever be sanctified in the full sense; that is, perfected in love? Nay, can he grow at all in grace, in the loving knowledge of our Lord Jesus Christ? Yea, can he retain the grace which God has already given him? Can he con-tinue in the faith which he has received, or in the favour of God? Do not you yourself allow all this, and continually assert it? But, if this be so, how can it be said that faith is the only condition of sanctification?"

5. I do allow all this, and continually maintain it as the truth of God. I allow there is a repentance consequent upon, as well as a repentance previous to, justification. It is incumbent on all that are justified to be zealous of good works. And these are so neces-sary, that if a man willingly neglect them, he cannot reasonably expect that he shall ever be sanctified; he cannot grow in grace, in the image of God, the mind which was in Christ Jesus; nay, he cannot retain the grace he has received; he cannot continue in faith, or in the favour of God.

What is the inference we must draw herefrom? Why, that both repentance, rightly understood, and the practice of all good works, works of piety, as well as works of mercy, (now properly so called, since they spring from faith,) are, in some sense, necessary to sanctification.

6. I say, repentance rightly understood; for this must not be confounded with the former repentance. The repentance consequent upon justification is widely different from that which is antecedent to it. This implies no guilt, no sense of condemnation, no consciousness of the wrath of God. It does not suppose any doubt of the favour of God, or any "fear that hath torment." It is properly a conviction, wrought by the Holy Ghost, of the sin which still remains in our heart; of the phronema sarkos, the carnal mind, which "does still remain," (as our Church speaks,) "even in them that are regenerate;" although it does no longer reign; it has not now dominion over them. It is a conviction of our proneness to evil, of an heart bent to backsliding, of the still continuing tendency of the flesh to lust against the spirit. Sometimes, unless we continually watch and pray, it lusteth to pride, sometimes to anger, sometimes to love of the world, love of ease, love of honour, or love of pleasure more than of God. It is a conviction of the tendency of our heart to self-will, to Atheism, or idolatry; and, above all, to unbelief, whereby, in a thousand ways, and under a thousand pretences, we are ever departing, more or less, from the living God.

7. With this conviction of the sin remaining in our hearts, there is joined a clear conviction of the sin remaining in our lives; still cleaving to all our words and actions. In the best of these we now discern a mixture of evil, either in the spirit, the matter, or the manner of them; something that could not endure the righteous judgment of God, were he extreme to mark what is done amiss. Where we least suspected it, we find a taint of pride, or self-will, of unbelief, or idolatry; so that we are now more ashamed of our best duties than formerly of our worst sins: And hence we cannot

but feel that these are so far from having any thing meritorious in them, yea, so far from being able to stand in sight of the divine justice, that for those also we should be guilty before God, were it not for the blood of the covenant.

8. Experience shows that, together with this conviction of sin remaining in our hearts, and cleaving to all our words and actions; as well as the guilt which on account thereof we should incur, were we not continually sprinkled with the atoning blood; one thing more is implied in this repentance; namely, a conviction of our helplessness, of our utter inability to think one good thought, or to form one good desire; and much more to speak one word aright, or to perform one good action, but through his free almighty grace, first preventing us, and then accompanying us every moment.

9. "But what good works are those, the practice of which you affirm to be necessary to sanctification?" First, all works of piety; such as public prayer, family prayer, and praying in our closet; receiving the supper of the Lord; searching the Scriptures, by hearing, reading, meditating; and using such a measure of fasting or abstinence as our bodily health allows.

10. Secondly, all works of mercy; whether they relate to the bodies or souls of men; such as feeding the hungry, clothing the naked, entertaining the stranger, visiting those that are in prison, or sick, or variously afflicted; such as the endeavouring to instruct the ignorant, to awaken the stupid sinner, to quicken the lukewarm, to confirm the wavering, to comfort the feebleminded, to succour the tempted, or contribute in any manner to the saving of souls from death. This is the repentance, and these the "fruits meet for repentance," which are necessary to full sanctification. This is the way wherein God hath appointed his children to wait for complete salvation.

11. Hence may appear the extreme mischievousness of that seemingly innocent opinion, that there is no sin in a believer; that all sin is destroyed, root and branch, the moment a man is justified. By totally preventing that repentance, it quite blocks up the way to sanctification. There is no place for repentance in him who believes there is no sin either in his life or heart: Consequently, there is no place for his being perfected in love, to which that repentance is indispensably necessary.

12. Hence it may likewise appear, that there is no possible danger in thus expecting full salvation. For suppose we were mistaken, suppose no such blessing ever was or can be attained, yet we lose nothing: Nay, that very expectation quickens us in using all the talents which God has given us; yea, in improving them all; so that when our Lord cometh, he will receive his own with increase.

13. But to return. Though it be allowed, that both this repentance and its fruits are necessary to full salvation; yet they are not necessary either in the same sense with faith, or in the same degree:—Not in the same degree; for these fruits are only necessary conditionally, if there be time and opportunity for them; otherwise a man may be sanctified without them. But he cannot be sanctified without faith. Likewise, let a man have ever so much of this repentance, or ever so many good works, yet all this does not at all avail: He is not sanctified till he believes. But the moment he believes, with or without those fruits, yea, with more or less of this repentance, he is sanctified.—Not in the same sense; for this repentance and these fruits are only remotely necessary, necessary in order to the continuance of his faith, as well as the increase of it; whereas faith is immediately and directly necessary to sanctification. It remains, that faith is the only condition which is immediately and proximately necessary to sanctification.

14. "But what is that faith whereby we are sanctified;—saved from sin, and perfected in love?" It is a divine evidence and con-

viction, First, that God hath promised it in the Holy Scripture. Till we are thoroughly satisfied of this, there is no moving one step further. And one would imagine there needed not one word more to satisfy a reasonable man of this, than the ancient promise, "Then will I circumcise thy heart, and the heart of thy seed, to love the Lord thy God with all thy heart, and with all thy soul, and with all thy mind." How clearly does this express the being perfected in love!—how strongly imply the being saved from all sin! For as long as love takes up the whole heart, what room is there for sin therein?

15. It is a divine evidence and conviction, Secondly, that what God hath promised he is able to perform. Admitting, therefore, that "with men it is impossible" to "bring a clean thing out of an unclean," to purify the heart from all sin, and to fill it with all holiness; yet this creates no difficulty in the case, seeing "with God all things are possible." And surely no one ever imagined it was possible to any power less than that of the Almighty! But if God speaks, it shall be done. God saith, "Let there be light; and there" is "light!"

16. It is, Thirdly, a divine evidence and Conviction that he is able and willing to do it now. And why not? Is not a moment to him the same as a thousand years? He cannot want more time to accomplish whatever is his will. And he cannot want or stay for any more worthiness or fitness in the persons he is pleased to honour. We may therefore boldly say, at any point of time, "Now is the day of salvation!" "Today, if ye will hear his voice, harden not your hearts!" "Behold, all things are now ready; come unto the marriage!"

17. To this confidence, that God is both able and willing to sanctify us now, there needs to be added one thing more, a divine evidence and conviction that he doeth it. In that hour it is done: God says to the inmost soul, "According to thy faith be it unto thee!" Then the soul is pure from every spot of sin; it is clean "from all

unrighteousness." The believer then experiences the deep meaning of those solemn words, "If we walk in the light as He is in the light, we have fellowship one with another, and the blood of Jesus Christ his Son cleanseth us from all sin."

18. "But does God work this great work in the soul gradually or instantaneously?" Perhaps it may be gradually wrought in some; I mean in this sense, they do not advert to the particular moment wherein sin ceases to be. But it is infinitely desirable, were it the will of God, that it should be done instantaneously; that the Lord should destroy sin "by the breath of his mouth," in a moment, in the twinkling of an eye. And so he generally does; a plain fact, of which there is evidence enough to satisfy any unprejudiced person. Thou therefore look for it every moment! Look for it in the way above described; in all those good works whereunto thou art "created anew in Christ Jesus." There is then no danger: You can be no worse, if you are no better, for that expectation. For were you to be disappointed of your hope, still you lose nothing. But you shall not be disappointed of your hope: It will come, and will not tarry. Look for it then every day, every hour, every moment! Why not this hour, this moment? Certainly you may look for it now, if you believe it is by faith. And by this token you may surely know whether you seek it by faith or by works. If by works, you want something to be done first, before you are sanctified. You think, I must first be or do thus or thus. Then you are seeking it by works unto this day. If you seek it by faith, you may expect it as you are; and if as you are, then expect it now. It is of importance to observe, that there is an inseparable connexion between these three points, expect it by faith, expect it as you are, and expect it now! To deny one of them, is to deny them all; to allow one, is to allow them all. Do you believe we are sanctified by faith? Be true then to your principle; and look for this blessing just as you are, neither better nor worse; as a poor sinner that has still nothing to pay, nothing to plead, but "Christ died." And if you look for it as you are, then expect it now. Stay for nothing:

The Scripture Way of Salvation

Why should you? Christ is ready; and He is all you want. He is waiting for you: He is at the door! Let your inmost soul cry out:

> *Come in, come in, thou heavenly Guest!*
> *Nor hence again remove;*
> *But sup with me, and let the feast*
> *Be everlasting love.*

Humble, Gentle, Patient Love
1767

The perfection revival began to cool in the mid-sixties but that did not end the controversy. John's extant letters to his brother Charles reveal a struggle within the societies (and brothers) over the doctrine's viability. Were the Methodist's going to jettison Wesley's most beloved teaching? Or, would Christian perfection survive and become a staple in Methodist identity? For us history answers the question. But in 1767, when John penned this letter to Charles, the question was still in debate. Thanks must be given to Wesley's dogged persistence for perfect love became part of Methodism's heart and soul. The definition of per-fection as humble, gentle, patient love *can be found sprinkled through-out Wesley's later writings. The phrase originates from the schism's major faults (as Wesley saw them) with the three adjectives serving as antonyms to three of the primary sinful tempers: pride, anger, and self-will.*[11] *Source: Telford.*

To Brother Charles
January 27, 1767

Dear Brother,

Some thoughts occurred to my mind this morning which I be-lieve it may be useful to set down: the rather because it may be a means of our understanding each other clearly; that we may agree as far as ever we can, and then let all the world know it.

I was thinking on Christian Perfection, with regard to the thing, the manner, and the time:

---

[11] The opposite of pride is humility, of anger is gentleness, of self-will and desire is patience. These also were the chief sins of the schismatics. Wesley came to emphasize these three qualities when defining perfect love. Cf. *A Plain Account of Christian Perfection: The Annotated Edition*, 64, 215 note 130.

Humble, Gentle, Patient Love

1. By perfection I mean the humble, gentle, patient love of God and man ruling all the tempers, words, and actions, the whole heart by the whole life. I do not include an impossibility of falling from it, either in part or in whole. Therefore I retract several expressions in our Hymns which partly express, partly imply, such an impossibility. And I do not contend for the term sinless, though I do not object against it.

Do we agree or differ here? If we differ, wherein?

2. As to the manner. I believe this perfection is always wrought in the soul by faith, by a simple act of faith, consequently in an instant. But I believe in a gradual work both preceding and following that instant.

Do we agree or differ here?

3. As to the time. I believe this instant generally is the instant of death, the moment before the soul leaves the body. But I believe it may be ten, twenty, or forty years before death.

Do we agree or differ here?

I believe it is usually many years after justification, but that it may be within five years or five months after it. I know no conclusive argument to the contrary. Do you? If it must be many years after justification, I would be glad to know how many. *Pretium quotus arrogat annus*? ("What year must claim the reward?")[12] And how many days or months or even years can you allow to be between perfection and death? How far from justification must it be? And how near to death?

If it be possible, let you and I come to a good understanding, both for our own sakes and for the sake of the people.

---

[12] Horace's Epistles, II. i. 35.

The Repentance of Believers
1767

This homily serves as a sequel to On Sin in Believers *and* The Scripture Way of Salvation. *Wesley's purpose is expressed in the opening paragraphs. His concern is to explain how repentance continues in the life of the believer en route to perfection. Sinful tempers remain in the believer requiring a further work of repentance for holiness to be realized experientially. Once again, note the specific sinful tempers Wesley addresses. These offer important insights into his understanding of the nature of perfect love. Then, take stock on how Wesley defines and delineates faith in the sanctification process. How does Wesley integrate his instantaneous motif with his gradualism? Compare what Wesley articulates here with what he expresses in* On Sin in Believers *and* The Scripture Way of Salvation. *Together, these three sermons present Wesley's fully developed gospel of two works of grace. Source: Works J 5:156-170.*

Repent and believe the gospel.

Mark 1:15

1. It is generally supposed, that repentance and faith are only the gate of religion; that they are necessary only at the beginning of our Christian course, when we are setting out in the way to the kingdom. And this may seem to be confirmed by the great Apostle, where, exhorting the Hebrew Christians to "go on to perfection," he teaches them to leave these "first principles of the doctrine of Christ;" "not laying again the foundation of repentance from dead works, and of faith towards God;" which must at least mean, that they should comparatively leave these, that at first took up all their thoughts, in order to "press forward toward the prize of the high calling of God in Christ Jesus."

2. And this is undoubtedly true, that there is a repentance and a faith, which are, more especially, necessary at the beginning: A repentance, which is a conviction of our utter sinfulness, and guiltiness, and helplessness; and which precedes our receiving

that kingdom of God, which, our Lord observes, is "within us;" and a faith, whereby we receive that kingdom, even "righteousness, and peace, and joy in the Holy Ghost."

3. But, notwithstanding this, there is also a repentance and a faith, (taking the words in another sense, a sense not quite the same, nor yet entirely different,) which are requisite after we have "believed the gospel;" yea, and in every subsequent stage of our Christian course, or we cannot "run the race which is set before us." And this repentance and faith are full as necessary, in order to our continuance and growth in grace, as the former faith and repentance were, in order to our entering into the kingdom of God.

But in what sense are we to repent and believe, after we are justified? This is an important question, and worthy of being considered with the utmost attention.

I. And, First, in what sense are we to repent?
1. Repentance frequently means an inward change, a change of mind from sin to holiness. But we now speak of it in a quite different sense, as it is one kind of self-knowledge, the knowing ourselves sinners, yea, guilty, helpless sinners, even though we know we are children of God.

2. Indeed when we first know this; when we first find redemption in the blood of Jesus; when the love of God is first shed abroad in our hearts, and his kingdom set up therein; it is natural to suppose that we are no longer sinners, that all our sins are not only covered but destroyed. As we do not then feel any evil in our hearts, we readily imagine none is there. Nay, some well-meaning men have imagined this not only at that time, but ever after; having persuaded themselves, that when they were justified, they were entirely sanctified: Yea, they have laid it down as a general rule, in spite of Scripture, reason, and experience. These sincerely believe, and earnestly maintain, that all sin is destroyed when we are justified; and that there is no sin in the heart of a believer; but

that it is altogether clean from that moment. But though we readily acknowledge, "he that believeth is born of God," and "he that is born of God doth not commit sin," yet we cannot allow that he does not feel it within: It does not reign, but it does remain. And a conviction of the sin which remains in our heart, is one great branch of the repentance we are now speaking of.

3. For it is seldom long before he who imagined all sin was gone, feels there is still pride in his heart. He is convinced both that in many respects he has thought of himself more highly than he ought to think, and that he has taken to himself the praise of something he had received, and gloried in it as though he had not received it; and yet he knows he is in the favor of God. He cannot, and ought not, to "cast away his confidence." "The Spirit" still "witnesses with" his "spirit, that he is a child of God."

4. Nor is it long before he feels self-will in his heart; even a will contrary to the will of God. A will every man must inevitably have, as long as he has an understanding. This is an essential part of human nature, indeed of the nature of every intelligent being. Our blessed Lord himself had a will as a man; otherwise he had not been a man. But his human will was invariably subject to the will of his Father. At all times, and on all occasions, even in the deepest affliction, he could say, "Not as I will, but as thou wilt." But this is not the case at all times, even with a true believer in Christ. He frequently finds his will more or less exalting itself against the will of God. He wills something, because it is pleasing to nature, which is not pleasing to God; and he nills (is averse from) something, because it is painful to nature, which is the will of God concerning him. Indeed, suppose he continues in the faith, he fights against it with all his might: But this very thing implies that it really exists, and that he is conscious of it.

5. Now self-will, as well as pride, is a species of idolatry; and both are directly contrary to the love of God. The same observation may be made concerning the love of the world. But this

likewise even true believers are liable to feel in themselves; and every one of them does feel it, more or less, sooner or later, in one branch or another. It is true, when he first "passes from death unto life," he desires nothing more but God. He can truly say, "All my desire is unto thee, and unto the remembrance of thy name." "Whom have I in heaven but thee, and there is none upon earth that I desire beside thee!" But it is not so always. In process of time he will feel again, though perhaps only for a few moments, either "the desire of the flesh," or "the desire of the eye," or "the pride of life." Nay, if he does not continually watch and pray, he may find lust reviving; yea, and thrusting sore at him that he may fall, till he has scarce any strength left in him. He may feel the assaults of inordinate affection; yea, a strong propensity to "love the creature more than the Creator;" whether it be a child, a parent, a husband or wife, or "the friend that is as his own soul." He may feel, in a thousand various ways, a desire of earthly things or pleasures. In the same proportion he will forget God, not seeking his happiness in him, and consequently being a "lover of pleasure more than a lover of God."

6. If he does not keep himself every moment, he will again feel the desire of the eye; the desire of gratifying his imagination with something great, or beautiful, or uncommon. In hour many ways does this desire assault the soul? Perhaps with regard to the poorest trifles, such as dress, or furniture; things never designed to satisfy the appetite of an immortal spirit. Yet, how natural is it for us, even after we have "tasted of the powers of the world to come," to sink again into these foolish, low desires of things that perish in the using! How hard is it, even for those who know in whom they have believed, to conquer but one branch of the desire of the eye, curiosity; constantly to trample it under their feet; to desire nothing merely because it is new!

7. And how hard is it even for the children of God wholly to conquer the pride of life! St. John seems to mean by this nearly the same with what the world terms the sense of honor. This is no

other than a desire of, and delight in, "the honor that cometh of men;" a desire and love of praise; and, which is always joined with it, a proportionable fear of dispraise. Nearly allied to this is evil shame; the being ashamed of that wherein we ought to glory. And this is seldom divided from the fear of man, which brings a thousand snares upon the soul. Now where is he, even among those that seem strong in faith, who does not find in himself a degree of all these evil tempers? So that even these are but in part "crucified to the world;" for the evil root still remains in their heart.

8. And do we not feel other tempers, which are as contrary to the love of our neighbor as these are to the love of God? The love of our neighbor "thinketh no evil." Do not we find anything of the kind? Do we never find any jealousies, any evil surmisings, any groundless or unreasonable suspicions? He that is clear in these respects, let him cast the first stone at his neighbor. Who does not sometimes feel other tempers or inward motions, which he knows are contrary to brotherly love? If nothing of malice, hatred, or bitterness, is there no touch of envy; particularly toward those who enjoy some real or supposed good, which we desire but cannot attain? Do we never find any degree of resentment, when we are injured or affronted; especially by those whom we peculiarly loved, and whom we had most labored to help or oblige? Does injustice or ingratitude never excite in us any desire of revenge? any desire of returning evil for evil, instead of "overcoming evil with good?" This also shows, how much is still in our heart, which is contrary to the love of our neighbor.

9. Covetousness, in every kind and degree, is certainly as contrary to this as to the love of God; whether philarguria, the love of money, which is too frequently "the root of all evil;" or pleonexia, literally, a desire of having more, or increasing in substance. And how few, even of the real children of God, are entirely free from both! Indeed one great man, Martin Luther, used to say, he "never had any covetousness in him" (not only in his converted state,

but) "ever since he was born." But, if so, I would not scruple to say, he was the only man born of a woman, (except him that was God as well as man,) who had not, who was born without it. Nay, I believe, never was any one born of God, that lived any considerable time after, who did not feel more or less of it many times, especially in the latter sense. We may therefore set it down as an undoubted truth, that covetousness, together with pride, and self-will, and anger, remain in the hearts even of them that are justified.

10. It is their experiencing this, which has inclined so many serious persons to understand the latter part of the seventh chapter to the Romans, not of them that are "under the law," that are convinced of sin, which is undoubtedly the meaning of the Apostle, but of them that are "under grace;" that are "justified freely through the redemption that is in Christ." And it is most certain, they are thus far right:—There does still remain, even in them that are justified, a mind which is in some measure carnal; (so the Apostle tells even the believers at Corinth, "Ye are carnal") an heart bent to backsliding, still ever ready to "depart from the living God;" a propensity to pride, self-will, anger, revenge, love of the world, yea, and all evil; a root of bitterness, which, if the restraint were taken off for a moment, would instantly spring up; yea, such a depth of corruption, as, without clear light from God, we cannot possibly conceive. And a conviction of all this sin remaining in their hearts is the repentance which belongs to them that are justified.

11. But we should likewise be convinced, that as sin remains in our hearts, so it cleaves to all our words and actions. Indeed it is to be feared, that many of our words are more than mixed with sin; that they are sinful altogether; for such undoubtedly is all uncharitable conversation; all which does not spring from brotherly love; all which does not agree with that golden rule, "What ye would that others should do to you, even so do unto them." Of this kind is all backbiting, all tale-bearing, all whispering, all

evil-speaking, that is, repeating the faults of absent persons; for none would have others repeat his faults when he is absent. Now how few are there, even among believers, who are in no degree guilty of this; who steadily observe the good old rule, "Of the dead and the absent, nothing but good!" And suppose they do, do they likewise abstain from unprofitable conversation? Yet all this is unquestionably sinful, and "grieves the Holy Spirit of God." Yea, and "for every idle word that men shall speak, they shall give an account in the day of judgment."

12. But let it be supposed, that they continually "watch and pray," and so do "not enter into this temptation;" that they constantly set a watch before their mouth, and keep the door of their lips; suppose they exercise themselves herein, that all their "conversation may be in grace, seasoned with salt, and meet to minister grace to the hearers;" yet do they not daily slide into useless discourse, notwithstanding all their caution? And even when they endeavor to speak for God, are their words pure, free from unholy mixtures? Do they find nothing wrong in their very intention? Do they speak merely to please God, and not partly to please themselves? Is it wholly to do the will of God, and not their own will also? Or, if they begin with a single eye, do they go on "looking unto Jesus," and talking with Him all the time they are talking with their neighbor? When they are reproving sin, do they feel no anger or unkind temper to the sinner? When they are instructing the ignorant, do they not find any pride, any self-preference? When they are comforting the afflicted, or provoking one another to love and to good works, do they never perceive any inward self-commendation: "Now you have spoke well?" Or any vanity, a desire that others should think so, and esteem them on the account? In some or all of these respects, how much sin cleaves to the best conversation even of believers! The conviction of which is another branch of the repentance which belongs to them that are justified.

13. And how much sin, if their conscience is thoroughly awake, may they find cleaving to their actions also! Nay, are there not many of these, which, though they are such as the world would not condemn, yet cannot be commended, no, nor excused, if we judge by the word of God? Are there not many of their actions, which, they themselves know, are not to the glory of God? Many, wherein they did not even aim at this; which were not undertaken with an eye to God? And of those that were, are there not many, wherein their eye is not singly fixed on God? wherein they are doing their own will, at least as much as His; and seeking to please themselves as much, if not more than to please God?— And while they are endeavoring to do good to their neighbor, do they not feel wrong tempers of various kinds? Hence their good actions, so called, are far from being strictly such; being polluted with such a mixture of evil: Such are their works of mercy. And is there not the same mixture in their works of piety? While they are hearing the word which is able to save their souls, do they not frequently find such thoughts as make them afraid lest it should turn to their condemnation, rather than their salvation? Is it not often the same case, while they are endeavoring to offer up their prayers to God, whether in public or private? Nay, while they are engaged in the most solemn service, even while they are at the table of the Lord, what manner of thoughts arise in them. Are not their hearts sometimes wandering to the ends of the earth; sometimes filled with such imaginations, as make them fear lest all their sacrifice should be an abomination to the Lord? So that they are now more ashamed of their best duties, than they were once of their worst sins.

14. Again: How many sins of omission are they chargeable with! We know the words of the Apostle: "To him that knoweth to do good, and doeth it not, to him it is sin." But do they not know a thousand instances, wherein they might have done good, to enemies, to strangers, to their brethren, either with regard to their bodies or their souls, and they did it not? How many omissions have they been guilty of, in their duty toward God! How many

opportunities of communicating, of hearing his word, of public or private prayers have they neglected! So great reason had even that holy man, Archbishop Usher, after all his labours for God, to cry out, almost with his dying breath, "Lord, forgive me my sins of omission!"

15. But, besides these outward omissions, may they not find in themselves inward defects without number? Defects of every kind: They have not the love, the fear, the confidence they ought to have, toward God. They have not the love which is due to their neighbor, to every child of man; no, nor even that which is due to their brethren, to every child of God, whether those that are at a distance from them, or those with whom they are immediately connected. They have no holy temper in the degree they ought; they are defective in every thing;—in a deep consciousness of which they are ready to cry out, with M. De Renty, "I am a ground all overrun with thorns;" or, with Job, "I am vile: I abhor myself, and repent as in dust and ashes."

16. A conviction of their guiltiness is another branch of that repentance which belongs to the children of God. But this is cautiously to be understood, and in a peculiar sense. For it is certain, "there is no condemnation to them that are in Christ Jesus," that believe in him, and, in the power of that faith, "walk not after the flesh, but after the Spirit." Yet can they no more bear the strict justice of God now, than before they believed. This pronounces them to be still worthy of death, an all the preceding accounts. And it would absolutely condemn them thereto, were it not for the atoning blood. Therefore they are thoroughly convinced, that they still deserve punishment, although it is hereby turned aside from them. But here there are extremes on one hand and on the other, and few steer clear of them. Most men strike on one or the other, either thinking themselves condemned when they are not, or thinking they deserve to be acquitted. Nay, the truth lies between: They still deserve, strictly speaking, only the damnation of hell. But what they deserve does not come upon them, because

they "have an Advocate with the Father." His life, and death, and intercession still interpose between them and condemnation.

17. A conviction of their utter helplessness is yet another branch of this repentance. I mean hereby two things: First, that they are no more able now of themselves to think one good thought, to form one good desire, to speak one good word, or do one good work, than before they were justified; that they have still no kind or degree of strength of their own; no power either to do good, or resist evil; no ability to conquer, or even withstand the world, the devil, or their own evil nature. They can, it is certain, do all these things; but it is not by their own strength. They have power to overcome all these enemies; for "sin hath no more dominion over them:" But it is not from nature, either in whole or in part; it is the mere gift of God: Nor is it given all at once, as if they had a stock laid up for many years; but from moment to moment.

18. By this helplessness I mean, Secondly, an absolute inability to deliver ourselves from that guiltiness or desert of punishment whereof we are still conscious; yea, and an inability to remove, by all the grace we have, (to say nothing of our natural powers,) either the pride, self-will, love of the world, anger, and general proneness to depart from God, which we experimentally know to remain in the heart, even of them that are regenerate; or the evil which, in spite of all our endeavours, cleaves to all our words and actions. Add to this, an utter inability wholly to avoid uncharitable, and, much more, unprofitable conversation; and an inability to avoid sins of omission, or to supply the numberless defects we are convinced of; especially the want of love, and other right tempers, both to God and man.

19. If any man is not satisfied of this, if any believes that whoever is justified is able to remove these sins out of his heart and life, let him make the experiment let him try whether, by the grace he has already received, he can expel pride, self-will, or inbred sin in general. Let him try whether he can cleanse his

words and actions from all mixture of evil; whether he can avoid all uncharitable and unprofitable conversation, with all the sins of omission; and, lastly, whether he can supply the numberless defects which he still finds in himself. Let him not be discouraged by one or two experiments, but repeat the trial again and again; and the longer he tries, the more deeply will he be convinced of his utter helplessness in all these respects.

20. Indeed this is so evident a truth, that well nigh all the children of God, scattered abroad, however they differ in other points, yet generally agree in this;—that although we may, "by the Spirit, mortify the deeds of the body;" resist and conquer both outward and inward sin; although we may weaken our enemies day by day;—yet we cannot drive them out. By all the grace which is given at justification we cannot extirpate them. Though we watch and pray ever so much, we cannot wholly cleanse either our hearts or hands. Most sure we cannot, till it shall please our Lord to speak to our hearts again, to speak the second time, "Be clean." And then only the leprosy is cleansed. Then only the evil root, the carnal mind, is destroyed; and inbred sin subsists no more. But if there be no such second change, if there be no instantaneous deliverance after justification, if there be none but a gradual work of God, (that there is a gradual work none denies,) then we must be content, as well as we can, to remain full of sin till death; and, if so, we must remain guilty till death, continually deserving punishment. For it is impossible the guilt, or desert of punishment, should be removed from us, as long as all this sin remains in our heart, and cleaves to our words and actions. Nay, in rigorous justice, all we think, and speak, and act, continually increases it.

II. 1. In this sense we are to repent, after we are justified. And till we do so, we can go no farther. For, till we are sensible of our disease, it admits of no cure. But, supposing we do thus repent, then are we called to "believe the gospel."

2. And this also is to be understood in a peculiar sense, different from that wherein we believed in order to justification. Believe the glad tidings of great salvation, which God hath prepared for all people. Believe that he who is "the brightness of his Father's glory, the express image of his person," is "able to save unto the uttermost all that come unto God through him." He is able to save you from all the sin that still remains in your heart. He is able to save you from all the sin that cleaves to all your words and actions. He is able to save you from sins of omission, and to supply whatever is wanting in you. It is true, this is impossible with man; but with God-Man all things are possible. For what can be too hard for Him who hath "all power in heaven and in earth?" Indeed his bare power to do this is not a sufficient foundation for our faith that he will do it, that he will thus exert his power, unless he hath promised it. But this he has done: He has promised it over and over, in the strongest terms.

He has given us these "exceeding great and precious promises," both in the Old and the New Testament. So we read in the law, in the most ancient part of the oracles of God, "The Lord thy God will circumcise thy heart, and the heart of thy seed, to love the Lord thy God, with all thy heart, and with all thy soul." (Dt 30:6) So in the Psalms, "He shall redeem Israel," the Israel of God, "from all his sins." So in the Prophet, "Then will I sprinkle clean water upon you, and ye shall be clean: From all your filthiness and from all your idols will I cleanse you. And I will put my Spirit within you, and ye shall keep my judgments and do them. I will also save you from all your uncleannesses." (Ezek 36:25, &c.)

So likewise in the New Testament, "Blessed be the Lord God of Israel, for he hath visited and redeemed his people, and hath raised up an horn of salvation for us, to perform the oath which he sware to our father Abraham, That he would grant unto us, that we, being delivered out of the hands of our enemies, should serve him without fear, in holiness and righteousness before him all the days of our life." (Luke 1:68, &c.)

255

3. You have therefore good reason to believe, he is not only able, but willing to do this; to cleanse you from all your filthiness of flesh and spirit; to "save you from all your uncleannesses." This is the thing which you now long for; this is the faith which you now particularly need, namely, that the Great Physician, the lover of my soul, is willing to make me clean. But is he willing to do this tomorrow or to-day? Let him answer for himself: "Today, if ye will hear" my "voice, harden not your hearts." If you put it off till to-morrow, you harden your hearts; you refuse to hear his voice. Believe, therefore, that he is willing to save you to-day. He is willing to save you now. "Behold, now is the accepted time." He now saith, "Be thou clean!" Only believe, and you also will immediately find, "all things are possible to him that believeth."

4. Continue to believe in him that loved thee, and gave himself for thee; that bore all thy sins in his own body on the tree; and he saveth thee from all condemnation, by his blood continually applied. Thus it is that we continue in a justified state. And when we go on "from faith to faith," when we have faith to be cleansed from indwelling sin, to be saved from all our uncleannesses, we are likewise saved from all that guilt, that desert of punishment, which we felt before. So that then we may say, not only,

> *Every moment, Lord, I want*
> *The merit of thy death!*
> *but, likewise, in the full assurance of faith,*
> *Every moment, Lord, I have*
> *The merit of thy death!*

For, by that faith in his life, death, and intercession for us, renewed from moment to moment, we are every whit clean, and there is not only now no condemnation for us, but no such desert of punishment as was before, the Lord cleansing both our hearts and lives.

5. By the same faith we feel the power of Christ every moment resting upon us, whereby alone we are what we are; whereby we are enabled to continue in spiritual life, and without which, notwithstanding all our present holiness, we should be devils the next moment. But as long as we retain our faith in him, we "draw water out of the wells of salvation." Leaning on our Beloved, even Christ in us the hope of glory, who dwelleth in our hearts by faith, who likewise is ever interceding for us at the right hand of God, we receive help from him to think, and speak, and act, what is acceptable in his sight. Thus does he "prevent" them that believe, in all their "doings, and further them with his continual help;" so that all their designs, conversations, and actions are "begun, continued, and ended in him." Thus doth he "cleanse the thoughts of their hearts, by the inspiration of his Holy Spirit, that they may perfectly love him, and worthily magnify his holy name."

6. Thus it is, that in the children of God, repentance and faith exactly answer each other. By repentance we feel the sin remaining in our hearts, and cleaving to our words and actions: By faith, we receive the power of God in Christ, purifying our hearts, and cleansing our hands. By repentance, we are still sensible that we deserve punishment for all our tempers, and words, and actions: By faith, we are conscious that our Advocate with the Father is continually pleading for us, and thereby continually turning aside all condemnation and punishment from us. By repentance we have an abiding conviction that there is no help in us: By faith, we receive not only mercy, "but grace to help in" every "time of need." Repentance disclaims the very possibility of any other help: Faith accepts all the help we stand in need of, from Him that hath all power in heaven and earth. Repentance says, "Without him I can do nothing." Faith says, "I can do all things through Christ strengthening me." Through Him I can not only overcome, but expel, all the enemies of my soul. Through Him I can "love the Lord my God with all my heart, mind, soul, and strength;"

yea, and "walk in holiness and righteousness before him all the days of my life."

III. 1. From what has been said, we may easily learn the mischievousness of that opinion, that we are wholly sanctified when we are justified; that our hearts are then cleansed from all sin. It is true, we are then delivered, as was observed before, from the dominion of outward sin; and, at the same time, the power of inward sin is so broken, that we need no longer follow, or be led by it: But it is by no means true, that inward sin is then totally destroyed; that the root of pride, self-will, anger, love of the world, is then taken out of the heart; or that the carnal mind, and the heart bent to backsliding, are entirely extirpated. And to suppose the contrary is not, as some may think, an innocent, harmless mistake. No: It does immense harm: It entirely blocks up the way to any farther change; for it is manifest, "they that are whole need not a Physician, but they that are sick." If, therefore, we think we are quite made whole already, there is no room to seek any farther healing. On this supposition it is absurd to expect a farther deliverance from sin, whether gradual or instantaneous.

2. On the contrary, a deep conviction that we are not yet whole; that our hearts are not fully purified; that there is yet in us a "carnal mind," which is still in its nature "enmity against God;" that a whole body of sin remains in our heart, weakened indeed, but not destroyed; shows, beyond all possibility of doubt, the absolute necessity of a farther change. We allow, that at the very moment of justification, we are born again: In that instant we experience that inward change from "darkness into marvelous light;" from the image of the brute and the devil, into the image of God; from the earthly, sensual, devilish mind, to the mind which was in Christ Jesus. But are we then entirely changed? Are we wholly transformed into the image of him that created us? Far from it: We still retain a depth of sin; and it is the consciousness of this which constrains us to groan, for a full deliverance, to Him that is mighty to save. Hence it is, that those believers who are not con-

vinced of the deep corruption of their hearts, or but slightly and, as it were, notionally convinced, have little concern about entire sanctification. They may possibly hold the opinion, that such a thing is to be, either at death, or some time, they know not when, before it. But they have no great uneasiness for the want of it, and no great hunger or thirst after it. They cannot, until they know themselves better, until they repent in the sense above described, until God unveils the inbred monster's face, and shows them the real state of their souls. Then only, when they feel the burden, will they groan for deliverance from it. Then, and not till then, will they cry out, in the agony of their soul,

> *Break off the yoke of inbred sin,*
> *And fully set my spirit free!*
> *I cannot rest till pure within,*
> *Till I am wholly lost in thee.*

3. We may learn from hence, Secondly, that a deep conviction of our demerit, after we are accepted, (which, in one sense, may be termed guilt,) is absolutely necessary, in order to our seeing the true value of the atoning blood; in order to our feeling that we need this as much, after we are justified, as ever we did before. Without this conviction we cannot but account the blood of the covenant as a common thing, something of which we have not now any great need, seeing all our past sins are blotted out. Yea, but if both our hearts and lives are thus unclean, there is a kind of guilt which we are contracting every moment, and which, of consequence, would every moment expose us to fresh condemnation, but that

> *He ever lives above,*
> *For us to intercede,*
> *His all-atoning love,*
> *His precious blood, to plead.*

It is this repentance, and the faith intimately connected with it, which are expressed in those strong lines,

> *I sin in every breath I draw,*
> *Nor do thy will, nor keep thy law*
> *On earth, as angels do above:*
> *But still the fountain open stands,*
> *Washes my feet, my heart, my hands,*
> *Till I am perfected in love.*

4. We may observe, Thirdly, a deep conviction of our utter helplessness, of our total inability to retain anything we have received, much more to deliver ourselves from the world of iniquity remaining both in our hearts and lives, teaches us truly to live upon Christ by faith, not only as our Priest, but as our King. Hereby we are brought to "magnify him," indeed; to "give him all the glory of his grace;" to "make him a whole Christ, an entire Saviour; and truly to set the crown upon his head." These excellent words, as they have frequently been used, have little or no meaning; but they are fulfilled in a strong and deep sense, when we thus, as it were, go out of ourselves, in order to be swallowed up in him; when we sink into nothing, that He may be all in all. Then, his almighty grace having abolished "every high thing which exalted itself against him," every temper, and thought, and word, and work "is brought to the obedience of Christ."

Londonderry, April 24, 1767

Section Five

The Late Period

1768 – 1791

Questions to Consider for
John Wesley's Late Period

1. How does Wesley integrate his doctrine of perfect love into his larger theology of the faith journey (*ordo salutis*)?

2. Compare Wesley's mature *ordo salutis* with earlier periods. Are there any changes or developments? If so, what has changed?

3. What parallels exist between Wesley's mature views on perfection with his earlier periods? What has changed? What has not?

4. Once again, note how Wesley defines perfection in his late period. What is the essential idea he is seeking to communicate?

5. Does *ars moriendi* (the art of dying) inform his mature doctrine of full salvation? If so, how? What has changed from prior periods?

6. Look at how Wesley defines sin in this period. Which kind of sin is removed in the gift of perfect love and which kind is not?

7. Note how Wesley understands infirmities and involuntary sin in this section. How do these views inform his mature understanding of degrees of perfection?

8. Reflect on how perfect love is attained. What is the relationship between divine grace and human agency? How would you state Wesley's position in your own words? Has his views changed over time? If so, what changed?

The Imperfection of Perfection
1772

In 1772 Wesley published An Extract of the Journal of Elizabeth Harper. *In the following preface he explains his reasons for doing so: to clarify further his doctrine of "involuntary transgressions" in relation to perfect love. The reader would do well to pay close attention to how Wesley distinguishes between the two, and how this distinction informs his mature explication of full salvation. Source: Works J 14:261.*

To The Reader:

1. To set the doctrine of Christian perfection too high is the ready way to drive it out of the world. Let a man only describe it as implying a freedom from mistakes and human infirmities; and whoever knows there is no such freedom in this life naturally concludes, "There is no perfection." Hence we should always carefully guard against this, by insisting, it is no more and no less than giving God all our heart; loving Him with all our heart, and our neighbour as ourselves.

2. This is well consistent with a thousand infirmities, which belong to every soul while in the body. To place this in the clearest and fullest light, I have published the following extract from the artless Journal of a plain woman, wrote merely for her own use. I have no doubt but God had all her heart. But yet how many were her infirmities! And these are the more apparent, because she was a person of no uncommon endowments; one that had just plain, natural understanding, without any advantage of education, and who wrote down daily just what she felt, with all possible artlessness and simplicity. The chief of these are wandering thoughts; (whether natural or preternatural;) listlessness in private prayer; (I believe, entirely owing to bodily disorder;) hurry in business; (it seems, not apparent to others, though frequently felt by herself;) want of a steady, invariable advertence to the presence of God;

speaking too many words, more than were strictly necessary; speaking, through ignorance, a word not strictly true; speaking sometimes too quick, so as to have the appearance of anger; omission of things which had better be done. Perhaps one might mention, likewise, under this head, such vehement temptations to anger, to impatience, to fretfulness, to immoderate sorrow, and to follow her own will, that at divers times she escaped with the skin of her teeth, and scarce knew whether she escaped or not. So particular a detail of these things may be of singular use to those who find the same temptations; and who may be encouraged thereby, to "hold the beginning of their confidence steadfast unto the end."

3. But it may be objected, "If perfection means only that love which is consistent with all these infirmities, then how does it differ from what is experienced by every believer?" I answer, (1.) Many are delivered from these infirmities, in a far greater measure than she was. I judge her to have been a real witness of Christian perfection, but only in a low degree. (2.) Whom do you know that experiences even what she did, that never-failing love of God and man; that uninterrupted calmness of mind; that invariable meekness, gentleness, humility; that continual hunger and thirst after righteousness, after the entire image of God; above all, that absolute, unreserved dependence upon Christ, as the fountain of every good and perfect gift, of all holiness and happiness? Does every believer experience this? I will be bold to say, not one in a thousand. I suppose, not one upon earth, unless he has received another gift, widely different from what he received when he was justified. At least, I know no one in the three kingdoms who comes up to this experience, (besides a few in their first love,) unless, after justification, he has found a second change wrought in a moment. However, concerning that circumstance we need not dispute, whether it be wrought gradually or instantaneously; only let the change be wrought; only let our souls be renewed in the whole image of God; only let all that mind be in us which was also in Christ Jesus; let Him reign in our hearts without a rival, at

all times, and in all places. Let us be all devoted to Him in soul and in body; and let all our thoughts, and words, and actions be continually offered up to God, as holy sacrifices acceptable to God through Christ.

4. A few more circumstances relating to this amiable woman may not be unacceptable to the reader. Elizabeth, the daughter of William and Joan Tuck, was born at Penzance, December 20, 1734. She was brought to Redruth when about four years old; and, as she grew up, lived as other harmless people did. June 30, 1755, she was married to one Andrew Harper, a shop-keeper of Redruth; and, three or four years after, she became weak and sickly. At the same time she grew distressed in her mind, which she strove to remove by various ways; but all to no purpose. In the latter end of the year 1763, a fever brought her to the brink of eternity. She was greatly afraid to die; and hearing there were some in the town who had no fear of death, she entreated her husband, without delay, to send for one of the Preachers. Conversing with him, she saw the way of conquering the fear of death. She soon recovered her health, and from that time sought the Lord with her whole heart, till, on Easter-day, (having joined the society before,) as she was receiving the Lord's supper, these words were strongly applied to her soul: "It is God that justifieth: Who is he that condemneth?" She went home, called her husband, and said, "Now all my sins are forgiven. I am not afraid to die now; for I love God, and I know He loves me."

5. From this time she walked closely with God, and was hearty and zealous in his cause. There was nothing in her power which she was not ready to do for the servants or children of God. She was exceedingly tempted, after she believed God had cleansed her from inbred sin. Of this she gives a large account in her Journal; but she did not cast away her confidence. When she saw death approaching she was not moved, but calmly looked up to God. She exhorted her husband, and all near her, not to love the world, or the things of the world. A little after she said, "'Lord,

thou knowest all things: Thou knowest that I love thee.' Thou knowest it hath been my only desire to please thee: Come, Lord Jesus! Come, and sanctify me throughout, spirit, soul, and body! O come quickly!" In a little time she cried, "He is come! He is come!" and presently fell asleep.

Pressing on to Perfection
1771-1784

The following series of letters illustrate the kind of counsel Wesley gave to seekers of heart holiness. Source: Telford.

To Mary Bishop
September 1, 1771.

My Dear Sister,

Concessions made in the chapel at Bath would not quench the flame kindled over the three kingdoms. Mr. Fletcher's Letters may do this in some measure; but the antidote cannot spread so fast as the poison. However, the Lord reigneth; and consequently all these things shall work together for the increase of his kingdom. Certainly simple faith is the very thing you want; that faith which lives upon Christ from moment to moment. I believe that sermon, *The Scripture Way of Salvation*, might at this time be very useful to you. It is a great thing to seize and improve the very now. What a blessing you may receive at this instant! Behold the Lamb of God!

What, if even before this letter comes to your hands; the Lord should come to your heart! Is He not nigh? Is He not now knocking at the door? What do you say? "Come in, my Lord, come in." Are you not ready? Are you not a mere sinner, and stripped of all? Therefore all is ready for you. Fear not; only believe, and enter into rest. How gracious is it in the kind Physician to humble you and prove you, and show you what is in your heart! Now let Christ and love alone be there...

To Miss J. C. March
June 3, 1774

You are living witness of two great truths: the one, that there cannot be a lasting, steady enjoyment of pure love without the direct testimony of the Spirit concerning it, without God's Spirit shining on His own work; the other, that setting perfection too high is the ready way to drive it out of the world. A third thing you may learn from your own experience is that the heart of man contains things that one would think incompatible. Such are the tempers and sensations of those especially that are renewed in love. Some of them seem to be quite inconsistent with others; so that, if we give way to reasoning on this head, if we will not believe what God has wrought till we can account for all the circumstances attending it, till we know how these things can be, we shall bewilder ourselves more and more, and—

Find no end, in wandering mazes lost

I believe one thing which has hurt you is that kind of silence. One use of your present journey may be this: Learn to speak for God without either fear or shame. You have need to be more simple. Look straight forward; eye one thing! Do not consider that you are a woman or a gentlewoman. Do not you bear an higher character? What! know you not that your very body is the temple of the Holy Ghost which is in you? Therefore glorify God with your body and with your spirit. Give Him the praise that is due unto His name.

I am glad you are going to Stroud. It is probable you will see that good young woman, A. Esther. If you do, I hope you will be enabled to encourage her, that she may hold fast the good gift of God. Her experience was exceeding clear when I talked with her last. If possible, guard her against evil reasoning, that she may never let go her simplicity.

Peace, be with all your spirits!

To Elizabeth Ritchie
June 3, 1774

My Dear Betsy,

Pressing on to Perfection

I shall much want to hear that you stand fast in the liberty wherewith Christ has made you free. It is absolutely certain that you never need lose anything of what God has wrought. He is able and He is willing to give you always what He has once given. He will do it, provided you watch unto prayer and stir up the gift of God which is in you. There is one invariable rule which God observes in all His dealings with the children of men: "Unto him that hath," uses what he hath, "shall be given, and he shall have more abundantly." When we are justified, He gives us one talent; to those that use this He gives more. When we are sanctified, He gives, as it were, five talents. And if you use the whole power which is then given, He will not only continue that power but increase it day by day. Meantime be not ignorant of Satan's devices: he will assault you on every side; he will cast temptations upon you,

Thick as autumnal leaves that strew the ground

But with every temptation there shall be a way to escape; and you shall be more than conqueror through Him that loves you. You can do, you can suffer His whole will. Go on in His name and in the power of His might; and fulfill the joy of,

Yours affectionately.

To Ann Bolton
September 27, 1777.

Shall not I speak to my dear friend all that is in my heart? I know no reason why I should not. I have done so from the time I knew you first, and more especially from the time you was with me in London. Then I took more intimate knowledge of you: I tasted of your spirit. I observed all your tempers, and marked you down as the 'sister of my choice.' As such I have looked upon you ever since without any intermission or variation. And sometimes you have been free and open to me; but at other times you

269

have been more shy and distant. My Nancy, let that time of distance and reserve return no more! Be to me always (if you can) what I am to you, a faithful and tender-hearted friend.

Undoubtedly Satan, who well understands the manner how the mind is influenced by the body, can, by means of those parts in the animal machine which are more immediately subservient to thinking, raise a thousand perceptions and emotions in the mind, so far as God is pleased to permit. I doubt not but he was the chief agent in your late painful exercises. And you gave him advantage by reasoning with him, that is, fighting him at his own weapons; instead of simply looking up and saying, "Thou shalt answer for me, O Lord, my God."

You undoubtedly want more thankfulness. And you want more simplicity; that grace, Cambray says, "which cuts the soul off from all unnecessary reflections upon itself." You are encompassed with ten thousand mercies; and the greatest of all is, "Christ in a pure and spotless heart!" Beware of ever admitting any doubt or reasoning concerning this! Whereunto you have attained hold fast! And use all the grace you have received. Warn every one, and exhort every one, especially those who groan after full salvation.

I cannot on any account pass an whole day without commending you to God in prayer. I thank you for writing to me so soon. Continue to love and pray for,

My dear Nancy,

Yours most affectionately

To Robert Carr Brackenbury
September 18, 1780.

Dear Sir,

The Lord knoweth the way wherein you go; and when you have been tried, you shall come forth as gold. It is true you have now full exercise for all your faith and patience; but by and by you will find good brought out of evil, and will bless God for the severe but wholesome medicine. I had all along a persuasion that God would deliver you, although I could not see which way it would be done; as I knew it was your desire not to do your own will, but the will of Him whose you are and whom you serve. May He still guide you in the way you should go, and enable you to give Him your whole heart! You must not set the great blessing afar off, because you find much war within. Perhaps this will not abate, but rather increase, till the moment your heart is set at liberty. The war will not cease before you attain, but by your attaining, the promise. And if you look for it by naked faith, why may you not receive it now? The cheerfulness of faith you should aim at in and above all things. Wishing you a continual supply of righteousness, peace, and joy,

  I am

        Your affectionate friend and brother

To Ann Loxdale
August 15, 1781.

My Dear Miss Loxdale,

  Your letter gave much satisfaction. Whereunto you have attained, hold fast; and "press on toward the mark, the prize of your high calling of God in Christ Jesus." I do not see any reason to doubt, but that you have tasted of the pure love of God. But you seem to be only a babe in that state, and have, therefore, need to go forward continually. It is by doing and suffering the whole will of our Lord, that we grow up in Him that is our Head; and if you diligently hearken to His voice, He will show you the way wherein you should go. But you have need to be exceeding faithful to the light He gives you. "While you have the light, walk in the light," and it will continually increase. Do not regard the judgment of the world, even of those called the religious world. You are not to conform to the judgment of others, but to follow your own light; that which the blessed Spirit gives you from time to time, which is truth and is no lie. That He may guide you and your sister into all truth and all holiness, is the prayer of,

My dear Miss Loxdale,

Yours most affectionately

April 12, 1782.

My Dear Miss Loxdale,

I advised formerly my dear Jenny Cooper, and so I advise you, frequently to read and meditate upon the thirteenth chapter of the First Epistle to the Corinthians. There is the true picture of Christian perfection! Let us copy after it with all our might. I believe it might likewise be of use to you to read more than once the *Plain Account of Christian Perfection*. Indeed, what is it more or less than *humble, gentle, patient love*! It is undoubtedly our privilege to "rejoice evermore," with a calm, still, heartfelt joy. Nevertheless, this is seldom long at one stay. Many circumstances may cause it to ebb and flow. This, therefore, is not the essence of religion; which is no other than *humble, gentle, patient love*. I do not know whether all these are not included in that one word, resignation. For the highest lesson our Lord (as man) learned on earth was to say, "Not as I will, but as thou wilt."— May He confirm you more and more!

Yours most affectionately.

To Isaac Andrews
January 4, 1784.

My Dear Brother,

After all I can say you will not conceive what I mean unless the Holy Spirit open your understanding.

Undoubtedly faith is *the work of God;* and yet it is the *duty of man* to believe. And every man may believe *if* he will, though not *when* he will. If he seek faith in the appointed ways, sooner or

272

later the power of the Lord will be present, whereby (1) God works, and by *His* power (2) man believes

In order of thinking God's working goes first; but not in order of time. Believing is the act of the human mind, strengthened by the power of God. What if you should find it now?

Your affectionate brother.

On Perfection
1784

*Controversy over Wesley's doctrine of Christian perfection contin-
ued throughout his life. So once again he wrote a sermon to answer his
critics and explain what Christian perfection is and what it is not. The
reader will notice that this homily incorporates those aspects of his
doctrine that developed as a response to the perfection revival and
schism in the 1760's; specifically, angelic and Adamic perfection. Note
how Wesley correlates involuntary transgressions and Christian perfection. Pay close attention to the objections and Wesley's responses.
Was he successful in answering these objections? Source: Works J
6:411-423.*

Let us go on to perfection.

Hebrews 6:1

The whole sentence runs thus: "Therefore, leaving the principles of the doctrine of Christ, let us go on unto perfection: Not
laying again the foundation of repentance from dead works, and
of faith toward God;" which he had just before termed, "the first
principles of the oracles of God," and "meat fit for babes," for
such as have just tasted that the Lord is gracious.

That the doing of this is a point of the utmost importance, the
Apostle intimates in the next words: "This will we do, if God
permit. For it is impossible for those who were once enlightened,
and have tasted of the good word of God, and the powers of the
world to come, and have fallen away, to renew them again to repentance." As if he had said, If we do not "go on to perfection,"
we are in the utmost danger of "falling away;" and if we do fall
away, it is "impossible," that is, exceeding hard, "to renew us
again to repentance."

In order to make this very important scripture as easy to be
understood as possible, I shall endeavor,

I. To show what perfection is
II. To answer some objections to it

274

On Perfection

III. To expostulate a little with the opposers of it

I. I will endeavor to show what perfection is.

1. And, First, I do not conceive the perfection here spoken of, to be the perfection of angels. As those glorious beings never "left their first estate," never declined from their original perfection, all their native faculties are unimpaired: Their understanding, in particular, is still a lamp of light, their apprehension of all things clear and distinct, and their judgment always true. Hence, though their knowledge is limited, (for they are creatures,) though they are ignorant of innumerable things, yet they are not liable to mistake: Their knowledge is perfect in its kind. And as their affections are all constantly guided by their unerring understanding, so that all their actions are suitable thereto; so they do, every moment, not their own will, but the good and acceptable will of God. Therefore it is not possible for man, whose understanding is darkened, to whom mistake is as natural as ignorance; who cannot think at all, but by the mediation of organs which are weakened and depraved, like the other parts of his corruptible body; it is not possible I say, for men always to think right, to apprehend things distinctly, and to judge truly of them. In consequence hereof, his affections, depending on his understanding, are variously disordered. And his words and actions are influenced, more or less, by the disorder both of his understanding and affections. It follows, that no man, while in the body, can possibly attain to angelic perfection.

2. Neither can any man, while he is in a corruptible body, attain to Adamic perfection. Adam, before his fall, was undoubtedly as pure, as free from sin, as even the holy angels. In like manner, his understanding was as clear as theirs, and his affections as regular. In virtue of this, as he always judged tight, so he was able always to speak and act right. But since man rebelled against God, the case is widely different with him. He is no longer able to avoid falling into innumerable mistakes; consequently, he cannot always avoid wrong affections; neither can he always think, speak,

and act right. Therefore man, in his present state, can no more attain Adamic than angelic perfection.

3. The highest perfection which man can attain, while the soul dwells in the body, does not exclude ignorance, and error, and a thousand other infirmities. Now, from wrong judgments, wrong words and actions will often necessarily flow: And, in some cases, wrong affections also may spring from the same source. I may judge wrong of you; I may think more or less highly of you than I ought to think; and this mistake in my judgment may not only occasion something wrong in my behavior but it may have a still deeper effect; it may occasion something wrong in my affection. From a wrong apprehension, I may love and esteem you either more or less than I ought. Nor can I be freed from liableness to such a mistake, while I remain in a corruptible body. A thousand infirmities, in consequence of this, will attend my spirit, till it returns to God who gave it. And, in numberless instances, it comes short of doing the will of God, as Adam did in paradise. Hence the best of men may say from the heart,

Every moment, Lord, I need
The merit of thy death,

for innumerable violations of the Adamic as well as the angelic law. It is well, therefore, for us, that we are not now under these, but under the law of love. "Love is" now "the fulfilling of the law," which is given to fallen man. This is now, with respect to us, "the perfect law." But even against this, through the present weakness of our understanding, we are continually liable to transgress. Therefore every man living needs the blood of atonement, or be could not stand before God.

4. What is then the perfection of which man is capable while he dwells in a corruptible body? It is the complying with that kind command, "My son, give me thy heart." It is the "loving the Lord his God with all his heart, and with all his soul and with all his

On Perfection

mind." This is the sum of Christian perfection: It is all comprised
in that one word, Love. The first branch of it is the love of God:
And as he that loves God loves his brother also, it is inseparably
connected with the second: "Thou shalt love thy neighbor as thyself:" Thou shalt love every man as thy own soul, as Christ loved
us. "On these two commandments hang all the Law and the
Prophets:" These contain the whole of Christian perfection.

5. Another view of this is given us in those words of the great
Apostle: "Let this mind be in you which was also in Christ Jesus." For although this immediately and directly refers to the humility of our Lord, yet it may be taken in a far more extensive
sense, so as to include the whole disposition of his mind, all his
affections, all his tempers, both toward God and man. Now, it is
certain that as there was no evil affection in him, so no good affection or temper was wanting. So that "whatsoever things are
holy, whatsoever things are lovely," are all included in "the mind
that was in Christ Jesus."

6. St. Paul, when writing to the Galatians, places perfection in yet
another view. It is the one undivided fruit of the Spirit, which he
describes thus: "The fruit of the Spirit is love, joy, peace, long-
suffering gentleness, goodness, fidelity," (so the word should be
translated here,) "meekness, temperance." What a glorious con-
stellation of graces is here! Now, suppose all these things to be
knit together in one, to be united together in the soul of a believer, this is Christian perfection.

7. Again: He writes to the Christians at Ephesus, of "putting on
the new man, which is created after God, in righteousness and
true holiness;" and to the Colossians, of "the new man renewed
after the image of him that created him;" plainly referring to the
words in Genesis, (1:27) "So God created man in his own image." Now, the moral image of God consists (as the Apostle observes) "in righteousness and true holiness." By sin this is totally

277

destroyed. And we never can recover it, till we are "created anew in Christ Jesus." And this is perfection.

8. St. Peter expresses it in a still different manner, though to the same effect: "As he that hath called you is holy, so be ye holy in all manner of conversation." (1 Pet 1:15) According to this Apostle, then, perfection is another name for universal holiness: Inward and outward righteousness: Holiness of life, arising from holiness of heart.

9. If any expressions can be stronger than these, they are those of St. Paul to the Thessalonians (1 Epistle 5:23): "The God of peace himself sanctify you wholly and may the whole of you, the spirit, the soul, and the body," (this is the literal translation,) "be preserved blameless unto the coming of our Lord Jesus Christ."

10. We cannot show this sanctification in a more excellent way, than by complying with that exhortation of the Apostle: "I beseech you, brethren, by the mercies of God, that is present your bodies" (yourselves, your souls and bodies; a part put for the whole, by a common figure of speech) "a living sacrifice unto God;" to whom ye were consecrated many years ago in baptism. When what was then devoted is actually presented to God, then is the man of God perfect.

11. To the same effect St. Peter says, "Ye are a holy priesthood, to offer up spiritual sacrifices, acceptable to God through Jesus Christ" (1 Pet 2:5). But what sacrifices shall we offer now, seeing the Jewish dispensation is at an end? If you have truly presented yourselves to God, you offer up to him continually all your thoughts, and words, and actions, through the Son of his love, as a sacrifice of praise and thanksgiving.

12 Thus you experience that He whose name is called JESUS does not bear that name in vain: That he does, in fact, "save his people from their sins;" the root as well as the branches. And this

salvation from sin, from all sin, is another description of perfection; though indeed it expresses only the least, the lowest branch of it, only the negative part of the great salvation.

II. I proposed, in the Second place, to answer some objections to this scriptural account of perfection.

1. One common objection to it is that there is no promise of it in the word of God. If this were so, we must give it up; we should have no foundation to build upon: For the promises of God is the only sure foundation of our hope. But surely there is a very clear and full promise that we shall all love the Lord our God with all our hearts. So we read, "Then will I circumcise thy heart, and the heart of thy seed, to love the Lord thy God with all thy heart, and with all thy soul" (Dt 30:6). Equally express is the word of our Lord, which is no less a promise, though in the form of a command: "Thou shalt love the Lord thy God with all thy heart, and with all thy soul, and with all thy mind" (Mt 22:37). No words can be more strong than these; no promise can be more express. In like manner, "Thou shalt love thy neighbor as thyself," is as express a promise as a command.

2. And indeed that general and unlimited promise which runs through the whole gospel dispensation, "I will put my laws in their minds, and write them in their hearts," turns all the commands into promises; and, consequently, that among the rest, "Let this mind be in you which was also in Christ Jesus." The command here is equivalent to a promise, and gives us full reason to expect that he will work in us what he requires of us.

3. With regard to the fruit of the Spirit, the Apostle, in affirming, "the fruit of the Spirit is love, joy, peace, longsuffering, gentleness, goodness, fidelity, meekness, temperance," does, in effect, affirm, that the Holy Spirit actually works love, and these other tempers, in those that are led by him. So that here also, we have firm ground to tread upon; this scripture likewise being equiva-

lent to a promise, and assuring us that all these shall be wrought in us, provided we are led by the Spirit.

4. And when the Apostle says to the Ephesians, "Ye have been taught, as the truth is in Jesus," to "be renewed in the spirit of your mind," and to "put on the new man, which is created after God,"—that is, after the image of God, "in righteousness and true holiness" (Eph 4:21-24), he leaves us no room to doubt, but God will thus "renew us in the spirit of our mind," and "create us anew" in the image of God, wherein we were at first created: Otherwise it could not be said, that this is "the truth as it is in Jesus."

5. The command of God, given by St. Peter, "Be ye holy, as he that hath called you is holy, in all manner of conversation," implies a promise that we shall be thus holy, if we are not wanting to ourselves. Nothing can be wanting on God's part: As he has called us to holiness, he is undoubtedly willing, as well as able, to work this holiness in us. For he cannot mock his helpless creatures, calling us to receive what he never intends to give. That he does call us thereto is undeniable; therefore he will give it if we are not disobedient to the heavenly calling.

6. The prayer of St. Paul for the Thessalonians, that God would "sanctify" them throughout, and "that the whole of them, the spirit, the soul, and the body, might be preserved blameless," will undoubtedly be heard in behalf of all the children of God, as well as of those at Thessalonica. Hereby, therefore, all Christians are encouraged to expect the same blessing from "the God of peace;" namely, that they also shall be "sanctified throughout, in spirit, soul, and body;" and that "the whole of them shall be preserved blameless unto the coming of our Lord Jesus Christ."

7. But the great question is, whether there is any promise in Scripture, that we shall be saved from sin. Undoubtedly there is. Such is that promise, "He shall redeem Israel from all his sins;"

On Perfection

exactly answerable to those words of the angel, "He shall save his people from their sins" (Ps 130:8). And surely "he is able to save unto the uttermost them that come unto God through him." Such is that glorious promise given through the Prophet Ezekiel: "Then will I sprinkle clean water upon you, and ye shall be clean: From all your filthiness, and from all your idols, will I cleanse you. A new heart also will I give you, and a new spirit will I put within you: And I will take away the stony heart out of your flesh, and I will give you an heart of flesh. And I will put my Spirit within you, and cause you to walk in my statutes, and ye shall keep my judgments, and do them" (Eze 36:25-27). Such (to mention no more) is that pronounced by Zechariah, "The oath which he sware to our father Abraham, that he would grant unto us, being delivered out of the hand of our enemies," (and such, doubtless, are all our sins,) "to serve him without fear, in holiness and right-eousness before him, all the days of our life" (Lk 1:73-75). The last part of this promise is peculiarly worthy of our observation. Lest any should say, "True, we shall be saved from our sins when we die," that clause is remarkably added, as if on purpose to ob-viate this pretence, all the days of our life. With what modesty then can any one affirm, that none shall enjoy this liberty till death?

8. "But," say some, "this cannot be the meaning of the words; for the thing is impossible." It is impossible to men: But the things impossible with men, are possible with God. "Nay, but this is im-possible in its own nature: For it implies a contradiction, that a man should be saved from all sin while he is in a sinful body."

There is a great deal of force in this objection. And perhaps we allow most of what you contend for. We have already allowed that while we are in the body we cannot be wholly free from mis-take. Notwithstanding all our care, we shall still be liable to judge wrong in many instances. And a mistake in judgment will very frequently occasion a mistake in practice. Nay, a wrong judgment may occasion something in the temper or passions which are not strictly right. It may occasion needless fear or ill-grounded hope,

281

unreasonable love or unreasonable aversion. But all this is no way inconsistent with the perfection above described.

9. You say, "Yes, it is inconsistent with the last article: It cannot consist with salvation from sin."

I answer, It will perfectly well consist with salvation from sin, according to that definition of sin, (which I apprehend to be the scriptural definition of it,) a voluntary transgression of a known law. "Nay, but all transgressions of the law of God, whether voluntary or involuntary, are sin: For St. John says, 'All sin is a transgression of the law.'" True, but he does not say, All transgression of the law is sin. This I deny: Let him prove it that can.

To say the truth, this is a mere strife of words. You say none is saved from sin in your sense of the word; but I do not admit of that sense, because the word is never so taken in Scripture. And you cannot deny the possibility of being saved from sin, in my sense of the word. And this is the sense wherein the word sin is over and over taken in Scripture.

"But surely we cannot be saved from sin, while we dwell in a sinful body." A sinful body? I pray observe, how deeply ambiguous, how equivocal, this expression is! But there is no authority for it in Scripture: The word sinful body is never found there. And as it is totally unscriptural, so it is palpably absurd. For no body or matter of any kind, can be sinful: Spirits alone are capable of sin. Pray in what part of the body should sin lodge? It cannot lodge in the skin, nor in the muscles, or nerves, or veins, or arteries; it cannot be in the bones, any more than in the hair or nails. Only the soul can be the seat of sin.

10. "But does not St. Paul himself say, 'They that are in the flesh cannot please God?'" I am afraid the sound of these words has deceived many unwary souls; who have been told, those words, they that are in the flesh, mean the same as they that are in the body. No; nothing less. The flesh, in this text, no more means the body than it does the soul. Abel, Enoch, Abraham, yea, all that cloud of witnesses recited by St. Paul in the eleventh of the He-

brews, did actually please God while they were in the body, as he himself testifies. The expression, therefore, here means neither more nor less than they that are unbelievers, they that are in their natural state, they that are without God in the world.

11. But let us attend to the reason of the thing. Why cannot the Almighty sanctify the soul while it is in the body? Cannot he sanctify you while you are in this house, as well as in the open air? Can the walls of brick or stone hinder him? No more can these walls of flesh and blood hinder him a moment from sanctifying you throughout. He can just as easily save you from all sin in the body as out of the body.

"But has he promised thus to save us from sin while we are in the body?" Undoubtedly he has: For a promise is implied in every commandment of God: Consequently in that, "Thou shalt love the Lord thy God with all thy heart, and with all thy soul, and with all thy mind." For this and every other commandment is given, not to the dead, but to the living. It is expressed in the words above recited, that we should walk "in holiness before him all the days of our life."

I have dwelt the longer on this, because it is the grand argument of those that oppose salvation from sin; and also, because it has not been so frequently and so fully answered: Whereas the arguments taken from Scripture have been answered a hundred times over.

12. But a still more plausible objection remains, taken from experience; which is, that there are no living witnesses of this salvation from sin. In answer to this, I allow,

(1.) That there are not many. Even in this sense, there are not many fathers. Such is our hardness of heart, such our slowness to believe what both the Prophets and Apostles have spoke, that there are few, exceeding few, true witnesses of the great salvation.

(2.) I allow that there are false witnesses, who either deceive their own souls, and speak of the things they know not, or "speak lies in hypocrisy." And I have frequently wondered that we have not more of both sorts. It is nothing strange, that men of warm imaginations should deceive themselves in this matter. Many do the same with regard to justification: They imagine they are justified, and are not. But though many imagine it falsely, yet there are some that are truly justified. And thus though many imagine they are sanctified, and are not, yet there are some that are really sanctified.

(3.) I allow that some who once enjoyed full salvation have now totally lost it. They once walked in glorious liberty, giving God their whole heart, "rejoicing, evermore, praying without ceasing, and in every thing giving thanks." But it is past. They now are shorn of their strength, and become like other men. Yet perhaps they do not give up their confidence; they still have a sense of his pardoning love. But even this is frequently assaulted by doubts and fears, so that they hold it with a trembling hand.

13. "Nay, this," say some pious and sensible men, "is the very thing which we contend for. We grant, it may please God to make some of his children for a time unspeakably holy and happy. We will not deny, that they may enjoy all the holiness and happiness which you speak of. But it is only for a time: God never designed that it should continue to their lives' end. Consequently, sin is only suspended: It is not destroyed."

This you affirm. But it is a thing of so deep importance, that it cannot be allowed without clear and cogent proof. And where is the proof? We know that, in general, "the gifts and calling of God are without repentance." He does not repent of any gifts which he hath bestowed upon the children of men. And how does the contrary appear, with regard to this particular gift of God? Why should we imagine, that he will make an exception with respect to the most precious of all his gifts on this side heaven? Is he not as able to give it us always, as to give it once? as able to give it for fifty years, as for one day? And how can it be proved, that he is not willing to continue this his lovingkindness? How is this supposition, that he is not willing, consistent with the positive assertion of the Apostle? who, after exhorting the Christians at Thessalonica, and in them all Christians in all ages, to "rejoice evermore, pray without ceasing, and in every thing give thanks,"—immediately adds, (as if on purpose to answer those who denied, not the power, but the will of God to work in them,) "For this is the will of God concerning you in Christ Jesus." Nay, and it is remarkable, that, after he had delivered that glorious promise, (such it properly is,) in the twenty-third verse, "The very God of peace shall sanctify you wholly: And the whole of you," (so it is in the original,) "the spirit, the soul, and the body, shall be preserved blameless unto the coming of the Lord Jesus Christ;" he adds again, "Faithful is he that hath called you, who also will do it." He will not only sanctify you wholly, but will preserve you in that state until he comes to receive you unto himself.

14. Agreeably to this is the plain matter of fact. Several persons have enjoyed this blessing, without any interruption, for many years. Several enjoy it at this day. And not a few have enjoyed it unto their death, as they have declared with their latest breath; calmly witnessing that God had saved them from all sin till their spirit returned to God.

15. As to the whole of the objections taken from experience, I desire it may be observed farther, either the persons objected to have attained Christian perfection, or they have not. If they have not, whatever objections are brought against them strike wide of the mark. For they are not the persons we are talking of: Therefore, whatever they are or do is beside the question. But if they have attained it, if they answer the description given under the

nine preceding articles, no reasonable objection can lie against them. They are superior to all censure; and "every tongue that riseth up against them will they utterly condemn."

16. "But I never saw one," continues the objector, "that answered my idea of perfection." It may be so. And it is probable (as I observed elsewhere) you never will. For your idea includes abundantly too much; even freedom from those infirmities which are not separable from a spirit that is connected with flesh and blood. But if you keep to the account that is given above, and allow for the weakness of human understanding, you may see at this day undeniable instances of genuine, scriptural perfection.

III. 1. It only remains, in the Third place, to expostulate a little with the opposers of this perfection.

Now permit me to ask, Why are you so angry with those who profess to have attained this? and so mad (I cannot give it any softer title) against Christian perfection?—against the most glorious gift which God ever gave to the children of men upon earth? View it in every one of the preceding points of light, and see what it contains that is either odious or terrible; that is calculated to excite either hatred or fear in any reasonable creature.

What rational objection can you have to the loving the Lord your God with all your heart? Why should you be afraid of it? Would it do you any hurt? Would it lessen your happiness, either in this world or the world to come? And why should you be unwilling that others should give him their whole heart? or that they should love their neighbors as themselves?—yea, "as Christ hath loved us?" Is this detestable? Is it the proper object of hatred? Or is it the most amiable thing under the sun? Is it proper to move terror? Is it not rather desirable in the highest degree?

2. Why are you so averse to having in you the whole "mind which was in Christ Jesus?"—all the affections, all the tempers and dispositions, which were in him while he dwelt among men? Why should you be afraid of this? Would it be any worse for you,

were God to work in you this very hour all the mind that was in him? If not, why should you hinder others from seeking this blessing? or be displeased at those who think they have attained it? Is any thing more lovely? any thing more to be desired by every child of man?

3. Why are you averse to having the whole "fruit of the Spirit"— "love, joy, peace, longsuffering, meekness, gentleness, fidelity, goodness, temperance?" Why should you be afraid of having all these planted in your inmost soul? As "against these there is no law," so there cannot be any reasonable objection. Surely nothing is more desirable, than that all these tempers should take deep root in your heart; nay, in the hearts of all that name the name of Christ; yea, of all the inhabitants of the earth.

4. What reason have you to be afraid of, or to entertain any aversion to, the being "renewed in the" whole "image of him that created you?" Is not this more desirable than any thing under heaven? Is it not consummately amiable? What can you wish for in comparison of this, either for your own soul, or for those for whom you entertain the strongest and tenderest affection? And when you enjoy this, what remains but to be "changed from glory to glory, by the Spirit of the Lord?"

5. Why should you be averse to universal holiness, the same thing under another name? Why should you entertain any prejudice against this, or look upon it with apprehension? whether you understand by that term the being inwardly conformed to the whole image and will of God, or an outward behavior in every point suitable to that conformity. Can you conceive any thing more amiable than this? Anything more desirable? Set prejudice aside, and surely you will desire to see it diffused over all the earth.

6. Is perfection (to vary the expression) the being "sanctified throughout, in spirit, soul, and body?" What lover of God and

man can be averse to this, or entertain frightful apprehensions of it? Is it not, in your best moments, your desire to be all of a piece?—all consistent with yourself?—all faith, all meekness, all love? And suppose you were once possessed of this glorious liberty, would not you wish to continue therein?—to be preserved "blameless unto the coming of our Lord Jesus Christ?"

7. For what cause should you that are children of God be averse to, or afraid of, presenting yourselves, your souls and bodies, as a living sacrifice, holy, acceptable to God?—to God your Creator, your Redeemer, your Sanctifier? Can any thing be more desirable than this entire self-dedication to him? And is it not your wish that all mankind should unite in this "reasonable service?" Surely no one can be averse to this, without being an enemy to all mankind. 8. And why should you be afraid of, or averse to, what is naturally implied in this; namely, the offering up all our thoughts, and words, and actions, as a spiritual sacrifice to God, acceptable to him through the blood and intercession of his well beloved Son? Surely you cannot deny that this is good and profitable to men, as well as pleasing to God. Should you not then devoutly pray that both you and all mankind may thus worship him in spirit and in truth?

9. Suffer me to ask one question more. Why should any man of reason and religion be either afraid of, or averse to, salvation from all sin? Is not sin the greatest evil on this side hell? And if so, does it not naturally follow, that an entire deliverance from it is one of the greatest blessings on this side heaven? How earnestly then should it be prayed for by all the children of God! By sin I mean a voluntary transgression of a known law. Are you averse to being delivered from this? Are you afraid of such deliverance? Do you then love sin that you are so unwilling to part with it? Surely no. You do not love either the devil or his works: You rather wish to be totally delivered from them; to have sin rooted out both of your life and your heart.

On Perfection

10. I have frequently observed, and not without surprise, that the opposers of perfection are more vehement against it when it is placed in this view, that in any other whatsoever. They will allow all you say of the love of God and man; of the mind which was in Christ; of the fruit of the Spirit; of the image of God; of universal holiness; of entire self-dedication; of sanctification in spirit, soul, and body; yea, and of the offering up of all our thoughts, words, and actions, as a sacrifice to God;—all this they will allow so we will allow sin, a little sin, to remain in us till death.

11. Pray compare this with that remarkable passage in John Bunyan's *Holy War*. "When Immanuel," says he, "had driven Diabolus and all his forces out of the city of Mansoul, Diabolus preferred a petition to Immanuel, that he might have only a small part of the city. When this was rejected, he begged to have only a little room within the walls." But Immanuel answered, he should have no place in it at all; no, not to rest the sole of his foot.

Had not the good old man forgot himself? Did not the force of truth so prevail over him here as utterly to overturn his own system?—to assert perfection in the clearest manner? For, if this is not salvation from sin, I cannot tell what is.

12. "No," says a great man, "this is the error of errors: I hate it from my heart. I pursue it through all the world with fire and sword." Nay, why so vehement? Do you seriously think there is no error under heaven equal to this? Here is something which I cannot understand. Why are those that oppose salvation from sin (few excepted) so eager, I had almost said, furious? Are you fighting *pro aris et focis*? "for God and your country?" for all you have in the world? for all that is near and dear unto you? for your liberty, your life? In God's name, why are you so fond of sin? What good has it ever done you? what good is it ever likely to do you, either in this world, or in the world to come? And why are you so violent against those that hope for a deliverance from it? Have patience with us, if we are in an error; yea, suffer us to enjoy our error. If we should not attain it, the very expectation of

289

this deliverance gives us present comfort; yea, and ministers strength to resist those enemies which we expect to conquer. If you could persuade us to despair of that victory, we should give over the contest. Now "we are saved by hope:" From this very hope a degree of salvation springs. Be not angry at those who are *felices errore suo*, "happy in their mistake." Else, be their opinion right or wrong, your temper is undeniably sinful. Bear then with us, as we do with you; and see whether the Lord will not deliver us!—whether he is not able, yea, and willing, "to save them to the uttermost that come unto God through him."

On Working Out Our Own Salvation
1785

This is the landmark sermon of Wesley's late period. Though the subject of full salvation is not its central focus, this sermon seeks to correlate his doctrine of perfect love within the larger question of divine grace and human agency. The roots of this homily lie in the Minute's Controversy *with the Calvinists.*

In 1770 Wesley published the Minutes *of the 1770 Conference in which he asserted with strong language the necessity of works for final salvation. The Calvinists were outraged at what they believed was salvation by human merit.[13] Of course, this was not Wesley's intent. An ensuing pamphlet war lasted for several years leading to John Fletcher publishing his famous* Five Checks *against Calvinist antinomianism. Finally, in 1785 Wesley published his mature thoughts in this homily.*

In this sermon Wesley seeks to clarify the roles that divine grace and human agency play in salvation, from the initial spark of spiritual awareness (prevenient grace) to the goal of perfect love (perfecting grace). In the end, all aspects of salvation rest on a synergism of grace and works. This homily deserves a careful reading to grasp how Wesley correlates grace and human agency within his mature perfection theology. Source: Works J 6:506-513.

Work out your own salvation with fear and trembling;
for it is God that worketh in you, both to will and to do
of his good pleasure.

Philippians 2:12-13

1. Some great truths, as the being and attributes of God, and the difference between moral good and evil, were known, in some measure, to the heathen world. The traces of them are to be found in all nations: So that, in some sense, it may be said to every child of man, "He hath showed thee, O man, what is good; even to do justly, to love mercy, and to walk humbly with thy God." With

---

[13] Cf. *John Wesley's Theology of Perfection: Developments in Doctrine & Theological System,* 206-210.

this truth he has, in some measure, "enlightened every one that cometh into the world." And hereby they that "have not the law," that have no written law, "are a law unto themselves." They show "the work of the law,"—the substance of it, though not the letter, "written in their hearts," by the same hand which wrote the commandments on the tables of stone: "Their conscience also bearing them witness," whether they act suitably thereto or not.

2. But there are two grand heads of doctrine, which contain many truths of the most important nature, of which the most enlightened Heathens in the ancient world were totally ignorant; as are also the most intelligent Heathens that are now on the face of the earth; I mean those which relate to the eternal Son of God, and the Spirit of God: To the Son, giving himself to be "a propitiation for the sins of the world;" and to the Spirit of God, renewing men in that image of God wherein they were created. For after all the pains which ingenious and learned men have taken (that great man, Chevalier Ramsay, in particular) to find some resemblance of these truths in the immense rubbish of heathen authors, the resemblance is so exceeding faint, as not to be discerned but by a very lively imagination. Beside that, even this resemblance, faint as it was, is only to be found in the discourses of a very few; and those were the most improved and deeply-thinking men, in their several generations; while the innumerable multitudes that surrounded them were little better for the knowledge of the philosophers, but remained as totally ignorant even of these capital truths as were the beasts that perish.

3. Certain it is, that these truths were never known to the vulgar, the bulk of mankind, to the generality of men in any nation, till they were brought to light by the gospel. Notwithstanding a spark of knowledge glimmering here and there, the whole earth was covered with darkness, till the Sun of righteousness arose and scattered the shades of night. Since this day-spring from on high has appeared, a great light hath shined unto those who, till then, sat in darkness and in the shadow of death. And thousands of

them in every age have known, "that God so loved the world, as to give his only Son, to the end that whosoever believeth on him should not perish, but have everlasting life." And being entrusted with the oracles of God, they have known that God hath also given us his Holy Spirit, who "worketh in us both to will and to do of his good pleasure."

4. How remarkable are those words of the Apostle, which precede these! "Let this mind be in you, which was also in Christ Jesus: Who, being in the form of God,"—the incommunicable nature of God from eternity, "counted it no act of robbery,"—(that is the precise meaning of the word,) no invasion of any other's prerogative, but his own unquestionable right, "to be equal with God." The word implies both the fullness and the supreme height of the Godhead; to which are opposed the two words, he emptied and he humbled himself. He "emptied himself" of that divine fullness, veiled his fullness from the eyes of men and angels; "taking," and by that very act emptying himself, "the form of a servant; being made in the likeness of man," a real man, like other men. "And being found in fashion as a man,"—a common man, without any peculiar beauty or excellency, "he humbled himself" to a still greater degree, "becoming obedient" to God, though equal with him, "even unto death; yea, the death of the cross:" The greatest instance both of humiliation and obedience.

Having proposed the example of Christ, the Apostle exhorts them to secure the salvation which Christ hath purchased for them: "Wherefore, work out your own salvation with fear and trembling: For it is God that worketh in you both to will and to do of his good pleasure."

In these comprehensive words we may observe,

I. That grand truth, which ought never to be out of our remembrance: "It is God that worketh in us both to will and to do of his own good pleasure."
II. The improvement we ought to make of it: "Work out your own salvation with fear and trembling."

III. The connexion between them: "It is God that worketh in you;" therefore, "work out your own salvation."

I. 1. First. We are to observe that great and important truth which ought never to be out of our remembrance: "It is God that worketh in us both to will and to do of his *good pleasure*." The meaning of these words may be made more plain by a small transposition of them: "It is God that of his good pleasure, worketh in you both to will and to do." This position of the words, connecting the phrase, of his *good pleasure*, with the word *worketh*, removes all imagination of merit from man, and gives God the whole glory of his work. Otherwise, we might have had some room for boasting, as if it were our own desert, some goodness in us, or some good thing done by us, which first moved God to work. But this expression cuts off all such vain conceits, and clearly shows his motive to work lay wholly in himself, in his own mere grace, in his unmerited mercy.

2. It is by this alone he is impelled to work in man both to will and to do. The expression is capable of two interpretations; both of which are unquestionably true. First, to will, may include the whole of inward, to do, the whole of outward, religion. And if it be thus understood, it implies, that it is God that worketh both inward and outward holiness. Secondly, to will, may imply every good desire; to do, whatever results therefrom. And then the sentence means, God breathes into us every good desire, and brings every good desire to good effect.

3. The original words, to thelein and to energein, seem to favor the latter construction: to thelein, which we render to will, plainly including every good desire, whether relating to our tempers, words, or actions; to inward or outward holiness. And to energein, which we render to do, manifestly implies all that power from on high, all that energy which works in us every right disposition, and then furnishes us for every good word and work.

294

4. Nothing can so directly tend to hide pride from man as a deep, lasting conviction of this. For if we are thoroughly sensible that we have nothing which we have not received, how can we glory as if we had not received it? If we know and feel that the very first motion of good is from above, as well as the power which conducts it to the end; if it is God that not only infuses every good desire, but that accompanies and follows it, else it vanishes away; then it evidently follows, that "he who glorieth" must "glory in the Lord."

II. 1. Proceed we now to the Second point: If God worketh in you, then work out your own salvation. The original word, rendered work out, implies the doing a thing thoroughly. Your own; for you yourselves must do this, or it will be left undone for ever. Your own salvation: Salvation begins with what is usually termed (and very properly) *preventing grace*; including the first wish to please God, the first dawn of light concerning his will, and the first slight transient conviction of having sinned against him. All these imply some tendency toward life; some degree of salvation; the beginning of a deliverance from a blind, unfeeling heart, quite insensible of God and the things of God. Salvation is carried on by *convincing grace*, usually in Scripture termed *repentance*; which brings a larger measure of self-knowledge, and a farther deliverance from the heart of stone. Afterwards we experience the proper Christian salvation; whereby, "through grace," we "are saved by faith;" consisting of those two grand branches, *justification* and *sanctification*. By justification we are saved from the guilt of sin, and restored to the favour of God; by sanctification we are saved from the power and root of sin, and restored to the image of God. All experience, as well as Scripture, show this salvation to be both instantaneous and gradual. It begins the moment we are justified, in the *holy, humble, gentle, patient love* of God and man. It gradually increases from that moment, as "a grain of mustard seed, which, at first, is the least of all seeds," but afterwards puts forth large branches, and becomes a great tree; till, in another instant, the heart is cleansed from all sin, and filled with pure love to God and man. But even that love increases more and more, till we "grow up in all things into Him that is our Head;" till we attain "the measure of the stature of the fullness of Christ."

2. But how are we to *work out* this salvation? The Apostle answers, "With fear and trembling." There is another passage of St. Paul, wherein the same expression occurs, which may give light to this: "Servants, obey your masters according to the flesh,"— according to the present state of things, although sensible that in a little time the servant will be free from his master, "with fear and trembling." This is a proverbial expression, which cannot be understood literally. For what master could bear, much less require, his servant to stand trembling and quaking before him? And the following words utterly exclude this meaning: "In singleness of heart;" with a single eye to the will and providence of God; "not with eye-service, as men-pleasers; but as servants of Christ, doing the will of God from the heart;" doing whatever they do as the will of God, and, therefore, with their might. (Eph 6:5, &c.) It is easy to see that these strong expressions of the Apostle clearly imply two things: First, that everything be done with the utmost earnestness of spirit, and with all care and caution: (Perhaps more directly referring to the former word, meta phobos, with fear:) Secondly, that it be done with the utmost diligence, speed, punctuality, and exactness; not improbably referring to the latter word, meta tromos, with trembling.

3. How easily may we transfer this to the business of life, the working out our own salvation! With the same temper, and in the same manner, that Christian servants serve their masters that are upon earth, let other Christians labour to serve their Master that is in heaven; that is, First, with the utmost earnestness of spirit, with all possible care and caution; and, Secondly, with the utmost diligence, speed, punctuality, and exactness.

4. But what are the steps which the Scriptures direct us to take, in the working out of our own salvation? The Prophet Isaiah gives

us a general answer, touching the first steps which we are to take: "Cease to do evil; learn to do well." If ever you desire that God should work in you that faith whereof cometh both present and eternal salvation, by the grace already given fly from all sin as from the face of a serpent; carefully avoid every evil word and work; yea, abstain from all appearance of evil. And "learn to do well:" Be zealous of good works, of works of piety, as well as works of mercy; family prayer, and crying to God in secret. Fast in secret, and "your Father which seeth in secret, he will reward you openly." "Search the Scriptures:" Hear them in public, read them in private, and meditate therein. At every opportunity, be a partaker of the Lord's Supper. "Do this in remembrance" of him; and he will meet you at his own table. Let your conversation be with the children of God; and see that it "be in grace, seasoned with salt." As ye have time, do good unto all men; to their souls and to their bodies. And herein "be ye steadfast, unmovable, always abounding in the work of the Lord." It then only remains, that ye deny yourselves and take up your cross daily. Deny yourselves every pleasure which does not prepare you for taking pleasure in God, and willingly embrace every means of drawing near to God, though it be a cross, though it be grievous to flesh and blood. Thus when you have redemption in the blood of Christ, you will "go on to perfection;" till "walking in the light as he is in the light," you are enabled to testify, that "he is faithful and just," not only to "forgive" your "sins," but to "cleanse" you "from all unrighteousness."

III. 1. "But," say some, "what connexion is there between the former and the latter clause of this sentence? Is there not rather a flat opposition between the one and the other? If it is God that worketh in us both to will and to do, what need is there of our working? Does not His working thus supersede the necessity of our working at all? Nay, does it not render our working impracticable, as well as unnecessary? For if we allow that God does all, what is there left for us to do?"

2. Such is the reasoning of flesh and blood. And, at first hearing, it is exceeding plausible. But it is not solid; as will evidently appear, if we consider the matter more deeply. We shall then see there is no opposition between these, "God works; therefore, do ye work;" but, on the contrary, the closest connexion; and that in two respects. For, First, God works; therefore you *can* work: Secondly, God works, therefore you *must* work.

3. First. God worketh in you; therefore, you *can* work: Otherwise it would be impossible. If he did not work, it would be impossible for you to work out your own salvation. "With man this is impossible," saith our Lord, "for a rich man to enter into the kingdom of heaven." Yea, it is impossible for any man, for any that is born of a woman, unless God work in him. Seeing all men are by nature, not only sick, but "dead in trespasses and in sins," it is not possible for them to do anything well till God raises them from the dead. It was impossible for Lazarus to come forth, till the Lord had given him life. And it is equally impossible for us to come out of our sins, yea, or to make the least motion toward it, till He who hath all power in heaven and earth calls our dead souls into life.

4. Yet this is no excuse for those who continue in sin, and lay the blame upon their Maker, by saying, "It is God only that must quicken us; for we cannot quicken our own souls." For allowing that all the souls of men are dead in sin by *nature*, this excuses none, seeing there is no man that is in a state of mere nature; there is no man, unless he has quenched the Spirit, that is wholly void of the grace of God. No man living is entirely destitute of what is vulgarly called *natural conscience*. But this is not natural: It is more properly termed, *preventing grace*. Every man has a greater or less measure of this, which waiteth not for the call of man. Every one has, sooner or later, good desires; although the generality of men stifle them before they can strike deep root, or produce any considerable fruit. Every one has some measure of that light, some faint glimmering ray, which, sooner or later,

more or less, enlightens every man that cometh into the world. And every one, unless he be one of the small number whose conscience is seared as with a hot iron, feels more or less uneasy when he acts contrary to the light of his own conscience. So that no man sins because he has not grace, but because he does not use the grace which he hath.

5. Therefore, inasmuch as God works in you, you are now able to work out your own salvation. Since he worketh in you of his own good pleasure, without any merit of yours, both to will and to do, it is possible for you to fulfil all righteousness. It is possible for you to "love God, because he hath first loved us;" and to "walk in love," after the pattern of our great Master. We know, indeed, that word of his to be absolutely true: "Without me ye can do nothing." But, on the other hand, we know, every believer can say, "I can do all things through Christ that strengtheneth me."

6. Meantime let us remember that God has joined these together in the experience of every believer; and therefore we must take care, not to imagine they are ever to be put asunder.

We must beware of that mock humility which teacheth us to say, in excuse for our willful disobedience, "O, I can do nothing!" and stops there, without once naming the grace of God. Pray, think twice. Consider what you say. I hope you wrong yourself; for if it be really true that you can do nothing, then you have no faith. And if you have not faith, you are in a wretched condition: You are not in a state of salvation. Surely it is not so. You can do something, through Christ strengthening you. Stir up the spark of grace which is now in you, and he will give you more grace.

7. Secondly. God worketh in you; therefore, you *must* work: You must be "workers together with him," (they are the very words of the Apostle,) otherwise he will cease working. The general rule on which his gracious dispensations invariably proceed is this: "Unto him that hath shall be given: But from him that hath

not,"—that does not improve the grace already given, "shall he taken away what he assuredly hath." (So the words ought to be rendered.) Even St. Augustine, who is generally supposed to favour the contrary doctrine, makes that just remark, *Qui fecit nos sine nobis, non salvabit nos sine nobis*: "He that made us without ourselves, will not save us without ourselves." He will not save us unless we "save ourselves from this untoward generation;" unless we ourselves "fight the good fight of faith, and lay hold on eternal life;" unless we "agonize to enter in at the strait gate," "deny ourselves, and take up our cross daily," and labour by every possible means to "make our own calling and election sure."

8. "Labour" then, brethren, "not for the meat that perisheth, but for that which endureth to everlasting life." Say with our blessed Lord, though in a somewhat different sense, "My Father worketh hitherto, and I work." In consideration that he still worketh in you, be never "weary of well doing." Go on, in virtue of the grace of God, preventing, accompanying, and following you, in "the work of faith, in the patience of hope, and the labour of love." "Be ye steadfast and immovable, always abounding in the work of the Lord." And "the God of peace, who brought again from the dead the great Shepherd of his sheep," (Jesus,) "make you perfect in every good work to do his will, working in you what is well-pleasing in his sight, through Jesus Christ; to whom be glory for ever and ever!"

Instantaneous & Gradual Perfection
1785-1786

Here is more counsel from the elderly Wesley to seekers of pure love. Source: Telford.

To George Gibbon
April 9, 1785.

Dear George,
    What you said was exactly right, the work of God is undoubtedly instantaneous with regard to sanctification as well as justification, and it is no objection at all that the work is gradual also. Whatever others do, it is our duty strongly and explicitly to exhort the believers to go on to perfection, and encourage them to expect perfect love by *simple faith*, and consequently to expect it *now*. This is the preaching which God always has blessed, and which He always will bless to those that are upright of heart.
    I am, dear George,

Your affectionate brother

To Mary Cooke
September 24, 1785

My Dear Sister,
    It is highly probable my letter to you was intercepted by some person of the same name, who, opened it (likely by a mistake) was afterwards ashamed to send it you. However, as you have now favored me better information, I hope there will be no such mistake the time to come. But I beg, when you write to do not write as to a stranger, but a friend. Be not afraid me because I have lived so much longer than you. I nothing upon that account, but wish to stand upon ground with you and to converse without either disguise reserve. I love you all three and not a little, especially your sisters spoke so freely to me; yet I do not say in the

301

same degree. There is a mildness and sweetness in your spirit, such as I wish to find in one that is more to me than a common friend. Not that I impute this to nature; whatever is truly amiable is not of nature, but from a higher principle. Cultivate this, my dear friend, to the uttermost. Still learn of Him who was meek and lowly in heart. Oh, what a blessing it is to be little and mean and vile in our own eyes! You are an amiable woman, it is true; but still you are a sinner, born to die! You are an immortal spirit come forth from God and speedily returning to Him. You know well that one thing, and one only, is needful for you upon earth - to ensure a better portion, to recover the favor and image of God. The former by His grace you have recovered; you have tasted of the love of God. See that you cast it not away. See that you hold fast the beginning of your confidence steadfast unto the end! And how soon may you be made a partaker of sanctification! And not only by a slow and insensible growth in grace, but by the power of the Highest overshadowing you in a moment, in the twinkling of an eye, so as utterly to abolish sin and to renew you in His whole image! If you are simple of heart, if you are willing to receive the heavenly gift, as a little child, without reasoning, why may you not receive it now? He is nigh that sanctifieth; He is with you; He is knocking at the door of your heart!

> *Come in, my Lord, come in,*
> *And seize her for Thine own*

This is the wish of, my dear friend,

Yours in tender affection

To Ann Bolton
December 15, 1786

My Dear Nancy,

There can be no possible reason to doubt concerning the happiness of that child. He did fear God, and according to his circumstances work righteousness. This is the essence of religion, according to St. Peter. His soul, therefore, was 'darkly safe with God,' although he was only under the Jewish Dispensation.

When the Son of Man shall come in his glory and assign every man his own reward, that reward will undoubtedly be proportioned, first to our inward holiness, our likeness to God, secondly to our works, and thirdly to our sufferings; therefore for whatever you suffer in time, you will be an unspeakable gainer in eternity. Many of your sufferings, perhaps the greatest part, are now past; but the joy is to come—Look up, my dear friend, look up, and see the Crown before you! A little longer, and you shall drink of the rivers of pleasure that flow at God's right hand for evermore.

My dear Nancy, Adieu!

To Samuel Mitchell
December 17, 1786

My Dear Brother,

You have great reason to praise God for his marvelous works, and to take care that you do not grieve His Holy Spirit by taking any glory to yourself. But I see a danger which you are not aware of. Many in England have thought they attained to something higher than loving God with all their hearts. But this all came to nothing. It is a snare of the Devil. I wish you could ask Dr. Crommelin's advice what kind of truss you should wear. Write to Mr. Rogers concerning a fourth preacher.

I am, dear Sammy,

Yours affectionately.

Degrees of Faith
1788

In the following sermon excerpts Wesley presents his mature ordo
salutis, *grounded on the principle of degrees of faith. In the 1740's
Wesley divided mankind into three states: natural, legal, and evangelical. The evangelical state was further divided into child, adolescent,
and adult. But by the 1780's his doctrine of prevenient grace took on a
larger role in shaping his thought and theology. Wesley now realized
the faith journey involves even more stages of spiritual development.
Perfect love is now placed within a larger framework of spiritual
growth. Source: Works J 7:195, 196-200, 236-238.*

Now faith is the evidence of things not seen.

Hebrews 11:1

Homily: On Faith

But what is Faith? It is a divine "evidence and conviction of
things not seen;" of things which are not seen now, whether they
are visible or invisible in their own nature. Particularly, it is a divine evidence and conviction of God, and of the things of God.
This is the most comprehensive definition of faith that ever was
or can be given; as including every species of faith, from the
lowest to the highest:

1. The lowest sort of faith, if it be any faith at all, is that of a *Materialist*, a man who, like the late Lord Kames, believes there is
nothing but matter in the universe. I say, if it be any faith at all;
for, properly speaking, it is not. It is not "an evidence or conviction of God," for they do not believe there is any; neither is it "a
conviction of things not seen," for they deny the existence of
such.

2. The Second sort of faith is the faith of a *Deist*. I mean, one
who believes there is a God, distinct from matter; but does not

304

believe the Bible. Of these we may observe two sorts. One sort are mere beasts in human shape, wholly under the power of the basest passions, and having "a downright appetite to mix with mud." Other Deists are, in most respects, rational creatures, though unhappily prejudiced against Christianity: Most of these believe the being and attributes of God; they believe that God made and governs the world; and that the soul does not die with the body, but will remain for ever in a state of happiness or misery.

3. The next sort of faith is the faith of *Heathens*, with which I join that of *Mahometans*. I cannot but prefer this before the faith of the Deists; because, though it embraces nearly the same objects, yet they are rather to be pitied than blamed for the narrowness of their faith. And their not believing the whole truth, is not owing to want of sincerity, but merely to want of light. When one asked Chicali, an old Indian Chief, "Why do not you red men know as much as us white men?" he readily answered, "Because you have the great Word, and we have not."

4. It cannot be doubted, but this plea will avail for millions of modern Heathens. Inasmuch as to them little is given, of them little will be required. As to the ancient Heathens, millions of them likewise were savages. No more therefore will be expected of them, than the living up to the light they had. But many of them, especially in the civilized nations, we have great reason to hope, although they lived among Heathens, yet were quite of another spirit; being taught of God, by his inward voice, all the essentials of true religion. Yea, and so was that Mahometan, and Arabian, who, a century or two ago, wrote the Life of *Hai Ebn Yokdan*. The story seems to be feigned; but it contains all the principles of pure religion and undefiled.

5. But, in general, we may surely place the faith of a *Jew* above that of a Heathen or Mahometan. By Jewish faith, I mean, the faith of those who lived between the giving of the law and the

coming of Christ. These, that is, those that were serious and sincere among them, believed all that is written in the Old Testament. In particular, they believed that, in the fulness of time, the Messiah would appear, "to finish the transgression, to make an end of sin, and bring in everlasting righteousness."

6. It is not so easy to pass any judgment concerning the faith of our modern Jews. It is plain, "the veil is still upon their hearts" when Moses and the Prophets are read. The god of this world still hardens their hearts, and still blinds their eyes, "lest at any time the light of the glorious gospel" should break in upon them. So that we may say of this people, as the Holy Ghost said to their forefathers, "The heart of this people is waxed gross, and their ears are dull of hearing, and their eyes have they closed; lest they should see with their eyes, and hear with their ears, and understand with their hearts, and should be converted, and I should heal them" (Acts 28:27). Yet it is not our part to pass sentence upon them, but to leave them to their own Master.

7. I need not dwell upon the faith of *John the Baptist*, the faith of the *Roman Catholics*, in general, seems to be above that of the ancient Jews. If most of these are volunteers in faith, believing more than God has revealed, it cannot be denied that they believe all which God has revealed, as necessary to salvation. In this we rejoice on their behalf. We are glad that none of those new Articles, which they added, at the Council of Trent, "to the faith once delivered to the saints," does so materially contradict any of the ancient Articles, as to render them of no effect.

8. The faith of the *Protestants*, in general, embraces only those truths as necessary to salvation, which are clearly revealed in the oracles of God. Whatever is plainly declared in the Old and New Testament is the object of their faith. They believe neither more nor less than what is manifestly contained in, and provable by, the Holy Scriptures. The word of God is "a lantern to their feet, and a light in all their paths." They dare not, on any pretence, go

from it, to the right hand or to the left. The written word is the whole and sole rule of their faith, as well as practice. They believe whatsoever God has declared, and profess to do whatsoever he hath commanded. This is the proper faith of Protestants: By this they will abide, and no other.

9. Hitherto faith has been considered chiefly as an evidence and conviction of such or such truths. And this is the sense wherein it is taken at this day in every part of the Christian world. But, in the mean time, let it be carefully observed, (for eternity depends upon it,) that neither the faith of a Roman Catholic, nor that of a Protestant, if it contains no more than this, no more than the embracing such and such truths, will avail any more before God, than the faith of a Mahometan or a Heathen; yea, of a Deist or Materialist. For can this "faith save him?" Can it save any man either from sin or from hell? No more than it could save Judas Iscariot: No more than it could save the devil and his angels; all of whom are convinced that every tittle of Holy Scripture is true.

10. But what is the faith which is properly saving; which brings eternal salvation to all those that keep it to the end? It is such a divine conviction of God, and the things of God, as, even in its *infant state*, enables every one that possesses it to "fear God and work righteousness." And whosoever, in every nation, believes thus far, the Apostle declares, is "accepted of him." He actually is, at that very moment, in a state of acceptance. But he is at present only a *servant* of God, not properly a son. Meantime, let it be well observed, that "the wrath of God" no longer "abideth on him."

11. Indeed, nearly fifty years ago, when the Preachers, commonly called Methodists, began to preach that grand scriptural doctrine, salvation by faith, they were not sufficiently apprized of the difference between a *servant* and a *child* of God. They did not clearly understand, that even one "who feareth God, and worketh righteousness, is accepted of him." In consequence of this, they

were apt to make sad the hearts of those whom God had not made sad. For they frequently asked those who feared God, "Do you know that your sins are forgiven?" And upon their answering, "No," immediately replied, "Then you are a child of the devil." No; that does not follow. It might have been said, (and it is all that can be said with propriety,) "Hitherto you are only a servant, you are not a child of God. You have already great reason to praise God that he has called you to his honourable service. Fear not. Continue crying unto him, 'and you shall see greater things than these.'"

12. And, indeed, unless the servants of God halt by the way, they will receive the adoption of sons. They will receive the faith of the *children* of God, by his revealing his only begotten Son in their hearts. Thus, the faith of a child is, properly and directly, a divine conviction, whereby every child of God is enabled to testify, "The life that I now live, I live by faith in the Son of God, who loved me, and gave himself for me." And whosoever hath this, the Spirit of God witnesseth with his spirit, that he is a child of God. So the Apostle writes to the Galatians: "Ye are the sons of God by faith. And because ye are sons, God hath sent forth the Spirit of his Son into your hearts, crying, Abba, Father;" that is, giving you a childlike confidence in him, together with a kind affection toward him. This then it is, that (if St. Paul was taught of God, and wrote as he was moved by the Holy Ghost) properly constitutes the difference between a servant of God, and a child of God. "He that believeth," as a child of God, "hath the witness in himself." This the servant hath not. Yet let no man discourage him; rather, lovingly exhort him to expect it every moment...

Homily: On The Discoveries of Faith

14. Exhort him (believer) to press on, by all possible means, till he passes "from faith to faith;" from the faith of a *servant* to the faith of a *son*; from the spirit of bondage unto fear, to the spirit of

childlike love: He will then have "Christ revealed in his heart," enabling him to testify, "The life that I now live in the flesh, I live by faith in the Son of God, who loved me, and gave himself for me,"—the proper voice of a child of God. He will then be "born of God;" inwardly changed by the mighty power of God, from "an earthly, sensual, devilish" mind, to the "mind which was in Christ Jesus." He will experience what St. Paul means by those remarkable words to the Galatians, "Ye are the sons of God by faith; and because ye are sons, God hath sent forth the Spirit of his Son into your hearts, crying, Abba, Father." "He that believeth," as a son, (as St. John observes,) "hath the witness in himself." "The Spirit itself witnesses with his spirit, that he is a child of God." "The love of God is shed abroad in his heart by the Holy Ghost which is given unto him."

15. But many doubts and fears may still remain, even in a child of God, while he is weak in faith; while he is in the number of those whom St. Paul terms "babes in Christ." But when his faith is strengthened, when he receives faith's abiding impression, realizing things to come; when he has received the abiding witness of the Spirit, doubts and fears vanish away. He then enjoys the plerophory, or "full assurance, of faith;" excluding all doubt, and all "fear that hath torment." To those whom he styles *young men,* St. John says, "I have written unto you, young men, because ye are strong, and the word of God abideth in you, and ye have overcome the wicked one." These, the Apostle observes in the other verse, had "the word of God abiding in them." It may not improbably mean the pardoning word, the word which spake all their sins forgiven; in consequence of which, they have the consciousness of the divine favour without any intermission.

16. To these more especially we may apply the exhortation of the Apostle Paul: "Leaving the first principles of the doctrine of Christ," namely, repentance and faith, "let us go on unto perfection." But in what sense are we to leave those principles? Not absolutely; for we are to retain both one and the other, the knowl-

edge of ourselves, and the knowledge of God, unto our lives' end: But only comparatively; not fixing, as we did at first, our whole attention upon them; thinking and talking perpetually of nothing else, but either repentance or faith. But what is the perfection here spoken of? It is not only a deliverance from doubts and fears, but from sin; from all inward as well as outward sin; from evil desires, and evil tempers, as well as from evil words and works. Yea, and it is not only a negative blessing, a deliverance from all evil dispositions, implied in that expression, "I will circumcise thy heart;" but a positive one likewise; even the planting all good dispositions in their place; clearly implied in that other expression, "To love the Lord your God with all your heart, and with all your soul."

17. These are they to whom the Apostle John gives the venerable title of *Fathers*, who "have known him that is from the beginning;" the eternal Three-One God. One of these expresses himself thus: "I bear about with me an experimental verity and a plenitude of the presence of the ever-blessed Trinity." And those who are fathers in Christ, generally, though I believe not always, enjoy the plerophory, or "full assurance, of hope;" having no more doubt of reigning with him in glory, than if they already saw him coming in the clouds of heaven. But this does not prevent their continually increasing in the knowledge and love of God. While they "rejoice evermore, pray without ceasing, and in everything give thanks," they pray in particular, that they may never cease to watch, to deny themselves, to take up their cross daily, to fight the good fight of faith; and against the world, the devil, and their own manifold infirmities; till they are able to "comprehend, with all saints, what is the length, and breadth, and height, and depth, and to know that love of Christ which passeth knowledge;" yea, to "be filled with all the fullness of God."

Counsel for One Made Perfect
1787-1790

Wesley was a firm believer in continued growth following the believer's perfection in love. In the following letters he counsels Jeannie Bisson to reach for even greater heights in Christ and the Holy Trinity. From what he counsels Miss Bisson we can glean insights into Wesley's mature understanding of this growth process. Source: Works J 4:395; Letters: Telford.

Journal

Sat. (August) 25 (1787) — Having now leisure, I finished a sermon on discerning the "Signs of the Times." This morning I had a particular conversation (as I had once or twice before) with Jeannie Bisson of this town; such a young woman as I have hardly seen elsewhere. She seems to be wholly devoted to God, and to have constant communion with him. She has a clear and strong understanding; and I cannot perceive the least tincture of enthusiasm. I am afraid she will not live long. I am amazed at the grace of God which is in her: I think she is far beyond Madame Guion, in deep communion with God; and I doubt whether I have found her fellow in England. Precious as my time is, it would have been worth my while to come to Jersey, had it been only to see this prodigy of grace.

Letters

September 7, 1787

My Dear Sister,

I have thought of you much since I had the satisfaction of conversing with you: And I will tell you every thought that passed through my mind, as I wish always to do. It seems to me

311

that our blessed Lord is willing to show all the power of his grace in you; even his power of saving to the uttermost those that come unto God through Him. But there is a mountain that stands in the way; and how you will get over it, I know not: I mean pride. O my sister, what can save you from this, but the mighty power of God! I almost tremble for you. If you give way to it, yea, but a little, your grace will wither away. But still, that God whom you serve is able to deliver you; and He really will, if you continue instant in prayer. That other temptation which did formerly beset you, I trust will assault you no more: Or, if it should, you are now better prepared for it; and you will know in whom your strength lieth.

When you have opportunity, my dear Jenny, write freely to,

Your affectionate brother

December 17, 1787

My Dear Sister,

I love to hear from you; especially when you send me that good news that you still stand fast in the liberty wherewith Christ has made you free. I have a good hope that you will never lose any of the things which He has wrought in you, but that you will receive a full reward! Do you always find a clear sense of the presence of the ever blessed Trinity? Are you enabled to rejoice evermore? In what sense do you pray without ceasing? And can you in everything give thanks; seeing it is the will of God concerning you in Christ Jesus? What you speak of your communion with Him comforts my heart. I love to read, to hear any part of your experience. If I doubted of anything you say, I would tell you so. I want to know everything wherein I can serve you. My dear Jenny, do not forget to pray for,

Yours

Counsel for One Made Perfect

October 2, 1788

My Dear Sister,

It gives me much pleasure to find you are still happy in God, leaning upon your Beloved. O may you increase therein more and more! May you be more and more holy, and you will be more and more happy! This I long for, even your perfection; your growing up in all things into Him that is our Head. O may you never endeavour:

> *Love's all-sufficient sea to raise*
> *By drops of creature-happiness!*

I sent you a little book or two by Mr. Clarke. If I can be of any service to you in anything, it would be an unspeakable satisfaction to,
My dear sister,
Yours affectionately

November 3, 1789

My Dear Sister,

When I heard Mr. Brackenbury give the first account of you, I had a great desire of having some conversation with you; and a much greater when I read the account of your experience which you had given him. How is it with you now, my dear friend? Is your soul now as much alive as ever? Do you still find deep and uninterrupted communion with God; with the Three-One God; with the Father, and the Son, through the Spirit? Do not you find anything deaden or flatten your soul? Do you now rejoice evermore? Do you pray without ceasing? Are you always conscious of the loving presence of God? Do you in everything give thanks, knowing it is the will of God concerning you in Christ Jesus?

Are you now as zealous of good works, and as active therein, as ever you was? And do you now live in eternity, and walk in eternity; and experience the life that is hid with Christ in God.

Have you one or more children? With whom do you now maintain the most intimate acquaintance? Do you sometimes visit our friends in Guernsey? Are there any books which you have a mind to have? Or is there anything else in which I can serve you? This would at all times be a pleasure to,

Yours very affectionately

February 13, 1790

My Dear Sister,

I love to see your name at the bottom of a letter; especially when it brings me the good news, that your spirit is still rejoicing in God your Saviour. My sight is so far decayed, that I cannot well read a small print by candlelight; but I can write almost as well as ever I could: And it does me no harm, but rather good, to preach once or twice a day. A few days since, I had a letter from one of our sisters in Scotland, whose experience agrees much with yours; only she goes farther: She speaks of being "taken up into heaven, surrounded with the blessed Trinity, and let into God the Father." I commend you to his care; and am,

Yours most affectionately

November 9, 1790

My Dear Sister,

How unsearchable are the counsels of God! How little are we able to account for his ways! When I saw the wonderful manner wherein He had dealt with you from your early years, when I talked with you in Jersey, and when I conversed more largely with you in Guernsey, I thought He was preparing you for a large sphere of action. Surely you was not then designed to be shut up in a little cottage, and fully taken up with domestic cares! I was in hopes of seeing all the graces which He had given you employed in far other things. However, although I cannot deny that you are now acting in a lower sphere than was originally designed you, yet I trust you still enjoy communion with God the Father, and

Counsel for One Made Perfect

his Son Jesus Christ. I hope you are still sensible, wherever you go, of the presence of the ever-blessed Trinity; and that you continually enjoy that loving-kindness which is better than life itself.

I wish you would inform me of your present outward and inward state. Have you all things that are needful for the body? Do your brethren and sisters treat you with tender affection, or with coldness? Are the Preachers free and loving to you? Is your soul as much alive as ever? Are the consolations of the Holy One small with you; or are they as frequent and as plentiful as ever? Write as particularly as you can,

Yours most affectionately

On The Wedding Garment
1790

This homily was written one year before Wesley's death and sum-marizes his core conviction that holiness is the "only qualification for glory." Only holiness fits one to enter God's holy celestial presence. The reader should compare what Wesley writes here with his early per-spective on ars moriendi. *Source: Works J 7:311-317.*

How camest thou in hither, not having a wedding garment?
Matthew 22:12

1. In the verses preceding the text we read, "After these things, Jesus spake to them again in parables, and said, A certain king made a supper for his son. And when the king came in to see the guests, he saw one who had not on a wedding garment. And he saith unto him, Friend, how camest thou in hither not having a wedding garment? And he was speechless. Then said the king to the servants, Bind him hand and foot, and cast him into outer darkness; there shall be weeping and gnashing of teeth."

2. Upon this parable one of our most celebrated expositors com-ments in the following manner:—"The design of this parable is to set forth that gracious supply made by God to men in and by the preaching of the gospel. To invite them to this, God sent forth his servants, the Prophets and Apostles."—And on these words, "Why camest thou in hither not having a wedding garment?" he proceeds thus: "The punishment of whom ought not to discour-age us, or make us turn our backs upon the holy ordinances." Certainly it ought not; but nothing of this kind can be inferred from this parable, which has no reference to the ordinances, any more than to baptism and marriage. And probably we should never have imagined it, but that the word supper occurred therein.

3. However, most of the English annotators have fallen into the same mistake with Mr. Burkitt. And so have thousands of their

316

On The Wedding Garment

readers. Yet a mistake it certainly is; and such a mistake as has not any shadow of foundation in the text. It is true, indeed, that none ought to approach the Lord's table without habitual, at least, if not actual, preparation; that is, a firm purpose to keep all the commandments of God, and a sincere desire to receive all his promises. But that obligation cannot be inferred from this text, though it may from many other passages of Scripture. But there is no need of multiplying texts; one is as good as a thousand: There needs no more to induce any man of a tender conscience to communicate at all opportunities, than that single commandment of our Lord, "Do this in remembrance of me."

4. But, whatever preparation is necessary in order to our being worthy partakers of the Lord's Supper, it has no relation at all to the "wedding garment" mentioned in this parable. It cannot: For that commemoration of his death was not then ordained. It relates wholly to the proceedings of our Lord, when he comes in the clouds of heaven to judge the quick and the dead; and to the qualifications which will then be necessary to their inheriting "the kingdom prepared for them from the foundation of the world."

5. Many excellent men, who are thoroughly apprized of this, who are convinced, the wedding garment here mentioned is not to be understood of any qualification for the Lord's Supper, but of the qualification for glory, interpret it of the righteousness of Christ; "which," say they, "is the sole qualification for heaven; this being the only righteousness wherein any man can stand in the day of the Lord. For who," they ask, "will then dare to appear before the great God, save in the righteousness of his well-beloved Son? Shall we not then at least, if not before, find the need of having a better righteousness than our own? And what other can that be than the righteousness of God our Saviour?" The late pious and ingenious Mr. Hervey descants largely upon this; particularly in his elaborate *Dialogues between Theron and Aspasio*.

6. Another elegant writer, now I trust with God, speaks strongly to the same effect, in the preface to his comment on St. Paul's Epistle to the Romans: "We certainly," says he, "shall need a better righteousness than our own, wherein to stand at the bar of God in the day of judgment." I do not understand the expression. Is it scriptural? Do we read it in the Bible, either in the Old Testament or the New? I doubt it is an unscriptural, awkward phrase, which has no determinate meaning. If you mean by that odd, uncouth question, "In whose righteousness are you to stand at the last day?"—for whose sake, or by whose merit, do you expect to enter into the glory of God? I answer, without the least hesitation, For the sake of Jesus Christ the Righteous. It is through his merits alone that all believers are saved; that is, justified—saved from the guilt, sanctified—saved from the nature, of sin; and glorified—taken into heaven.

7. It may be worth our while to spend a few more words on this important point. Is it possible to devise a more unintelligible expression than this, "In what righteousness are we to stand before God at the last day?" Why do you not speak plainly, and say, "For whose sake do you look to be saved?" Any plain peasant would then readily answer, "For the sake of Jesus Christ." But all those dark, ambiguous phrases tend only to puzzle the cause, and open a way for unwary hearers to slide into Antinomianism.

8. Is there any expression similar to this of the "wedding garment" to be found in Holy Scripture? In the Revelation we find mention made of "linen, white and clean, which is the righteousness of the saints." And this, too, many vehemently contend, means the righteousness of Christ. But how then are we to reconcile this with that passage in the seventh chapter, "They have washed their robes, and made them white in the blood of the Lamb?" Will they say, "The righteousness of Christ was washed and made white in the blood of Christ?" Away with such Antinomian jargon! Is not the plain meaning this:—It was from the

atoning blood that the very righteousness of the saints derived its value and acceptableness with God?

9. In the nineteenth chapter of the Revelation, at the ninth verse, there is an expression which comes much nearer to this:—"The wedding supper of the Lamb." There is a near resemblance between this and the marriage supper mentioned in the parable. Yet they are not altogether the same: There is a clear difference between them. The supper mentioned in the parable belongs to the Church Militant; that mentioned in the Revelation, to the Church Triumphant: The one, to the kingdom of God on earth; the other, to the kingdom of God in heaven. Accordingly, in the former, there may be found those who have not a "wedding garment." But there will be none such to be found in the latter: No, not "in that great multitude which no man can number, out of every kindred, and tongue, and people, and nation." They will all be "kings and priests unto God, and shall reign with him for ever and ever."

10. Does not that expression, "the righteousness of the saints," point out what is the "wedding garment" in the parable? It is the "holiness without which no man shall see the Lord." The righteousness of Christ is doubtless necessary for any soul that enters into glory: But so is personal holiness too, for every child of man. But it is highly needful to be observed, that they are necessary in different respects. The former is necessary to entitle us to heaven; the latter to qualify us for it. Without the righteousness of Christ we could have no claim to glory; without holiness we could have no fitness for it. By the former we become members of Christ, children of God, and heirs of the kingdom of heaven. By the latter "we are made meet to be partakers of the inheritance of the saints in light."

11. From the very time that the Son of God delivered this weighty truth to the children of men, that all who had not the "wedding garment" would be "cast into outer darkness, where are weeping and gnashing of teeth,"—the enemy of souls has been

labouring to obscure it, that they might still seek death in the error of their life; and many ways has he tried to disguise the holiness without which we cannot be saved. How many things have been palmed, even upon the Christian world, in the place of this! Some of these are utterly contrary thereto, and subversive of it. Some were noways connected with or related to it; but useless and insignificant trifles. Others might be deemed to be some part of it, but by no means the whole. It may be of use to enumerate some of them, lest ye should be ignorant of Satan's devices.

12. Of the first sort, things prescribed as Christian holiness, although flatly contrary thereto, is idolatry. How has this, in various shapes, been taught, and is to this day, as essential to holiness! How diligently is it now circulated in a great part of the Christian Church! Some of their idols are silver and gold, or wood and stone, "graven by art, and man's device;" some, men of like passions with themselves, particularly the Apostles of our Lords and the Virgin Mary. To these they add numberless saints of their own creation, with no small company of angels.

13. Another thing as directly contrary to the whole tenor of true religion, is, what is diligently taught in many parts of the Christian Church; I mean the spirit of persecution; of persecuting their brethren even unto death; so that the earth has been often covered with blood by those who were called Christians, in order to "make their calling and election sure." It is true, many, even in the Church of Rome, who were taught this horrid doctrine, now seem to be ashamed of it. But have the heads of that community as openly and explicitly renounced that capital doctrine of devils, as they avowed it in the Council of Constance, and practiced it for many ages? Till they have done this, they will be chargeable with the blood of Jerome of Prague, basely murdered, and of many thousands, both in the sight of God and man.

14. Let it not be said, "This does not concern us Protestants: We think and let think. We abhor the spirit of persecution; and main-

tain, as an indisputable truth, that every rational creature has a right to worship God as he is persuaded in his own mind." But are we true to our own principles? So far, that we do not use fire and faggot. We do not persecute unto blood those that do not subscribe to our opinions. Blessed be God, the laws of our country do not allow of this; but is there no such thing to be found in England as domestic persecution? The saying or doing anything unkind to another for following his own conscience is a species of persecution. Now, are we all clear of this? Is there no husband who, in this sense, persecutes his wife? who uses her unkindly, in word or deed, for worshipping God after her own conscience? Do no parents thus persecute their children? no masters or mistresses, their servants? If they do this, and think they do God service therein, they must not cast the first stone at the Roman Catholics.

15. When things of an indifferent nature are represented as necessary to salvation, it is a folly of the same kind, though not of the same magnitude. Indeed, it is not a little sin to represent trifles as necessary to salvation; such as going of pilgrimages, or anything that is not expressly enjoined in the Holy Scripture. Among these we may undoubtedly rank orthodoxy, or right opinions. We know, indeed, that wrong opinions in religion naturally lead to wrong tempers, or wrong practices; and that, consequently, it is our bounden duty to pray that we may have a right judgment in all things. But still a man may judge as accurately as the devil, and yet be as wicked as he.

16. Something more excusable are they who imagine holiness to consist in things that are only a part of it; (that is, when they are connected with the rest; otherwise they are no part of it at all;) suppose in doing no harm. And how exceeding common is this! How many take holiness and harmlessness to mean one and the same thing! whereas were a man as harmless as a post, he might be as far from holiness as heaven from earth. Suppose a man, therefore, to be exactly honest, to pay every one his own, to cheat no man, to wrong no man, to hurt no man, to be just in all his

dealings; suppose a woman to be uniformly modest and virtuous in all her words and actions; suppose the one and the other to be steady practisers of morality, that is, of justice, mercy, and truth; yet all this, though it is good as far as it goes, is but a part of Christian holiness. Yea, suppose a person of this amiable character to do much good wherever he is; to feed the hungry, clothe the naked, relieve the stranger, the sick, the prisoner; yea, and to save many souls from death; it is possible he may still fall far short of that holiness without which he cannot see the Lord.

17. What, then, is that holiness which is the true "wedding garment," the only qualification for glory? "In Christ Jesus," (that is, according to the Christian institution, whatever be the case of the heathen world,) "neither circumcision availeth any thing, nor uncircumcision; but a new creation,"—the renewal of the soul "in the image of God wherein it was created." In "Christ Jesus neither circumcision availeth anything, nor uncircumcision, but faith which worketh by love." It first, through the energy of God, worketh love to God and all mankind; and, by this love, every holy and heavenly temper, in particular, lowliness, meekness, gentleness, temperance, and longsuffering. "It is neither circumcision,"—the attending on all the Christian ordinances, "nor uncircumcision,"—the fulfilling of all heathen morality, but "the keeping the commandments of God;" particularly those, "Thou shalt love the Lord thy God with all thy heart, and thy neighbour as thyself." In a word, holiness is the having "the mind that was in Christ," and the "walking as Christ walked."

18. Such has been my judgment for these threescore years, without any material alteration. Only, about fifty years ago I had a clearer view than before of justification by faith; and in this, from that very hour, I never varied, no, not an hair's breadth. Nevertheless, an ingenious man has publicly accused me of a thousand variations. I pray God, not to lay this to his charge! I am now on the borders of the grave; but, by the grace of God, I still witness the same confession. Indeed, some have supposed, that when I

began to declare, "By grace ye are saved through faith," I retracted what I had before maintained: "Without holiness no man shall see the Lord." But it is an entire mistake: These scriptures well consist with each other; the meaning of the former being plainly this, By faith we are saved from sin, and made holy. The imagination, that faith supersedes holiness, is the marrow of Antinomianism.

19. The sum of all is this: The God of love is willing to save all the souls that he has made. This he has proclaimed to them in his word, together with the terms of salvation, revealed by the Son of his love, who gave his own life that they that believe in him might have everlasting life. And for these he has prepared a kingdom, from the foundation of the world. But he will not force them to accept of it; he leaves them in the hands of their own counsel; he saith, "Behold, I set before you life and death, blessing and cursing: Choose life, that ye may live." Choose holiness, by my grace; which is the way, the only way, to everlasting life. He cries aloud, "Be holy, and be happy; happy in this world, and happy in the world to come." "Holiness becometh his house for ever!" This is the wedding garment of all that are called to "the marriage of the Lamb." Clothed in this, they will not be found naked: "They have washed their robes and made them white in the blood of the Lamb." But as to all those who appear in the last day without the wedding garment, the Judge will say, "Cast them into outer darkness; there shall be weeping and gnashing of teeth."

Ars Moriendi Perfected
1791

The journey is now complete. It began in 1725 as the young John Wesley made the momentous decision to pursue holiness of heart and life. At the time his goal was to prepare himself to face death with complete confidence. After a checkered faith journey covering nearly seven decades, this is what Wesley finally attains: peace in the face of death and willingness to leave this world for the glories of heaven. Wesley rests solely on Christ crucified. He first tasted this assurance 53 years earlier at an Aldersgate society meeting, and now this same faith sustains him through his final trial. Source: Works J 5:42-44

On Thursday, February 17, 1791, Wesley preached at Lambeth, but on his return seemed much indisposed, and said he had taken cold. On the following Sunday he was so unwell as to be unable to engage in his usual public exercises; but on Monday he was so much better, that he went to Wickenham to dine with Lady Fitzgerald. He preached on Tuesday evening at City-road; and on Wednesday he went to Leatherhead, and preached to a small company what proved to be his last sermon, from, "Seek ye the Lord while he may be found, call ye upon him while he is near." On Friday he became so alarmingly ill, that Dr. Whitehead was sent for; but his skill proved unavailing. Mr. Wesley got rapidly worse, and felt that his end was drawing nigh. In this solemn crisis this eminent servant of God experienced the supporting influence of that religion which he had been the honored instrument of reviving in this land, and in America, to so great an extent as had been his labors in the cause of Christ, they were no more the foundation of his hope in death, than they had been in life.

Eight years before, when at Bristol, he had an alarming attack; and then, while contemplating his critical situation, he said to Mr. Bradford, "I have been reflecting on my past life; I have been wandering up and down between fifty and sixty years, endeavoring in my poor way to do a little good to my fellow-creatures; and now it is probable, that there are but a few steps between me and death; and what have I done to trust to for salvation? I can see nothing which I have done or suffered that will bear looking at. I have no other plea than this:

I the chief of sinners am,
But Jesus died for me.

This was his language to the last... And on one asking, "Is this the present language of your heart, and do you feel now as you did then?" he answered, "Yes;" and afterwards added, in reference to Christ, "He is all! He is all!" The day following, he reverted to the same subject, and said, "How necessary it is for every one to be on the right foundation!" and then quoted again his favorite stanza, expressive of the entire dependence of his soul on the sacrificial death of Christ. And he strikingly proved how available is that plea. The most cheering manifestations of the divine presence were vouchsafed to him. On another occasion, he had called for pen and ink, but when they were brought, being unable to write, one said to him, "Let me write for you, Sir; tell me what you would say." He replied, "Nothing, but that God is with us;" and not long after he broke out in a manner which, considering his weakness, astonished all present, in singing:

I'll praise my Maker while I've breath;
And when my voice is lost in death,
Praise shall employ my nobler powers;
My days of praise shall ne'er be past,
While life and thought and being last,
Or immortality endures.

Shortly after he had sung this verse, he became evidently worse and his voice failed in endeavoring to sing part of another hymn. Having rested awhile, he desired those who were with him to "pray and praise." They kneeled down, and the room seemed to be filled with the divine presence.

Having given directions respecting his funeral, he again begged they would pray and praise. Several friends who were in the house being called up, they all kneeled down again, and he joined with them in great fervor of spirit; but in particular parts of the prayer, his whole soul seemed to be engaged in a manner which evidently showed how ardently he longed for the full accomplishment of their united desires. And when one of the Preachers prayed, that if God were about to take away their father to his eternal rest, He would be pleased to continue and increase his blessing upon the doctrine and discipline which He had long made his servant the means of propagating and establishing in the world; Mr. Wesley responded, "Amen," with such a fervor and strength of voice as indicated how intense was his desire that the petition should be answered. In the course of the same day, he attempted to speak to one who came into his room; but perceiving that he did not make himself understood, he paused a little, and then, with all the remaining strength he had, cried out, *"The best of all is, God is with us!"*

Soon after, lifting up his dying arm in token of victory, and raising his feeble voice with a holy triumph not to be described, he again repeated the heart-reviving words, *"The best of all is, God with us!"* During the night following, he frequently attempted to repeat the psalm, part of which he had before sung; but such was his weakness he could only utter, "I'll praise... I'll praise."

On Wednesday morning, March 2nd, it was evident that the closing scene drew near; and Mr. Bradford having prayed with him, he was heard to articulate, "Farewell!" This was the last word he uttered; and while several of his friends were kneeling around his bed, he passed without a groan or struggle into the joyful presence of his Lord.

LaVergne, TN USA
15 July 2010
189600LV00002B/7/P